Pocket

BARCELONA

this third edition updated by
LAURIE ISOLA

Contents

<< CASTELLERS OUTSIDE LA SEU
< THE DRAGON STAIRWAY, PARC GÜELL

INTRODUCTION TO

Barcelona

It's tempting to say that there's nowhere quite like Barcelona – there's certainly not another city in Spain to touch it for sheer style, looks or energy. The glossy mags and travel press dwell enthusiastically on its outrageous architecture, designer shopping, cool bars and vibrant cultural scene, but Barcelona is more than just this year's fad. It's a confident, progressive city, one that is tirelessly self-renewing while preserving all that's best about its past. As old neighbourhoods bloom, and landmark museums and sights are restored with panache, there's still an enduring embrace of the good things in life, from the daily market to the late-night café.

RESTAURANTS IN THE PLAÇA REIAL

Best places for a Barcelona picnic

Parc de la Ciutadella is the city centre's favourite green space, while the gardens of Montjuïc offer some fantastic views. Any time the sun shines, the beach between Barceloneta and Port Olímpic makes for a great alfresco lunch, though for a real in-the-know experience stock up at the market and head for the Collserola hills.

The province of Catalunya (Catalonia in English), of which Barcelona is the capital, has a historical identity going back as far as the ninth century, and through the long period of domination by outside powers, as well as during the Franco dictatorship, it proved impossible to stifle the Catalan spirit. The city reflects this independence, being at the forefront of Spanish political activism, radical design and architecture, and commercial dynamism.

This is seen most perfectly in the glorious *modernista* (Art Nouveau) buildings that stud the city's streets and avenues. Antoni Gaudí is the most famous of those who have left their mark on Barcelona in this way: his Sagrada Família church is rightly revered, but just as fascinating are the (literally) fantastic houses, public buildings and parks that he and his contemporaries designed.

The city also boasts an extensive medieval Old Town – full of pivotal buildings from an earlier age of expansion – and a stupendous artistic legacy, from national (ie, Catalan) collections of Romanesque, Gothic and contemporary art to major galleries containing the life's work of the Catalan artists Joan Miró and Antoni Tàpies (not to mention a celebrated showcase of the work of Pablo Picasso).

Barcelona is equally proud of its cutting-edge restaurants – featuring some of the best chefs in Europe – its late-night bars, even its football team, the mercurial, incomparable FC Barcelona. Add a spruced-up waterfront, five kilometres of resort-standard sandy beach, and Olympic-rated sports and leisure facilities, and you have a city that entertains and cossets locals and visitors alike.

Despite its size, Spain's second city is a surprisingly easy place to find your way around. In effect, it's a series of self-contained neighbourhoods stretching out from the harbour, flanked by parks, hills and woodland. Much of what there is to see in the centre – Gothic cathedral, Picasso museum, markets,

CARVED DOOR AT CASA BATLLÓ

Gaudí buildings and art galleries – can be reached on foot, while a fast, cheap, integrated public transport system takes you directly to the peripheral attractions and suburbs. Meanwhile, bike tours, sightseeing buses and cruise boats all offer a different way of seeing the city.

True, for all its go-ahead feel, Barcelona has its problems, not least a petty crime rate that occasionally makes the international news. But there's no need to be unduly paranoid, and it would be a shame to stick solely to the main tourist sights since you'll miss so much. Tapas bars hidden down decrepit alleys, designer boutiques in gentrified Old Town quarters, street opera singers belting out an aria, bargain lunches in workers' taverns, neighbourhood funicular rides, unmarked gourmet restaurants, craft workshops, restored medieval palaces and specialist galleries – all are just as much Barcelona as the Ramblas or Gaudí's Sagrada Família.

When to visit

Barcelona is an established city-break destination with a year-round tourist, business and convention trade. Different seasons have different attractions, from spring dance festivals to Christmas markets, but there's always something going on. As far as the weather is concerned, the best times to go are spring and autumn, when the temperatures are comfortably warm and walking the streets isn't a chore. In summer, the city can be very hot and humid while August sees many shops, bars and restaurants close as the locals head out of the city in droves. It's worth considering a winter break, as long as you don't mind the prospect of occasional rain. It's generally still warm enough to sit out at a café, for example, even in December or January.

BARCELONA AT A GLANCE

>>EATING

In the popular Old Town areas food and service can be indifferent and expensive. There are some great bars and restaurants in tourist-heavy **La Ribera** and the **Barri Gòtic**, but you really need to explore the up-and-coming neighbourhoods of **Sant Pere**, **El Raval** and **Poble Sec** for the best local finds, from traditional taverns to chic contemporary tapas bars. Michelin stars and big bills are mostly found in the **Eixample**, while for the best fish and seafood head for harbourside **Barceloneta** or the **Port Olímpic**. The suburb of **Gràcia** is also a nice, village-like place to spend the evening, with plenty of good mid-range restaurants.

>>DRINKING

It should probably be called Bar-Celona – whatever you're looking for, you'll find it here, from bohemian boozer to cocktail bar. **Passeig del Born** (La Ribera) is one of the hottest destinations, with Sant Pere close on its heels, while there's an edgier scene in **El Raval** and around **Carrer de Blai** (Poble Sec). The main concentration of designer bars (as well as the city's gay scene) is in the **Esquerra de l'Eixample**, while the theme bars of **Port Olímpic** are mainstream summer-night playgrounds for locals and visitors. Bars usually stay open till any time between 11pm and 2 or 3am.

>>SHOPPING

Designer and high-street fashion can be found in the Eixample along **Passeig de Gràcia** and **Rambla de Catalunya**, though for new names and boutiques the best hunting ground is in the Old Town streets around **Passeig del Born** (La Ribera). Secondhand and vintage clothing stores line **c/de la Riera Baixa** (El Raval), there's music and streetwear along nearby **c/dels Tallers**, and for antiques and curios it's best in the streets near **c/Banys Nous** (Barri Gòtic). The markets, meanwhile, are king, from the heavyweight **Boqueria** to lesser-known gems like the **Mercat Santa Caterina** in trendy Sant Pere or Gràcia's **Mercat de la Llibertat**.

>>NIGHTLIFE

Clubs in Barcelona start late and go on until 5 or 6am, and while Thursday to Sunday sees the most action, there are **DJs** on the decks every night. The big name venues tend to be found out in the old industrial zones like **Poble Nou**; downtown music clubs are often jazz-orientated, though local rock, pop, indie and even flamenco get regular airings in venues across the **Barri Gòtic** and El Raval. For typically Catalan surroundings, a concert at Sant Pere's **Palau de la Música Catalana** can't be beaten, while the principal venue up in the Eixample is the contemporary city concert hall, **L'Auditori**.

OUR RECOMMENDATIONS FOR WHERE TO EAT, DRINK AND SHOP ARE LISTED AT THE END OF EACH PLACES CHAPTER.

Day One in Barcelona

1 The Ramblas > p.34. Everyone starts with a stroll down Barcelona's most emblematic street.

2 Mercat de la Boqueria > p.36. Wander through the stalls of one of Europe's best markets and soak up the vibrant atmosphere.

3 La Seu > p.42. The calm cloister of Barcelona's cathedral is a haven amid the bustle of the Gothic Quarter.

4 Museu d'Història de Barcelona > p.46. This place holds the archeological history of Roman Barcelona – right under your feet.

🍴 **Lunch** > p.53. Stop near the church of Santa María del Pi for alfresco drinks and a market-fresh meal at *Taller de Tapas*.

5 Museu Picasso > p.78. Walk through the tight-knit medieval streets of La Ribera to the must-see museum, housed in the city where Picasso developed his inimitable style.

6 Parc de la Ciutadella > p.86. Take time out in the museums, palm-houses and gardens of the city's favourite park.

7 Port Olímpic > p.100. The beach, boardwalk and seafront promenade set the scene for a sundowner drink.

🍴 **Dinner** > p.70. Some of the city's coolest places to eat and drink are in El Raval; try the creative cuisine at stylish *Biblioteca*'s open kitchen.

Day Two in Barcelona

1 Sagrada Família > p.114. To avoid the worst of the bustling crowds, arrive at Gaudí's masterpiece at opening time.

2 Passeig de Gràcia > p.104. Europe's most extraordinary urban architecture decorates the modern city's main avenue.

3 Museu Egipci de Barcelona > p.107 A captivating collection including mummies, amulets and sarcophagi transports you back to ancient Egypt.

4 Vinçon > p.110. Design, style and shopping opportunities, all under one roof.

Lunch > p.113. There's fabulous food at *Tapas, 24*, a classy uptown bar-diner.

5 Museu Nacional d'Art de Catalunya > p.93. The triumphant landscaped approach to Montjuïc culminates in the extraordinary Catalan National Art Gallery.

6 Fundació Joan Miró > p.96. The modernist building on the hill houses the life's work of Catalan artist Joan Miró.

7 Ride the Trasbordador Aeri > p.59. A thrilling cable car sweeps you across the inner harbour from Montjuïc to Port Vell.

8 Barceloneta > p.58. For marina or beach views, grab a table at an outdoor café in the old fishermen's quarter.

Dinner > p.85. After cold beer and tapas in up-and-coming Sant Pere, dine in Catalan style at La Ribera's *Senyor Parellada*.

Modernista Barcelona

Visionary *modernista* architects, like Antoni Gaudí, changed the way people looked at buildings. Their style, a sort of Catalan Art Nouveau, left Barcelona with an extraordinary architectural legacy that goes far beyond the famous sights of the Sagrada Família church and Parc Güell.

1 Hospital de la Santa Creu i de Sant Pau > p.115. Don't miss Lluís Domènech i Montaner's innovative public hospital, near the Sagrada Família.

2 La Pedrera > p.109. Inventive design permeates every aspect of Gaudí's fantastical "stone quarry" apartment building.

3 Casa Amatller > p.106. Catch a guided tour of this stunning house belonging to a nineteenth-century chocolate manufacturer.

🍴 **Lunch** > p.112. Take a lunch stop at *Casa Calvet*, an early Gaudí townhouse, now a classy Catalan restaurant.

4 Palau de la Música Catalana > p.74. Book in advance for a tour of this dramatic concert hall, or buy a ticket for an evening performance.

5 Arc de Triomf > p.86. Gateway to the Ciutadella park is this giant red-brick arch.

6 Castell dels Tres Dragons > p.88. The park's eye-catching "castle" is a *modernista* showcase for the city's natural science museum.

🍴 **Dinner** > p.132. In summer, Parc Güell is open until well into the evening – and the bars and restaurants of fashionable Gràcia are close at hand.

Budget Barcelona

Barcelona may be one of Europe's most fashionable cities, but it remains remarkably good value as far as most visitors are concerned. You certainly don't need to spend a fortune to eat well, see the major sights and enjoy yourself.

1 The Ramblas > p.34. Barcelona's greatest show – a stroll down the Ramblas – is a free spectacle around the clock.

2 MNAC > p.93. The ticket for the showpiece National Art Gallery is valid for two full days, and there's free entry on the first Sunday of every month.

Lunch > p.52. Virtually every restaurant offers a weekday *menú del día*, so lunch is a bargain at places like *Café de l'Acadèmia* where dinner might cost three times as much.

3 Relax at the beach > p.101. Enjoy five miles of sand, boardwalks and promenades.

4 Font Màgica > p.91. There's no charge to watch this magnificent display of water and light.

5 Caixa Forum > p.91. Entry to this dazzling arts and cultural centre costs less than a cocktail.

6 Parc de la Ciutadella > p.86. Unfurl a picnic blanket in the city's green lung.

Dinner > p.77. Many of Barcelona's markets also have stylish restaurants attached – like *Cuines Santa Caterina* in Sant Pere's dramatic Mercat Santa Caterina.

Big sights

1 Sagrada Família The most famous unfinished church in the world — the "Sacred Family" temple is the essential visit for Gaudí fans. **> p.114**

3 Parc Güell A public park without compare, where contorted stone pavilions, gingerbread buildings and surreal ceramics combine unforgettably. **> p.130**

2 La Seu Pride of the Gothic era, the city's majestic medieval cathedral anchors the Old Town. **> p.42**

4 Museu Nacional d'Art de Catalunya (MNAC) The National Museum of Art celebrates the glories of a thousand years of Catalan painting and sculpture. **> p.93**

5 The Ramblas The city's iconic central thoroughfare, where hawkers, stall-holders, eccentrics and tourists collide to gleeful effect. **> p.34**

Shopping

1 Mercat de la Boqueria The city's finest food market is a show in its own right, busy with locals and tourists from dawn to dusk. **> p.36**

2 Casa Gispert A hideaway treasure-trove of nuts, dried goods, coffee and spices in the heart of La Ribera. **> p.82**

3 Vinçon The most eminent showcase in town for Catalan household style, design and furnishings. **> p.110**

4 Custo Barcelona Barcelona's brightest designer brand injects colour and fun into shop windows across the city. **> p.82**

5 L'Arca Vintage heaven in the Gothic Quarter. **> p.50**

Restaurants

1 Biblioteca Creative, market-led Catalan cuisine is on the menu at fashionable *Biblioteca*. > **p.70**

2 Flash, Flash A fun retro Gràcia landmark that specializes in tortillas of all tastes, savoury to sweet. > **p.132**

4 Cinc Sentits Delight all five senses at Jordi Artal's Michelin-starred restaurant. > **p.124**

3 La Tomaquera Food cooked on the chargrill (*a la brasa*) is the speciality at this bustling tavern. > **p.98**

5 Senyor Parellada To eat home-style food with the locals, make time for this ravishingly handsome Old Town restaurant. > **p.85**

Museums

1 Museu del Disseny The city's applied art collections have a shiny, new home at the sleek *Disseny Hub* building. **> p.118**

3 Museu Frederic Marès Don't miss the museum dedicated to the "mad collector" to beat them all. > **p.43**

2 Museu Egipci Break off from your uptown shopping to view this select showing of fascinating Egyptian antiquities. > **p.107**

4 CosmoCaixa A science museum complete with its own rainforest. > **p.147**

5 Camp Nou and FC Barcelona Tour one of Europe's most magnificent stadiums, home to the local football heroes. > **p.137**

Art galleries

1 Fundació Joan Miró There's no more beautiful gallery in the city than the house on the hill presenting the life's work of Joan Miró. **> p.96**

2 Caixa Forum There's always an exhibition worth seeing in the city's best arts and cultural centre — not to mention concerts, films and other events. > **p.91**

3 Fundació Antoni Tàpies Acquaint yourself with the work of the master Catalan abstract artist, contained within a striking Eixample mansion. > **p.107**

4 Museu d'Art Contemporani de Barcelona (MACBA) Post-war contemporary art (Spanish, Catalan and international) has a home in a stunning building in El Raval. > **p.62**

5 Museu Picasso The city's most visited art collection traces Picasso's career in its entirety. > **p.78**

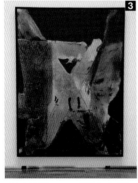

Tapas bars

1 Tickets A chance to taste some of Ferran Adrià's famous dishes at the *elBulli* chef's (relatively) affordable tapas joint. > **p.98**

2 Bodega La Plata Stand-up snacks and wine from the barrel are the staples at this famous Old Town bar. > **p.52**

3 Dos Palillos East meets West – and hipsters meet each other – in El Raval's cool Asian fusion tapas bar *Dos Palillos.* > **p.70**

5 Bar Pinotxo The best tapas bar in the best market — the Boqueria's *Pinotxo*, no contest. > **p.41**

4 El Xampanyet Step into this La Ribera institution for a glass of Catalan fizz and a bite or two before dinner. > **p.85**

Bars and clubs

1 Kahala The heady drinks at this Polynesian-themed cocktail bar will have you saying "¡*Aloha, Barcelona!*" **> p.143**

3 Café del Sol Sip *copas* and people watch from the *terrassa* of this Plaça del Sol institution. **> p.134**

2 Moog The city's techno club of choice for aficionados, open from midnight for nonstop dancing. **> p.73**

4 Resolis Resolis is the signature boho bar in the thriving El Raval neighbourhood. **> p.72**

5 Milk Mixology at its finest in the Barri Gòtic's most welcoming bar and bistro. **> p.54**

27

Music, dance and theatre

1 **Sidecar** This rootsy Plaça Reial rock club presents a varied roster of gigs and club nights, with indie and global sounds to the fore. > **p.55**

2 Palau de la Música Catalana
The city's finest concert hall, a *modernista* classic encased in a contemporary shell. > **p.74**

3 Tarantos The best place for flamenco sessions — the after-show dancing carries on into the small hours. > **p.55**

5 Gran Teatre del Liceu Book ahead for opera tickets at this renowned city landmark, though the guided tours are open to all. > **p.38**

4 Café Teatre Llantiol It's mime, magic and much, much more at Barcelona's long-established cabaret venue. > **p.73**

Outdoor Barcelona

1 Parc Zoològic Barcelona's zoo packs the world's fauna into the rolling grounds of the Ciutadella park. **> p.88**

2 City beaches The great urban escape is to the city's 5km of sand-fringed ocean, dotted with parks and playgrounds. > **p.101**

3 Jardí Botànic de Barcelona The impressive botanical gardens spread across a hillside above the Olympic Stadium. > **p.97**

4 Parc de la Ciutadella Whatever the season, the city's nicest park always springs a surprise. > **p.86**

5 Port Olímpic Twin towers and the landmark Frank Gehry fish dominate Barcelona's liveliest resort area. > **p.100**

Along the Ramblas

No day in the city seems complete without a stroll along the Ramblas, Spain's most famous thoroughfare. Cutting through Barcelona's Old Town areas, and connecting Plaça de Catalunya with the harbour, it's at the heart of the city's self-image – lined with cafés, restaurants, souvenir shops, flower stalls and newspaper kiosks. The name (from the Arabic *ramla* or "sand") refers to a seasonal stream bed that was paved over in medieval times. Since the nineteenth century it's been a fashionable promenade, and today the show goes on, as human statues, portrait painters, buskers and card sharps add to the vibrancy of Barcelona's most enthralling street. There are metro stops at Catalunya (top of the Ramblas), Liceu (middle) and Drassanes (bottom), or you can walk the entire length in about twenty minutes.

PLAÇA DE CATALUNYA

Ⓜ Catalunya. MAP P.36, POCKET MAP D10

The huge formal square at the top of the Ramblas stands right at the heart of the city. It's not only the focal point of events and demonstrations – notably a mass party on New Year's Eve – but also the site of prominent landmarks like the main city tourist office, the white-faced El Corte Inglés department store and El Triangle shopping centre (with the popular *Zurich* outdoor café beneath it).

The Ramblas itself actually comprises five separate named sections, starting with the northern stretch, Rambla Canaletes, nearest Plaça de Catalunya, which is marked by an iron fountain – a drink from this supposedly means you'll never leave Barcelona. Further down is the bird market on Rambla Estudis and the sudden profusion of flower stalls on Rambla Sant Josep, near the Boqueria market.

PLAÇA DE CATALUNYA

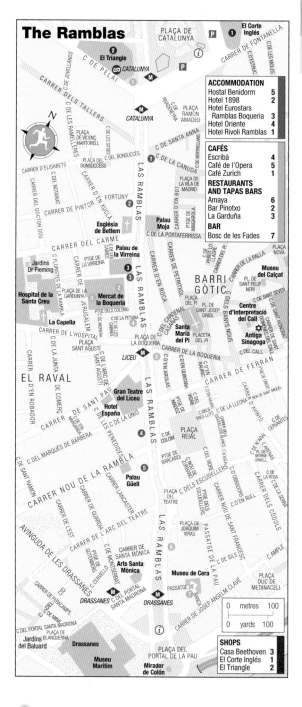

The Ramblas

PLAÇA DE CATALUNYA

El Corte Inglés

CARRER DE FONTANELLA

CARRER DE LES MOLES

C DE ESTRUC

El Triangle

C DE PELAI

CATALUNYA

C DE RIVADENEYRA

PLAÇA RAMON AMADEU

CARRER DELS TALLERS

C DE LES SITGES

C DE LES RAMELLERES

PLAÇA DE VICENÇ MARTORELL

CARRER D'ELISABETS

PLAÇA DEL BONSUCCÉS

C DEL BONSUCCÉS

C DE SANTA ANNA

C DE LA CANUDA

DE BERTRELLANS

PLAÇA DE LA VILA DE MADRID

CARRER DEL NOTARIAT

C DEL DOCTOR DOU

CARRER DE PINTOR FORTUNY

CARRER D'EN XUCLÀ

LAS RAMBLAS

C DE N BOT

PLAÇA DE MAGARÒLA

Palau Moja

C DE LA PORTAFERRISSA

Església de Betlem

Palau de la Virreina

CARRER DEL CARME

C DE FLORISTES DE LA RAMBLA

PTGE DE LA VIRREINA

LAS RAMBLAS

CARRER DE PETRITXOL

C D'EN PLANELL

C DE LA FRUITA

PLAÇA DE LA PALLA

PLAÇA NOVA

Museu del Calçat

Jardins Dr Fleming

Hospital de la Santa Creu

PLAÇA DE LA GARDUNYA

JERUSALEM

Mercat de la Boqueria

CARRER DE L'HOSPITAL

La Capella

C DE MORERA

PTGE DE LA PETXINA

C DE LA PETXINA

C DELS CABRES

PLAÇA DE LA BOQUERIA

C DEL CARDENAL CASAÑAS

CARRER D'EN ROCA

BARRI GÒTIC

PL. DE SANT FELIP NERI

PL. DEL PI

PL. DE SANT JOSEP ORIOL

Santa Maria del Pi

CARRER DE LA BOQUERIA

PLACETA DEL PI

CARRER DE SANT SEVER

C DE SANT SEVER

Centre d'Interpretació del Call

Antiga Sinagoga

C DE SANT HONORAT

C DE SANT DOMÈNEC DEL CALL

C DEL CALL

PLAÇA DE SANT AGUSTÍ

LICEU

C DE L'ARC DE SANT AGUSTÍ

EL RAVAL

CARRER D'EN ROBADOR

Gran Teatre del Liceu

Hotel España

CARRER DE SANT PAU

C DE LA UNIÓ

CARRER DE FERRAN

C D'EN QUINTANA

C D'EN RAURIC

C D'EN RAURIC

PTGE DE LA LLEONA

3ª PASª DE SANT MIQUEL

C D'EN AVINYÓ

C DE CERVANTES

PTGE DE MADOZ

C DEL VIDRE

C TRES LLITS

C DE LA LLEONA

DE COMERÇ

CARRER DE GUARDIA

C DE LES PENEDIDES

C DE COLOM

PLAÇA REIAL

C DE VIDRE

C DE N'ARAI

PTGE DE BACARDÍ

C DE NARAY

C DE LA ROSA

C DE LA SERRA

GEORGE ORWELL

Palau Güell

CARRER NOU DE LA RAMBLA

CARRER DE LANCASTER

C DEL MARQUÈS DE BARBERÀ

C DE SANT RAMON

CARRER DE GUÀRDIA

PTGE DE GUTTEMBERG

LAS RAMBLAS

C DELS ESCUDELLERS

PTGE DELS ESCUDELLERS

C D'EN RULL

CARRER DELS CÒDOLS

AVINGUDA DE LES DRASSANES

CARRER DE L'EST

CID

CARRER DE PERACAMPS

C DE MINA

CARRER DE L'ARC DEL TEATRE

C DE MONTSERRAT

C DE CERVELLÓ

Arts Santa Mònica

CARRER DE SANTA MÒNICA

DRASSANES

C DEL PORTAL SANTA MADRONA

Museu de Cera

DRASSANES

PASSATGE DE LA PAU

C DE SILS

PASSATGE DE LA BANCA

PLAÇA DE JOAQUIM XIRAU

PLAÇA DEL TEATRE

PASSATGE DE LA PAU

CARRER DE JOSEP ANSELM CLAVÉ

PLAÇA DUC DE MEDINACELI

C DEL PORTAL SANTA MADRONA

Jardins del Baluard

PLAÇA DE MINA

Drassanes

Museu Marítim

PLAÇA DEL PORTAL DE LA PAU

Mirador de Colón

BLANQUERNA

ACCOMMODATION

Hostal Benidorm	5
Hotel 1898	2
Hotel Eurostars Ramblas Boqueria	3
Hotel Oriente	4
Hotel Rivoli Ramblas	1

CAFÉS

Escribà	4
Café de l'Opera	5
Café Zurich	1

RESTAURANTS AND TAPAS BARS

Amaya	6
Bar Pinotxo	2
La Garduña	3

BAR

Bosc de les Fades	7

0	metres	100
0	yards	100

SHOPS

Casa Beethoven	3
El Corte Inglés	1
El Triangle	2

ESGLÉSIA DE BETLEM

Ramblas 107 Ⓜ Liceu. Daily 8am–1.30pm & 6–9pm. MAP P.35, POCKET MAP C11

It seems hard to believe, but the Ramblas was a war zone during the Spanish Civil War as the city erupted into factionalism in 1937. George Orwell was caught in the crossfire (an episode recorded in his *Homage to Catalonia*) and, with anarchists sacking the city's churches at will, the rich interior of the Baroque Església de Betlem was completely destroyed. However, the main facade on c/del Carme still sports a fine sculpted portal.

PALAU MOJA

Ramblas 188 Ⓜ Liceu ☎ 933 162 740. Tours available by appointment only. MAP P.35, POCKET MAP D11

The arcaded Palau Moja dates from the late eighteenth century and still retains an exterior staircase and elegant great hall. The palace's gallery (entrance is around the corner in c/Portaferrissa) is occasionally open for exhibitions relating to all things Catalan. Take a look, too, at the illustrated tiles above the

fountain at the start of c/de la Portaferrissa, which show the medieval gate (the *Porta Ferriça*) and market that were once sited here.

PALAU DE LA VIRREINA

Ramblas 99 Ⓜ Liceu ☎ 933 161 000, Ⓦ www.bcn.cat/cultura. Galleries Tues–Sun noon–8pm; for current exhibitions see Ⓦ lavirreina.bcn.cat; information office daily 10am–8.30pm. MAP P.35, POCKET MAP C12

Graceful eighteenth-century Palau de la Virreina is the HQ of the cultural department of the Ajuntament (city council), and there's a ground-floor information centre where you can find out about upcoming events and buy tickets. Various galleries and studios house changing exhibitions of contemporary art and photography, while at the back of the palace courtyard you can usually see the city's enormous Carnival giants (*gegants*), representing the thirteenth-century Catalan king Jaume I and his wife Violant. The origin of these ornate, five-metre-high figures is unclear, though they probably first enlivened medieval travelling fairs and are now an integral part of Barcelona's festival parades.

MERCAT DE LA BOQUERIA

Ramblas 91 Ⓜ Liceu ☎ 933 182 584, Ⓦ www.boqueria.info. Mon–Sat 8am–8.30pm. MAP P.35, POCKET MAP C12

Other markets might protest, but the city's glorious main food market really can claim to be the best in Spain. It's officially called the Mercat Sant Josep, though everyone knows it as La Boqueria. A riot of noise and colour, it's as popular with locals who come here to shop daily as with snap-happy tourists. Everything radiates out from the central fish and seafood

An insider's guide to the Ramblas

There are pavement cafés and restaurants all the way down the Ramblas, but the food can be indifferent and the prices high, so be warned. (For better value, go into the Boqueria market, where the traders eat.) The strolling crowds, too, provide perfect cover for pickpockets – keep a wary eye on your possessions at all times, especially when watching the buskers or shopping at the kiosks. And – however easy it looks to win – if you're going to play cards or dice with a man on a street, you've only yourself to blame if you get ripped off.

stalls – bunches of herbs, pots of spices, baskets of wild mushrooms, mounds of cheese and sausage, racks of bread, hanging hams and overloaded meat counters. It's easy to get waylaid at the entrance by the fruit cartons and squeezed juices, but the flagship fruit and veg stalls here are pricey. It's better value further in, in particular in the small outdoor square just beyond the north side of the market where the local allotment holders and market-gardeners gather. Everyone has a favourite market stall, but don't miss *Petras* and its array of wild mushrooms (it's at the back, by the market restaurant, *La Garduña*) or *Frutas y Verduras Jesús y Carmen*, which is framed with colourful bundles of exotic chillies. And of course, there are some

excellent stand-up tapas bars in the market as well, open from dawn onward for the traders.

PLAÇA DE LA BOQUERIA

Ⓜ Liceu. MAP P.35, POCKET MAP C12

The halfway point of the Ramblas is marked by Plaça de la Boqueria, with its large round pavement **mosaic by Joan Miró**. It's become something of a symbol for the city and is one of a number of public works in Barcelona by the artist, who was born just a couple of minutes' away in the Barri Gòtic. Over at Ramblas 82, **Casa Bruno Quadros** – the lower floor is now the Caixa Sabadell – was built in the 1890s to house an umbrella store, which explains its delightful facade, decorated with Oriental designs, dragons and parasols.

MERCAT DE LA BOQUERIA

GRAN TEATRE DEL LICEU

GRAN TEATRE DEL LICEU

Ramblas 51–59 Ⓜ Liceu Ⓦ www.liceu
barcelona.cat. Box office ☎ 934 859 913;
tours ☎ 934 859 914, daily (except Aug) at
10am, 11.30am, noon, 12.30pm & 1pm.
Guided tour €11.50, other tours €5.50.
MAP P.35, POCKET MAP C13

Barcelona's celebrated opera
house was first founded in 1847
and rebuilt after a fire in 1861
to become Spain's grandest
theatre. Regarded as a bastion
of the city's late nineteenth-
century commercial and
intellectual classes, the Liceu
was devastated again in 1893
when an anarchist threw two
bombs into the stalls during a
production of *William Tell*
– twenty people died. It then
burned down for the third time
in 1994, when a workman's
blowtorch set fire to the
scenery of an opera set. The
latest restoration of the lavishly
decorated interior took five
years, and the opera house
opened again in 1999, complete
with a modern extension, the
Espai Liceu, which also houses
a music and gift shop and a
café. You'll see and learn most

on the more expensive,
hour-long 10am guided tour
(the other, shorter, cheaper
tours are self-guided).
Highlights include the Salon of
Mirrors and the impressive
gilded auditorium containing
almost 2300 seats, making it
one of the world's largest opera
houses. Some tours also include
the option of visiting the
glorious *modernista*-styled
rooms of the Cercle del Liceu,
the opera house's private
members' club.

For Liceu performances,
check the website for details
and make bookings well in
advance. The traditional
meeting place for audience and
performers alike, meanwhile,
is the famous *Café de l'Opera*,
just across the Ramblas.

ARTS SANTA MÒNICA

Ramblas 7 Ⓜ Drassanes ☎ 935 671 110,
Ⓦ www.artsantamonica.cat. Tues–Sat
11am–9pm, Sun & hols 11am–5pm. Free.
MAP P.35, POCKET MAP C14

Down from the Liceu, the
bottom part of the Ramblas
(Rambla de Santa Mònica) was

The Ramblas statues

Time stands still for no man – not even for the famed human statues of the Ramblas, who make a living out of doing just that. A motley crew of figures once flanked the length of the street, but change is inevitable, and in 2012 – in an effort to keep pedestrian traffic moving, and prevent pickpockets from preying on the gathering crowds – the city moved the human statues to the wide stretch of Rambla de Santa Mònica. The number of statues was then capped to thirty a year, with performers being required to audition for the permit-only slots. Despite the cutback in territory and number, the remaining human statues are still an attraction. Be it Galileo or a horned demon, these stalwarts of the Ramblas continue to climb upon their plinths and strike a pose. What else is a statue going to do?

historically a theatre and red-light district, and it still has a rough edge or two. Flagship building is the Augustinian convent of Santa Mònica, which dates originally from 1626, making it the oldest building on the Ramblas. It was remodelled in the 1980s as a contemporary arts centre, and hosts regularly changing exhibitions – it's an unusual gallery space dedicated to "artistic creation, science, thought and communication" so there's usually something worth seeing, from an offbeat art installation to a show of archive photographs. Meanwhile, pavement artists and palm readers set up stalls outside on the Ramblas, augmented on weekend afternoons by a street market selling jewellery, beads, bags and ornaments.

MUSEU DE CERA

Ramblas 4–6, entrance on Ptge. de Banca Ⓜ Drassanes ☎ 933 172 649, Ⓦ www .museocerabcn.com. July–Sept daily 10am–10pm; Oct–June Mon–Fri 10am–1.30pm & 4–7.30pm, Sat & Sun 11am–2pm & 4.30–8.30pm. €15.
MAP P.35, POCKET MAP C14

You'd have to be hard-hearted indeed not to derive some pleasure from the city's wax museum. Located in a nineteenth-century bank building, it presents an ever more ludicrous series of tableaux in cavernous salons and gloomy corridors, depicting recitals, meetings and parlour gatherings attended by an anachronistic – not to say perverse – collection of characters, from Hitler to Princess Diana. Needless to say, it's enormously amusing, culminating in cheesy underwater tunnels and space capsules and an unpleasant "Terror Room". Even if this doesn't appeal it is definitely worth poking your head into the museum's extraordinary grotto bar, the *Bosc de les Fades*.

STREET PERFORMER, RAMBLAS

Shops

CASA BEETHOVEN

Ramblas 97 Ⓜ Liceu. Mon–Fri 9am–2pm &
4–8pm, Sat 9am–2pm & 5–8pm; closed Aug.
MAP P.35, POCKET MAP C12

Wonderful old shop selling
sheet music from wooden
library stacks, plus CDs and
music reference books – not
just classical, but also rock, jazz
and flamenco.

EL CORTE INGLÉS

Pl. de Catalunya 14 Ⓜ Catalunya Ⓦ www
.elcorteingles.es. Mon–Sat 9.30am–9.30pm.
MAP P.35, POCKET MAP E10

The city's biggest department
store has nine retail floors
(fashion, cosmetics, household
goods, toys), a good basement
supermarket and – best of all
– a top-floor café with terrific
views. For music, books,
computers and sports gear,
head for the nearby branch at
Av. Portal de l'Angel 19.

EL TRIANGLE

Pl. de Catalunya 4 Ⓜ Catalunya
Ⓦ eltriangle.es. Mon–Sat 10am–10pm.
MAP P.35, POCKET MAP D10

Shopping centre dominated
by the flagship FNAC store,
which specializes in books
(good English-language

selection), music, film and
computer stuff. Also a
Camper (for shoes), Habitat
(homeware) and Sephora
(cosmetics), plus lots of
boutiques, and a café on the
ground floor next to the
extensive newspaper and
magazine section.

Cafés

CAFÉ DE L'OPERA

Ramblas 74 Ⓜ Liceu ☎ 933 177 585.
Ⓦ www.cafeoperabcn.com. Daily
8.30am–2.30am. MAP P.35, POCKET MAP C12

If you're going to pay through
the nose for a seat on the
Ramblas, it may as well be at
this famous old café-bar
opposite the opera house,
which retains a *fin-de-siècle*
feel. Surprisingly, it's not a
complete tourist-fest and locals
pop in day and night for
drinks, cakes and tapas.

CAFÉ ZURICH

Pl. Catalunya 1 Ⓜ Catalunya ☎ 933 179 153.
Mon–Fri 8am–11pm, Sat 11am–midnight, Sun
9am–11pm. MAP P.35, POCKET MAP D10

The most famous meet-and-
greet café in town, right at
the top of the Ramblas and
underneath El Triangle
shopping centre. It's good for
croissants and breakfast
sandwiches and there's a huge
pavement terrace, but sit
inside if you don't want to be
bothered by endless rounds of
buskers and beggars.

ESCRIBÀ

Ramblas 83 Ⓜ Liceu ☎ 933 016 027.
Ⓦ www.escriba.es. Daily 9am–9pm. MAP P.35,
POCKET MAP C12

Wonderful pastries and cakes
from the renowned Escribà
family business in a classy
Art Nouveau shop. Many
rate this as the best bakery
in Barcelona.

ESCRIBÀ

BAR PINOTXO

Mercat de la Boqueria, Ramblas 91
Ⓜ Liceu ☎ 933 171 731, ⓦ pinotxobar.com.
Mon–Sat 6.30am–4pm; closed Aug. MAP P.35,
POCKET MAP C12

The market's most renowned refuelling stop – just inside the main entrance on the right – attracts traders, chefs, tourists and celebs, who stand three deep at busy times. A coffee, a grilled sandwich and a glass of *cava* is the local breakfast of choice, or let the cheery staff steer you towards the tapas and daily specials (€5–15), anything from a slice of tortilla to fried baby squid.

LA GARDUÑA

Mercat de la Boqueria, c/Jerusalem 18
Ⓜ Liceu ☎ 647 223 776. Mon–Sat
9am–11pm. MAP P.35, POCKET MAP C12

Tucked away at the back of the frenetic Boqueria market, this is an especially enticing place for lunch when there's a good-value *menú del dia* – basically, you'll be offered the best of the day's produce at pretty reasonable prices, and if you're lucky you'll get an outdoor seat with market views. At dinner, most mains are €9–20.

Restaurants and tapas bars

AMAYA

Ramblas 20–24 Ⓜ Drassanes ☎ 933 021 037,
ⓦ www.restauranteamaya.com. Daily 1.30–4pm
& 7–11.30pm. MAP P.35, POCKET MAP C14

There aren't too many reliable places on the Ramblas itself, but *Amaya* – a fixture since 1941 – fits the bill for a meal. The restaurant (its *terrassa* offers front-row seats to the action on the Ramblas) serves Basque seafood specialities, from octopus to anchovies, as well as rice dishes, *canelons* (Catalan–style cannelloni) and rich oxtail stew. The lunch and tapas menus offer the cheapest and most enjoyable introduction to the cuisine; otherwise, main dishes cost €14–20.

Bar

BOSC DE LES FADES

Ptge. de Banca 5 Ⓜ Drassanes ☎ 933 172
649. Mon–Thurs 10am–1am, Fri 10am–1.30am,
Sat 11am–2am, Sun 11am–1am. MAP P.35,
POCKET MAP C14

Down an alley by the wax museum, the "Forest of the Fairies" is festooned with gnarled plaster tree trunks, hanging branches, fountains and stalactites. It's a bit cheesy, which is perhaps why it's a huge hit with the twenty-something crowd who huddle in the grottoes with a cocktail or two.

Barri Gòtic

The Barri Gòtic, or Gothic Quarter, on the east side of the Ramblas forms the heart of Barcelona's Old Town. Its buildings date principally from the fourteenth and fifteenth centuries, and culminate in the extraordinary Gothic cathedral known as La Seu. Around here are hidden squares, some fascinating museums, the city's old Jewish quarter and the remains of the Roman walls. It takes the best part of a day to see everything – longer if you factor in the abundant cafés, antique shops, boutiques and galleries. Note that the southern area, en route to the harbour, is rather less gentrified than the cathedral district – take care at night in the poorly lit streets. Metros Liceu (west), Jaume I (east) and Drassanes (south) provide access to the neighbourhood.

LA SEU

Pl. de la Seu Ⓜ Jaume I. Mon–Fri 8am–12.45pm & 5.15–7.30pm, Sat 8am–12.45pm & 5.15–7.30pm, Sun & hols 8am–1.45pm & 5.15–7.30pm. Free during general admission times, otherwise tourist admission charge obligatory (Mon–Sat 1–5pm, Sun 2–5pm), €6, includes entrance to all sections. MAP P.44–45, POCKET MAP E12

Barcelona's cathedral is one of the great Gothic buildings of Spain, dedicated to Santa Eulàlia, who was martyred by the Romans for daring to prefer Christianity – her ornate tomb rests in a crypt beneath the high altar. A magnificent fourteenth-century **cloister** looks over a lush tropical garden complete with soaring palm trees and honking white geese. There's also glittering church treasure on show in the cathedral museum.

Performances of the Catalan national dance, the *sardana*, take place in front of the cathedral (usually Sun at noon, plus Easter–Nov Sat at 6pm), while the pedestrianized Avinguda de la Catedral hosts an antiques market every Thursday, and a Christmas craft fair in December.

MUSEU DIOCESÀ

Av. Catedral 4 Ⓜ Jaume I ☎ 933 152 213. Tues–Fri 11am–6pm, Sat 11am–2pm & 2.30–6pm, Sun 11am–2pm. €6. MAP P.44–45, POCKET MAP E12

Stand back to look at the cathedral buildings and it's easy to see the line of Roman towers that originally stood on this spot incorporated into the later medieval structures. One such tower formed part of the

LA SEU

PLAÇA DEL REI

cathedral almshouse, now the Museu Diocesà, whose soaring spaces have been beautifully adapted to show an impressive collection of religious art and church treasures. The ticket also includes entrance into the temporary art and architecture exhibitions held here.

REIAL CERCLE ARTÍSTIC

C/Arcs 5 ⓜ Jaume I ☎ 933 181 774, ⓦ www.dalibarcelona.com. Daily 10am–10pm. €10. MAP P.44–45, POCKET MAP D12

The handsome Gothic palace housing the Royal Art Circle hosts various free exhibitions and concerts, though the big draw is the collection of 44 original sculptures by Salvador Dalí, completed in the 1970s. A lovely terrace restaurant above the Gothic streets also offers a pricey lunch, while on your way to or from the cathedral spare a glance for the graffiti-like frieze surmounting the nearby **Collegi d'Arquitectes** on Plaça Nova – designed by that other inimitable master, Pablo Picasso.

PLAÇA DEL REI

ⓜ Jaume I. MAP P.44–45, POCKET MAP E12

The harmonious enclosed square of Plaça del Rei was once the palace courtyard of the Counts of Barcelona. Stairs climb from here to the palace's main hall, the fourteenth-century **Saló del Tinell**. It was here that Ferdinand and Isabella received Christopher Columbus on his triumphant return from his famous voyage of 1492. At one time the Spanish Inquisition met in the hall, taking full advantage of the popular belief that the walls would move if a lie was spoken. Nowadays it hosts temporary exhibitions, while concerts are occasionally held in the hall or outside in the square. The palace buildings include the beautiful fourteenth-century **Capella de Santa Agata**, and the romantic Renaissance **Torre del Rei Martí**. There's no public access to the tower, but the interiors of the hall and chapel can usually be seen during a visit to the adjacent Museu d'Història de Barcelona.

MUSEU FREDERIC MARÈS

Pl. de Sant Iu 5–6 ⓜ Jaume I ☎ 932 563 500, ⓦ www.museumares.bcn.cat. Tues–Sat 10am–7pm, Sun & hols 11am–8pm. €4.20, free Sun after 3pm & first Sun of the month. MAP P.44–45, POCKET MAP E12

Don't miss a visit to one of the Old Town's most fascinating museums, which occupies a wing of the old royal palace. It celebrates the diverse passions of sculptor, painter and restorer Frederic Marès (1893–1991), whose beautifully presented collection of ancient and medieval sculpture does little to prepare visitors for Marès's true obsession, namely a kaleidoscopic array of curios and collectibles. Entire rooms are devoted to keys and locks, cigarette cards and snuffboxes, fans, gloves and brooches, walking sticks, dolls' houses, old gramophones and archaic bicycles – to list just a sample of what's in the collection.

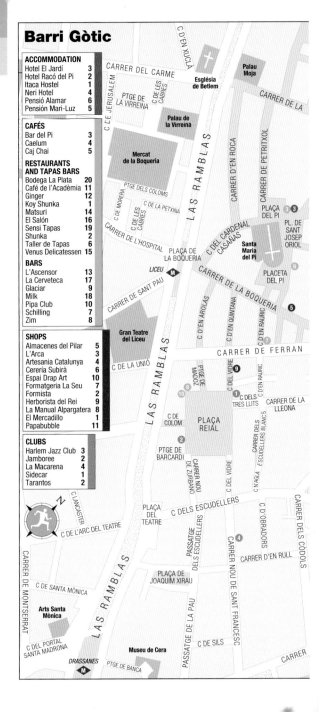

Barri Gòtic

ACCOMMODATION
Hotel El Jardí	3
Hotel Racó del Pi	2
Itaca Hostel	1
Neri Hotel	4
Pensió Alamar	6
Pensión Mari-Luz	5

CAFÉS
Bar del Pi	3
Caelum	4
Caj Chai	5

RESTAURANTS AND TAPAS BARS
Bodega La Plata	20
Café de l'Acadèmia	11
Ginger	12
Koy Shunka	1
Matsuri	14
El Salón	16
Sensi Tapas	19
Shunka	2
Taller de Tapas	6
Venus Delicatessen	15

BARS
L'Ascensor	13
La Cerveteca	17
Glaciar	9
Milk	18
Pipa Club	10
Schilling	7
Zim	8

SHOPS
Almacenes del Pilar	5
L'Arca	3
Artesania Catalunya	4
Cerería Subirà	6
Espai Drap Art	10
Formatgeria La Seu	7
Formista	2
Herborista del Rei	9
La Manual Alpargatera	8
El Mercadillo	1
Papabubble	11

CLUBS
Harlem Jazz Club	3
Jamboree	2
La Macarena	4
Sidecar	1
Tarantos	2

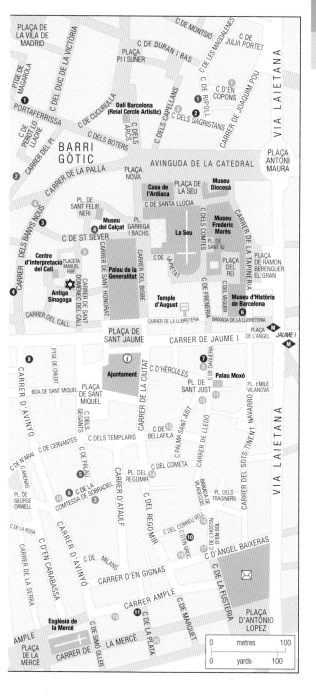

PLAÇA DE
LA VILA DE
MADRID

C DE MONTSIÓ

C DE
JULIA PORTET

C DE DURAN I BAS

PLAÇA
PI I SUNER

PTGE DE
MAGAROLA

C DEL DUC DE LA VICTORIA

C DE LES MAGDALENES

C DE RIPOLL

C D'EN
COPONS

VIA LAIETANA

PORTAFERRISSA

C DE CUCURULLA

C DE JOAQUIM POU

Dali Barcelona
(Reial Cercle Artistic)

C DE
PEROT LO
LLADRE

C DELS CAPELLANS

C DELS SAGRISTANS

C DELS BOTERS

PLAÇA
ANTONI
MAURA

BARRI
GÒTIC

C DELS
ARCS

AVINGUDA DE LA CATEDRAL

CARRER DEL PI

CARRER DE LA PALLA

PLAÇA
NOVA

Casa de
l'Ardiaca

PLAÇA DE
LA SEU

Museu
Diocesà

CARRER DE PEROTLO

C DE SANTA LLÚCIA

Museu
Frederic
Marès

PL. DE
SANT FELIP
NERI

Museu
del Calçat

PL.
GARRIGA
I BACHS

La Seu

C DELS COMTES

CARRER DE LA TAPINERIA

CARRER DELS BANYS NOUS

C DE ST SEVER

PL. DE
SANT IU

PLAÇA
DE RAMON
BERENGUER
EL GRAN

Centre
d'Interpretació
del Call

PLACETA
MANUEL
RIBE

CARRER DE SANT SEVER

C DE
LA PIETAT

PLAÇA
DEL
REI

Palau de la
Generalitat

CARRER DEL BISBE

Museu d'Història
de Barcelona

Antiga
Sinagoga

CARRER DE SANT
DOMENEC DEL CALL

Temple
d'August

C DE FRENERIA

C DEL VEGUER

CARRER DEL CALL

CARRER DE LA LLIBRETERIA

BAIXADA DE LA LLIBRETERIA

PLAÇA DE
SANT JAUME

CARRER DE JAUME I

PLAÇA
DE L'ÀNGEL

JAUME I

Ajuntament

C D'HÉRCULES

C DE DAGUERIA

Palau Moxó

PL. EMILE
VILANOVA

PTGE DE CREDIT

CARRER DE LA CIUTAT

PL. DE
SANT JUST

CARRER D'AVINYO

BDA DE SANT MIQUEL

PLAÇA
DE SANT
MIQUEL

C DELS
GEGANTS

C DE
BELLAFILA

C DE LLEDÓ

CARRER DEL SOTS-TINENT NAVARRO

C DELS TEMPLARIS

C PALMA SANT JUST

VIA LAIETANA

C DE N'ARAI

ARENAS

C DE CERVANTES

C DE PALAU

PL. DEL
REGOMIR

C DEL COMETA

PL. DE
GEORGE
ORWELL

C DE LA
COMTESSA DE SOBRADIEL

CARRER D'ATAULF

BAIXADA DE
VILADECOLS

PL. DELS
TRAGINERS

C DE LA ROSA

C DEL REGOMIR

C DEL CORREU VELL

CARRER DE LA SERRA

CARRER D'EN CARABASSA

C DE. MILANS

C D'EN GROC

C DE L'HOSTAL
D'EN SOL

C D'ÀNGEL BAIXERAS

CARRER D'EN GIGNAS

CARRER AMPLE

C DE LA FUSTERIA

Església de
la Mercè

C DE SIMÓ OLLER

LA MERCÈ

C DE MARQUET

C DE LA PLATA

PLAÇA
D'ANTÒNIO
LOPEZ

AMPLE

PLAÇA
DE LA
MERCÈ

CARRER DE

| 0 | metres | 100 |
| 0 | yards | 100 |

45

MUSEU D'HISTÒRIA DE BARCELONA (MUHBA)

Pl. del Rei, entrance on c/del Veguer
Ⓜ Jaume I ☎ 932 562 100, Ⓦ www
.museuhistoria.bcn.cat. Tues–Sat 10am–7pm,
Sun 10am–8pm. €7. MAP P.44–45, POCKET MAP E12

The Barcelona History Museum comprises half a dozen sites across the city, though its principal hub is what's known as the "Conjunt Monumental" (or monumental ensemble) of Plaça del Rei, whose crucial draw is an amazing underground archeological section – nothing less than the remains of the Roman city of Barcino (first century BC to the sixth century AD), which stretch under the surrounding streets as far as the cathedral. Excavations and explanatory diagrams show the full extent of the streets and buildings – from lookout towers to laundries – while models, mosaics, murals and finds help flesh out the reality of daily life in Barcino.

There's a well-stocked book and gift shop on site (entrance on c/Llibreteria), while the museum ticket also allows entry to the other MUHBA sites, notably the Poble Sec air-raid shelter and Pedralbes monastery. Roman fans should also take the opportunity to see the four remarkable Roman columns of the Temple d'August in the courtyard of the nearby Centre Excursionista de Catalunya (c/Paradis 10; closed Mon).

ESGLÉSIA DE SANTA MARÍA DEL PI

Pl. Sant Josep Oriol Ⓜ Liceu. April–Oct
Mon–Sat 10am–7pm, Sun & hols 4–8pm;
Nov–March Mon–Sat 10am–6pm, Sun & hols
4–7pm. €4. MAP P.44–45, POCKET MAP D12

The fourteenth-century church of Santa María is known for its marvellous stained glass, particularly a 10m-wide rose window (often claimed, rather boldly, to be the largest in the world). The church flanks Plaça Sant Josep Oriol, the prettiest of three delightful adjacent squares and an ideal place for an outdoor coffee and a browse around the weekend **artists' market** (Sat 11am–8pm, Sun 11am–2pm).

The church is named – like the squares on either side, Plaça del Pi and Plaçeta del Pi – after the pine tree that once stood here. A **farmers' market** spills across Plaça del Pi on the first and third Friday,

EXHIBIT AT THE MUSEU D'HISTORIA DE BARCELONA

ESGLÉSIA DE SANTA MARIA DEL PI

Saturday and Sunday of the month, while the characteristic cafés of narrow **Carrer de Petritxol** (off Plaça del Pi) are the places to head to for a cup of hot chocolate – *Dulcinea* at no. 2 is the traditional choice – and a browse around the street's commercial art galleries. The most famous is **Sala Parés** at c/Petritxol 5, well known as the site of Picasso's first solo exhibition.

MUSEU DEL CALÇAT

Pl. Sant Felip Neri 5 ⓜ Liceu ☎ 933 014 533. Tues–Sun & hols 11am–2pm. €2.50. MAP P.44–45, POCKET MAP D12

The former headquarters of the shoemakers' guild (founded in 1202) houses a one-room footwear museum, containing originals dating back to the 1600s as well as oddities like the world's biggest shoe, made for the city's Columbus statue at the bottom of the Ramblas. The museum flanks one side of pretty Plaça Sant Felip Neri, where in summer you can eat outside at the restaurant of the boutique *Neri Hotel*, which sets out candlelit tables in the square.

ANTIGA SINAGOGA

C/Marlet 5, corner with c/Sant Domènec del Call ⓜ Liceu ☎ 933 170 790, ⓦ www.calldebarcelona.org. June–Aug Mon–Fri 10.30am–6.30pm, Sat & Sun 10.30am–2.30pm; Sept–May Mon–Fri 11am–5.30pm, Sat & Sun 11am–3pm. €2.50. MAP P.44–45, POCKET MAP D12

Barcelona's medieval Jewish quarter was centred on c/Sant Domènec del Call, where a synagogue existed from as early as the third century AD until the pogrom of 1391, but even after that date the building survived in various guises and has since been sympathetically restored. The city authorities have signposted a few other points of interest in what's known as "El Call Major", including the **Centre d'Interpretació del Call** in nearby Plaçeta Manuel Ribé (Tues–Fri 11am–2pm, Sat & Sun 11am–7pm; free), whose informative storyboards (in English) shed more light on Barcelona's fascinating Jewish heritage.

PALAU DE LA GENERALITAT

Pl. de Sant Jaume ⓜ Jaume I ☎ 934 024 600. Tours on 2nd and 4th Sun of the month (not Aug), every hour, 10am–noon; also on April 23, and Sept 11 & 24. Passport or ID required. Free. MAP P.44–45, POCKET MAP D12/13

The home of the Catalan government presents its oldest aspect around the side, where the fifteenth-century c/del Bisbe facade contains a medallion portraying Sant Jordi (St George, patron saint of Catalunya). Inside, there's a beautiful first-floor cloister, the intricately worked chapel and salon of Sant Jordi as well as an upper courtyard planted with orange trees. You can visit the interior on a one-hour guided tour on alternate Sundays (only one or two tours each day are in English), while the Generalitat is also open on public holidays, particularly April 23 – the **Dia de Sant Jordi** (St George's Day). A nationalist holiday in Catalunya, this is also a local Valentine's Day, when it's traditional to exchange books and roses.

PLAÇA DE SANT JAUME

ⓜ Jaume I. MAP P.44–45, POCKET MAP D13

The spacious square at the end of the main c/de Ferran is at the heart of city and regional government business, and the traditional place for demonstrations and local festivals. Whistle-happy local police try to keep things moving, while taxis and bike-tour groups weave between the pedestrians.

AJUNTAMENT DE BARCELONA

Pl. de Sant Jaume ⓜ Jaume I ☎ 934 027 000. Public admitted Sun 10am–1.30pm, entrance on c/Font de Sant Miquel. Free. MAP P.44–45, POCKET MAP D13

On the south side of Plaça de Sant Jaume stands Barcelona's city hall. On Sundays you're allowed into the building for a self-guided tour around the splendid marble galleries and staircases. The highlights are the magnificent fourteenth-century council chamber, known as the **Saló de Cent**, and the dramatic historical murals in the **Saló de les Cròniques** (Hall of Chronicles).

PALAU MOXÓ

Pl. de Sant Just 4 ⓜ Jaume I ☎ 933 152 238, ⓦ palaumoxo.com. Guided tours for groups by reservation only. €13. MAP P.44–45, POCKET MAP E13

The Palau Moxó has been in the hands of the same family since 1770, which makes it unique in Barcelona – especially since most other palatial Baroque residences were destroyed during the Civil War. You'll see grand salons and intimate chambers on the weekly guided tours, while regular concerts provide another taste of the noble life.

PLAÇA REIAL

ⓜ Liceu. MAP P.44–45, POCKET MAP C13

The elegant Plaça Reial – hidden behind an archway off the Ramblas – is studded with palm trees and decorated iron

PALAU DE LA GENERALITAT

lamps (designed by the young Antoni Gaudí), and bordered by pastel-coloured arcaded buildings. Sitting in the square certainly puts you in mixed company – buskers, eccentrics, tramps and bemused visitors – though most of the really unsavoury characters have been driven off over the years and predatory waiters are usually the biggest nuisance these days. Don't expect to see too many locals until night falls, when the surrounding bars come into their own. Passing through on a Sunday morning, look in on the **coin and stamp market** (10am–2pm).

CARRER D'AVINYÓ

Ⓜ Liceu. MAP P.44–45, POCKET MAP D13/14

Carrer d'Avinyó, running south from c/de Ferran towards the harbour, cuts through the most atmospheric part of the southern Barri Gòtic. Formerly a red-light district, it still looks the part – lined with dark overhanging buildings – but the funky cafés, streetwear shops and boutiques tell the story of its creeping gentrification. A few rough edges still show, particularly around **Plaça George Orwell**, a favoured hangout for locals with its cheap cafés, restaurants and bars, some of which offer seating on the lively square.

LA MERCÈ

Ⓜ Drassanes. MAP P.44–45, POCKET MAP D14

In the eighteenth century, the harbourside neighbourhood known as La Mercè was home to the nobles and merchants enriched by Barcelona's maritime trade. Most moved north to the more fashionable Eixample later in the nineteenth century, and since then Carrer de la Mercè and surrounding streets (particularly Ample, d'en Gignàs and Regomir) have been home to a series of old-style taverns known as *tascas* or *bodegas* – a glass of wine from the barrel and a plate of tapas here is one of the Old Town's more authentic experiences.

At Plaça de la Mercè, the **Església de la Mercè** is the focus of the city's biggest annual bash, the Festes de la Mercè every September, dedicated to the co-patroness of Barcelona, whose image is paraded from the church. It's an excuse for a week of partying, parades, special events and concerts, culminating in spectacular pyrotechnics along the seafront.

Shops

ALMACENES DEL PILAR

C/Boqueria 43 ⓜ Liceu ⓦ www
.almacenesdelpilar.com. Mon–Sat 10am–2pm
& 4.30–8pm; closed Aug. MAP P.44–45,
POCKET MAP D13

A world of frills, lace, cloth and material used in the making of Spain's traditional regional costumes. You can pick up a decorated fan for just a few euros, though quality items go for a lot more.

L'ARCA

C/Banys Nous 20 ⓜ Liceu ⓦ www.larcadelavia
.com. Mon–Fri 10am–2pm & 5–8pm, Sat 11am–
2pm; closed Aug. MAP P.44–45, POCKET MAP D12

Catalan brides used to fill up their nuptial trunk (l'arca) with embroidered linen and lace, and this shop is a treasure-trove of vintage and antique textiles. Period costumes can be hired or purchased as well – one of Kate Winslet's *Titanic* costumes came from here.

ARTESANIA CATALUNYA

C/Banys Nous 11 ⓜ Liceu ⓦ www.artesania
-catalunya.com. Mon–Sat 10am–8pm, Sun &
hols 10am–2pm. MAP P.44–45, POCKET MAP D12

It's always worth a look in the showroom of the arts and crafts

L'ARCA

promotion board. Exhibitions change but most of the work is contemporary in style, from basketwork to glassware, though traditional methods are still very much encouraged.

CERERÍA SUBIRÀ

Bxda. Llibreteria 7 ⓜ Jaume I. Mon–Thurs
9am–1.30pm & 4–8pm, Fri 9.30am–8pm, Sat
10am–8pm. MAP P.44–45, POCKET MAP E13

Barcelona's oldest shop (it's been here since 1760) boasts a beautiful interior, selling unique handcrafted candles.

ESPAI DRAP ART

C/Groc 1 ⓜ Jaume I ⓦ www.drapart.net.
Tues–Fri 11am–2pm & 5–8pm, Sat 6–9pm.
MAP P.44–45, POCKET MAP E14

The Drap Art creative recycling organisation has a shop and exhibition space for artists to show their wildly inventive wares, from trash bangles to tin bags.

FORMATGERIA LA SEU

C/Dagueria 16 ⓜ Jaume I ⓦ www
.formatgerialaseu.com. Tues–Thurs 10am–2pm
& 5–8pm, Fri & Sat 10am–3.30pm & 5–8pm;
closed Aug. MAP P.44–45, POCKET MAP E13

Sells the best farmhouse cheeses from independent producers all over Spain. Chatty Scottish owner Katherine is usually on hand to advise, and you can try before you buy with a €3 tasting plate – ask about the "formatgelat", a cheese-ice cream fusion that's unique to the shop.

FORMISTA

C/Sagristans 9 ⓜ Jaume I ⓦ www
.formista.com. Mon–Sat noon–9pm.
MAP P.44–45, POCKET MAP E12

Gallery-shop hybrid selling unique handmade objects by international designers and artists. There are sleek leather handbags alongside porcelain jewellery, hand-printed textiles and more.

HERBORISTA DEL REI

C/del Vidre 1 ⓜ Liceu ☎ 933 180 512,
ⓦ herboristadelrei.com. Tues–Fri 4–8pm,
Sat 10am–8pm. MAP P.44–45, POCKET MAP D13
A renowned early nineteenth-century herbalist's shop, tucked off Plaça Reial, which stocks more than 250 medicinal herbs designed to combat all complaints.

LA MANUAL ALPARGATERA

C/d'Avinyó 7 ⓜ Liceu ⓦ www.lamanual
alpargatera.com. Mon–Fri 9.30am–1.30pm &
4.30–8pm, Sat 10am–1.30pm & 4.30–8pm.
MAP P.44–45, POCKET MAP D13
In this traditional workshop they make and sell *alpargatas* (espadrilles) to order, as well as producing other straw, rope and basket work.

EL MERCADILLO

C/Portaferrissa 17 ⓜ Liceu. Mon–Sat
11am–8.30pm. MAP P.44–45, POCKET MAP D12
The camel at the entrance marks this hippy-dippy indoor street market of shops and stalls selling T-shirts, skate-wear, vintage gear and jewellery.

PAPABUBBLE

C/Ample 28 ⓜ Jaume I ⓦ www.papabubble
.com. Mon–Fri 10am–2pm & 4–8.30pm, Sat
10am–8.30pm, Sun 11am–7.30pm; closed
Aug. MAP P.44–45, POCKET MAP D14
Groovy young things roll out home-made candy to a chill-out soundtrack. Come and watch them at work, sample a sweet, and take home a gorgeously wrapped gift.

Cafés

BAR DEL PI

Pl. Sant Josep Oriol 1 ⓜ Liceu ☎ 933 022
123. Tues–Fri 9am–11pm, Sat 9.30am–11pm,
Sun 10am–10pm. MAP P.44–45, POCKET MAP D12
Best known for its terrace tables on one of Barcelona's prettiest squares. Linger over drinks and sandwiches as the Old Town reveals its charms, especially during the weekend artists' market.

CAELUM

C/Palla 8 ⓜ Liceu ☎ 933 026 993,
ⓦ www.caelumbarcelona.com. Mon–Thurs
10am–8.30pm, Fri & Sat 10.30am–11.30pm,
Sun 11.30am–8.30pm; open afternoons in Aug.
MAP P.44–45, POCKET MAP D12
The lovingly packaged confections in this upscale café-deli (the name is Latin for "heaven") are made in convents and monasteries across Spain. Choose from marzipan sweets from Seville, Benedictine preserves or Cistercian cookies.

CAJ CHAI

C/Sant Domènec del Call 12 ⓜ Liceu
☎ 933 019 592, ⓦ www.cajchai.com.
Mon 3–10pm, Tues–Sun 10.30am–10pm.
MAP P.44–45, POCKET MAP D12
This refined back-street boudoir offers a menu of painstakingly prepared teas, from Moroccan mint to organic Nepalese *oolong*, plus brownies, *baklava* and sandwiches.

Restaurants and tapas bars

BODEGA LA PLATA

C/de la Mercè 28 Ⓜ Drassanes ☎ 933 151 009. Mon–Sat 9am–3pm & 6.30–11pm.
MAP P.44–45, POCKET MAP E14

A classic taste of the Old Town, with a marble tapas counter open to the street (anchovies are the speciality) and dirt-cheap wine straight from the barrel.

CAFÉ DE L'ACADÈMIA

C/Lledó 1 Ⓜ Jaume I ☎ 933 198 253. Mon–Fri 1.30–4pm & 8.30–11.30pm; closed 2 weeks in Aug. MAP P.44–45, POCKET MAP E13

Great for a date or a lazy lunch, with creative Catalan dishes served in a romantic stone-flagged restaurant or outside in the medieval square. Expect classy grills, fresh fish, rice dishes, seasonal game and a taste of local favourites like salt cod, wild mushrooms or grilled veg. Prices are pretty reasonable (mains €11–18) and

DRINKER AT BODEGA LA PLATA

it's always busy, so dinner reservations are essential. A no-choice *menú del dia* is a bargain for the quality (and it's even cheaper eaten at the bar).

GINGER

C/Palma Sant Just 1 Ⓜ Jaume I ☎ 933 105 309. Ⓦ www.ginger.cat. Tues–Sat 7.30pm–3am; closed 2 weeks in Aug.
MAP P.44–45, POCKET MAP E13

Cocktails and fancy tapas in a slickly updated 1970s-style setting. It's a world away from *patatas bravas* and battered squid – think roast duck vinaigrette, stuffed aubergine rolls, tuna tartare and vegetarian satay for around €6.50–9 a pop.

KOY SHUNKA

C/Copons 7 Ⓜ Jaume I ☎ 934 127 939. Ⓦ www.koyshunka.com. Tues–Sat 1.30–3pm & 8.30–11.30pm, Sun 1.30–3pm. MAP P.44–45, POCKET MAP E12

The city's hottest Japanese chef, Hideki Matsuhisa, has branched out from his original *Shunka* restaurant with a rather more hip, nearby sister joint, where peerless sushi and dishes like grilled Wagyu beef and roast black cod await. With pricey rice rolls, mains around €20, and €82 and €118 tasting menus, it's a more rarefied experience all round, and you'll definitely need to book.

MATSURI

Pl. Regomir 1 Ⓜ Jaume I ☎ 932 681 535. Ⓦ www.matsuri-restaurante.com. Daily 8pm–midnight. MAP P.44–45, POCKET MAP E13

A soothing place for creative Southeast-Asian cuisine, with a large menu concentrating on Thai-style noodles, salads and curries, as well as sushi, sashimi and tempura dishes. A daily specials list has some more unusual choices, and staff offer friendly advice. Around €30 a head.

EL SALÓN

C/l'Hostal d'en Sol 6–8 Ⓜ Jaume I ☎ 933 152 159, Ⓦ www.elsalon.es. Mon–Sat 8pm–midnight. MAP P.44–45, POCKET MAP E14

It's easy to fall for the cosy charms of *El Salón*, with its candlelit tables in a Gothic dining room and summer terrace in the nearby square. The contemporary Mediterranean menu changes every few months, with inventive salads giving way to things like grilled aubergine, pepper and onion served with goat's cheese, or lamb with mustard and honey sauce. Salads and starters are from €8, with most mains in the range of €10 to €16.

SENSI TAPAS

C/Ample 26 Ⓜ Jaume I ☎ 932 956 588, Ⓦ www.sensi.es. Daily 7pm–midnight. MAP P.44–45, POCKET MAP D14

Best to make reservations as this intimate space in stone and dark wood and splashes of red quickly fills with diners looking for tapas with an exotic spin. There are impeccably executed classics like buttery *patatas bravas*, but the stars of the show, such as the tender Iberian pork *tataki*, take their cues from further afield (€5–12).

SHUNKA

C/Sagristans 5 Ⓜ Jaume I ☎ 934 124 991. Tues–Sun 1.30–3.30pm & 8.30–11.30pm; closed 4 weeks in Aug & Sept. MAP P.44–45. POCKET MAP E12

Locals think this is the best Japanese restaurant in the Old Town – it's certainly always busy, so advance reservations are essential, though you might strike lucky if you're prepared to eat early or late. The open kitchen and bustling staff are half the show, while the food – sushi to udon noodles – is really good. Around €40.

GINGER

TALLER DE TAPAS

Pl. Sant Josep Oriol 9 Ⓜ Liceu ☎ 933 018 020, Ⓦ www.tallerdetapas.com. Daily noon–midnight (Fri & Sat until 1am). MAP P.44–45, POCKET MAP D12

The fashionable "tapas workshop" sucks in tourists with its pretty location by the church of Santa María del Pi. There's a year-round outdoor terrace, while the open kitchen turns out reliable, market-fresh dishes, with fish a speciality at dinner, from grilled langoustine to seared tuna (most tapas €4–12). There are other branches around town, (including one at c/Argenteria 51 in the Born), though this was the first.

VENUS DELICATESSEN

C/d'Avinyó 25 Ⓜ Liceu ☎ 936 760 315. Mon–Fri 8.30am–1am, Sat & Sun 10am–2am. MAP P.44–45, POCKET MAP D13

Not a deli, despite the name, but it's a handy place serving Mediterranean bistro cuisine throughout the day and night. It's also good for vegetarians, with things like lasagne, couscous, moussaka and salads, mostly meat-free and costing around €7–10.

Bars

L'ASCENSOR

C/Bellafila 3 Ⓜ Jaume I ☎ 933 185 347.
Daily 6pm–2am. MAP P.44–45, POCKET MAP E13
Sliding antique wooden
elevator doors signal the
entrance to "The Lift", but it's
no theme bar – just an
easy-going local hangout, great
for a late-night drink.

LA CERVETECA

C/d'en Gignàs 25 Ⓜ Jaume I ☎ 933 150 407,
Ⓦ www.lacerveteca.com. Mon–Thurs & Sun
6–11pm, Fri & Sat 6pm–midnight. MAP P.44–45,
POCKET MAP E14
La Cerveteca offers the city's
best world beer selection,
available to drink in or take
out. Brews are taken seriously
here, but it's not a beard-and-
sandals beer-fest, more a
modern art, Muddy Waters,
Latino-beat kind of place for
ale enthusiasts.

GLACIAR

Pl. Reial 3 Ⓜ Liceu ☎ 933 021 163.
Mon–Thurs noon–2.30am, Fri & Sat
noon–3am, Sun 11am–2.30am. MAP P.44–45,
POCKET MAP C13
At this traditional Barcelona
meeting point the terrace
seating is packed most sunny
evenings and at weekends, and
the comings and goings in the
Old Town's funkiest square are
half the entertainment.

MILK

C/d'en Gignàs 21 Ⓜ Jaume I ☎ 932 680 922,
Ⓦ www.milkbarcelona.com. Daily 9am–2am.
MAP P.44–45, POCKET MAP E14
Irish-owned bar and bistro
that's carved a real niche as a
welcoming neighbourhood
hangout. Decor, they say, is that
of a "millionaire's drawing
room", with its sofas, cushions
and antique chandeliers. Get
there early for the famously
relaxed brunch (daily

9am–4.30pm), or there's dinner
and cocktails every night to a
funky soundtrack.

PIPA CLUB

Pl. Reial 3 Ⓜ Liceu ☎ 933 024 732,
Ⓦ www.bpipaclub.com. Daily 10pm–3am.
MAP P.44–45, POCKET MAP C13
Historically a pipe-smoker's
haunt, it's a wood-panelled,
jazzy, late-night kind of place
– ring the bell to be let in and
make your way up the stairs.

SCHILLING

C/de Ferran 23 Ⓜ Liceu ☎ 933 176 787,
Ⓦ www.cafeschilling.com. Daily 10am–3am.
MAP P.44–45, POCKET MAP D13
Something of a haven on this
heavily touristed drag, *Schilling*
has a certain European
"grand-café" style, with its high
ceilings, big windows and
upmarket feel. It has a loyal gay
following, but it's a mixed,
chilled place to meet friends,
grab a *copa* and move on.

ZIM

C/Dagueria 20 Ⓜ Jaume I. Mon–Sat 6–11pm;
closed Aug. MAP P.44–45, POCKET MAP E13
The owner of the adjacent
Formatgeria La Seu (cheese
shop) offers up this tiny,
hole-in-the-wall tasting bar

L'ASCENSOR

for selected wines from boutique producers. It can be a real squeeze, and hours are somewhat flexible, but for a reviving glass or two accompanied by farmhouse cheese, cured meat and artisan-made bread, you can't beat it.

Clubs

HARLEM JAZZ CLUB

C/Comtessa de Sobradiel 8 Ⓜ Jaume I
☎ 933 100 755, ⓦ www.harlemjazzclub.es.
Closed Aug. MAP P.44–45, POCKET MAP D13

For many years *the* hot place for jazz, where every style gets an airing, from African and Gypsy to flamenco and fusion. Live music Tues–Sun at 10.30pm and midnight (weekends 11.30pm & 2am). Entry €5–10, depending on the night and the act.

JAMBOREE

Pl. Reial 17 Ⓜ Liceu ☎ 933 191 789, ⓦ www
.masimas.com. MAP P.44–45, POCKET MAP C13

They don't get the big jazz names here that they used to, but the nightly gigs (at 8pm & 10pm; from €12) still pull in the crowds, while the wild Monday night WTF jazz, funk and hip-hop jam session (from 8pm; €5) is a city fixture. Stay on for the club, which kicks in after midnight (entry €10) and you get funky sounds and retro pop, rock and disco until 5am.

LA MACARENA

C/Nou de Sant Francesc 5 Ⓜ Drassanes
ⓦ www.macarenaclub.com. Mon–Thurs & Sun 11.45pm–5am, Fri & Sat 11.45pm–6am.
MAP P.44–45, POCKET MAP D14

Once a place where flamenco tunes were offered up to La Macarena, the Virgin of Seville – now, a heaving temple to all things electro. Entry free until around 1am, then from €5.

PERFORMER AT TARANTOS

SIDECAR

Pl. Reial 7 Ⓜ Liceu ☎ 933 177 666,
ⓦ www.sidecarfactoryclub.com. Mon–Thurs 7pm–5am, Fri & Sat 7pm–6am. MAP P.44–45, POCKET MAP C13

Hip music club – pronounced "See-day-car" – with gigs (usually at 10.30pm) and DJs (from 12.30am) that champion rock, indie, roots and fusion acts, so a good place to check out the latest Catalan hip-hop, rumba and flamenco sounds. Entry €7–10, though some gigs up to €20.

TARANTOS

Pl. Reial 17 Ⓜ Liceu ☎ 933 191 789, ⓦ www
.masimas.com. MAP P.44–45, POCKET MAP C13

Jamboree's sister club is the place for short, exuberant flamenco tasters, where young singers, dancers and guitarists perform nightly at 8.30pm, 9.30pm & 10.30pm (with extra sessions in July and August). Purists are a bit sniffy, but it's a great introduction to the scene. Entry €10.

Port Vell and Barceloneta

Barcelona has an urban waterfront that merges seamlessly with the Old Town, providing an easy escape from the claustrophobic medieval streets. The harbour at the bottom of the Ramblas has been thoroughly overhauled in recent years and Port Vell (Old Port), as it's now known, presents a series of heavyweight tourist attractions, from sightseeing boats and maritime museum to aquarium and IMAX cinema. By way of contrast, Barceloneta – the wedge of land to the east, backing the marina – retains its eighteenth-century character, and the former fishing quarter is still the most popular place to come and eat paella, fish and seafood. Metro Drassanes, at the bottom of the Ramblas, is the best starting point for Port Vell; Barceloneta has its own metro station.

MIRADOR DE COLÓN

Pl. Portal de la Pau ⓜ Drassanes ☎ 933 025 224. March–Sept daily 8.30am–8.30pm; Oct–Feb daily 8.30am–7.30pm. €4. MAP P.58–59, POCKET MAP C15

The monument at the foot of the Ramblas commemorates the visit made by Christopher Columbus in June 1493, when the navigator received a royal welcome in Barcelona. Columbus tops a grandiose iron column, 52m high, guarded by lions, and you can ride the lift up to the panoramic viewing platform at Columbus's feet. Meanwhile, from the quayside in front of the Columbus monument, Las Golondrinas sightseeing boats depart on regular trips throughout the year around the inner harbour.

MUSEU MARÍTIM

Av. de les Drassanes ⓜ Drassanes ☎ 933 429 920, ⓦ www.mmb.cat. Daily 10am–8pm. MAP P.58–59, POCKET MAP B14/15

Barcelona's medieval shipyards, or Drassanes, were in continuous use – fitting and arming Catalunya's war fleet or trading vessels – until well into the eighteenth century. The stone-vaulted buildings make a fitting home for the city's excellent Maritime Museum, though a large-scale renovation project means access is restricted, probably until sometime in 2015. In the meantime, there's cut-price admission (free on Sun after

3pm) to one or two changing exhibitions that draw on the museum collections, and continued access to museum activities, shop and café. The ticket also includes a short tour of the *Santa Eulàlia*, a vintage three-masted schooner moored down on the Moll de la Fusta harbourside (closed Mon, check hours at the museum).

L'AQUÀRIUM

Moll d'Espanya ⓜ Drassanes ☎ 932 217 474, ⓦ www.aquariumbcn.com. Daily: July & Aug 9.30am–11pm; June & Sept 9.30am–9.30pm; Oct–May 9.30am–9pm; until 9.30pm at weekends. €20. MAP P.58–59, POCKET MAP G8–H8

Port Vell's high-profile aquarium drags in families and school parties throughout the year to see "a magical world, full of mystery". Or, to be more precise, to see 11,000 fish and sea creatures in 35 themed tanks representing underwater caves, tropical reefs and other maritime habitats. It's vastly overpriced, and despite the claims of excellence it offers few new experiences, save perhaps the 80-metre-long walk-through underwater tunnel, which brings you face to face with gliding rays and cruising sharks.

MAREMÀGNUM

Moll d'Espanya ⓜ Drassanes. Daily 10am–10pm. MAP P.58–59, POCKET MAP G8

From near the Columbus statue, the wooden Rambla de Mar swing bridge strides across the harbour to the Maremàgnum mall and leisure centre on Moll d'Espanya. It's a typically bold piece of Catalan design, its soaring glass lines tempered by the undulating wooden walkways that provide scintillating views back across the harbour to the city. Inside are two floors of gift shops and boutiques, plus a range of cafés and fast-food outlets.

IMAX PORT VELL

Moll d'Espanya ⓜ Drassanes ☎ 932 251 111, ⓦ www.imaxportvell.com. Screenings 11am–10pm, later at weekends. Tickets €9.75 or €13.70 for 2 films. MAP P.58–59, POCKET MAP G8–H8

Barcelona's IMAX theatre has three screens showing films virtually hourly in 3D or giant-screen format. The themes are familiar – forces of nature, heroic exploration, alien adventure, etc, and some Hollywood 3D blockbusters are shown, but films are in Spanish or Catalan only.

THE CROSS-HARBOUR CABLE CAR

a museum tracing the history of Catalunya from the Stone Age to the present day. Poke around the interior of a Roman grain ship or compare the rival nineteenth-century architectural plans for the Eixample. The top-floor café-bar boasts a glorious view of the city from its terrace – no museum ticket needed – while the flash restaurants in the **Palau de Mar** arcade below overlook the busy marina.

BARCELONETA

Ⓜ Barceloneta. MAP P.58–59, POCKET MAP H8–J7

There's no finer place for lunch on a sunny day than Barceloneta, an eighteenth-century neighbourhood of tightly packed gridded streets with bustling harbour on one side and sandy beach on the other. There's a local market, the **Mercat de la Barceloneta**

MUSEU D'HISTÒRIA DE CATALUNYA

Palau de Mar, Pl. de Pau Vila 3
Ⓜ Barceloneta ☎ 932 254 700, ⓦ www
.mhcat.net. Tues–Sat 10am–7pm (Wed until 8pm), Sun & hols 10am–2.30pm. €4.50; last Tues of month free. MAP P.58–59, POCKET MAP F15

A dramatic harbourside warehouse conversion contains

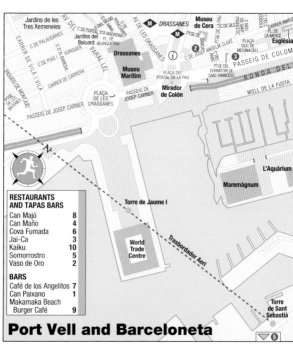

RESTAURANTS AND TAPAS BARS	
Can Majó	8
Can Maño	4
Cova Fumada	6
Jai-Ca	3
Kaiku	10
Somorrostro	5
Vaso de Oro	2

BARS	
Café de los Angelitos	7
Can Paixano	1
Makamaka Beach Burger Café	9

Port Vell and Barceloneta

The cross-harbour cable car

The most thrilling ride in the city is across the harbour on the Trasbordador Aeri, or cable car, which sweeps from the Sant Sebastià tower at the foot of Barceloneta to Montjuïc. Departures are every 15min (daily: March–May & Sept–Oct 11am–7pm; June–Aug 11am–8pm; Nov–Feb 11am–5.30pm; €11 one-way, €16.50 return), but expect queues in summer and at weekends as the cars only carry about twenty people at a time.

(Mon–Thurs & Sat 7am–3pm, Fri 7am–8pm), with a couple of excellent bars and restaurants, while Barceloneta's famous seafood restaurants are found across the neighbourhood, but most characteristically lined along the harbourside Passeig Joan de Borbó.

PLATJA DE SANT SEBASTIÀ

Ⓜ Barceloneta. MAP P.58–59, POCKET MAP G9–K8

Barceloneta's beach – the first in a series of sandy city beaches – curves from the flanks of the neighbourhood, past the swimming pools of the Club Natació and out to the landmark sail-shaped *W Barcelona* hotel. Closer to the Barceloneta end there are beach bars, outdoor cafés and sculptures, while a double row of palms backs the esplanade that runs above the sands as far as the Port Olímpic (a 15min walk). Bladers, skaters, joggers and cyclists have one of the Med's best views for company.

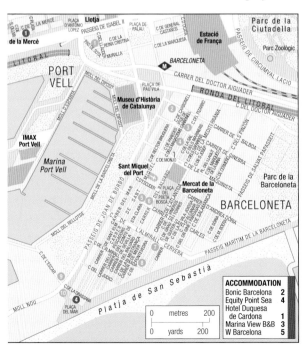

ACCOMMODATION	
Bonic Barcelona	2
Equity Point Sea	4
Hotel Duquesa de Cardona	1
Marina View B&B	3
W Barcelona	5

59

Restaurants and tapas bars

SEAFOOD TAPAS

CAN MAJÓ

C/Almirall Aixada 23 Ⓜ Barceloneta ☎ 932
215 455, Ⓦ www.canmajo.es. Tues–Sat 1–4pm
& 8–11.30pm, Sun 1–4pm. MAP P.58–59,
POCKET MAP H8

This ticks all the boxes for a
quality seafood meal, with a
bonus of a lovely summer
terrassa by the beach
promenade where you can tuck
into wonderful rice dishes,
fideuà (noodles with seafood),
suquet (fish stew) or grilled
fish. Expect to spend €40–50
a head.

CAN MAÑO

C/Baluard 12 Ⓜ Barceloneta ☎ 933 193 082.
Mon 8–11pm, Tues–Fri 8.15–11am, 12.15–4pm
& 8–11pm, Sat 8.15–11am & 12.45–4pm;
closed Aug. MAP P.58–59, POCKET MAP F15

There's rarely a tourist in sight
in this classic old-fashioned
diner. Basically, your choice is
fried or grilled fish,
supplemented by a few daily
seafood specials and basic
meat dishes. It's an authentic,
no-frills experience that's
likely to cost you less than €15
a head.

COVA FUMADA

C/Baluard 56 Ⓜ Barceloneta ☎ 932 214 061.
Mon–Wed 9am–3.20pm, Thurs & Fri
9am–3.20pm & 6–8.20pm, Sat 9am–1.30pm;
closed Aug. MAP P.58–59, POCKET MAP H8

Behind brown wooden doors
on the market square (there's
no sign) is this rough-and-
ready tavern with battered
marble tables and antique
barrels. That it's always packed
is a testament to the quality
of the market-fresh tapas
(€2–10), from the griddled
prawns to the *bomba* (spicy
potato meatball).

JAI-CA

C/Ginebra 9 & 13 Ⓜ Barceloneta ☎ 932 683
265. No.9 Mon & Wed–Sun noon–midnight;
No.13 Tues–Sun 9am–midnight. MAP P.58–59,
POCKET MAP F15

A great choice for tapas (dishes
up to €10), with bundles of
razor clams, stuffed mussels,
crisp baby squid and other
seafood platters.

KAIKU

Pg. de Joan de Borbó 74 Ⓜ Barceloneta
☎ 932 219 082. May–Sept Tues–Sat
1.30–3.30pm & 7–10pm, Sun 1.30–3.30pm;
Oct–April Tues–Sun 1.30–3.30pm; closed Aug.
MAP P.58–59, POCKET MAP H8

Great lunch-only joint on the
seafront terrace for fantastic,
Basque-influenced seafood
meals (dishes €8–17, cheaper
set menu served Tues–Fri).
Tastes are out-of-the-ordinary
– think smoked vegetable rice
with mushrooms and rocket, or
steamed mussels with thyme
– and you'll need to book.

SOMORROSTRO

C/Sant Carles 11 Ⓜ Barceloneta ☎ 932 250
010, Ⓦ www.restaurantesomorrostro.com.
Mon & Thurs–Sat 8pm–11.30pm, Sun 2–4pm.
MAP P.58–59, POCKET MAP H8

It takes two

You want a seafood paella or an *arròs negre* (black rice, with squid ink), or maybe a garlicky *fideuà* (noodles with seafood) – of course you do. Problem is, you're on your own and virtually every restaurant that offers these classic Barcelona dishes does so for a minimum of two people (often you don't find out until you examine the menu's small print). Solution? Ask the waiter upfront, as sometimes the kitchen will oblige single diners, or look for the dishes on a *menú del dia* (especially on Thurs, traditionally rice day), when there should be no minimum. Probably best not to grab a stranger off the street to share a paella, however desperate you are.

Creative "boat-to-table" Mediterranean cuisine with a mission: preserving and promoting the livelihood and traditions of this fishing community. The three-course evening menu (€17; available to the first 15 customers) is great value, and it's good fun watching the open kitchen in action.

VASO DE ORO

C/Balboa 6 Ⓜ Barceloneta ☎ 933 193 098. Daily 9am–midnight. MAP P.58–59, POCKET MAP F15

An old favourite for stand-up tapas (€4–15) – there's no menu, but order the *patatas bravas*, some thick slices of fried sausage, grilled shellfish and a dollop of tuna salad and you've touched all the bases. Unusually, they also brew their own beer, light and dark.

Bars

CAFÉ DE LOS ANGELITOS

C/l'Almirall Cervera 26 Ⓜ Barceloneta ☎ 932 211 224, Ⓦ www.cafedelosangelitos.es. Mon–Thurs 5pm–2am, Fri 5pm–3am, Sat 3pm–3am, Sun 3pm–2am. MAP P.58–59, POCKET MAP H8

It's easy to lose track of time at this congenial and cosy neighbourhood bar, where attentive bartenders craft classic cocktails, from martinis to manhattans (from €6), and serve up simple yet delicious tapas.

CAN PAIXANO

C/de la Reina Cristina 7 Ⓜ Barceloneta ☎ 933 100 839, Ⓦ www.canpaixano.com. Mon–Sat 9am–10.30pm; closed 2 weeks in Aug. MAP P.58–59, POCKET MAP E14

A must on everyone's itinerary is this counter-only joint where the drink of choice – all right, the only drink – is *cava* by the glass or bottle. It's popular, so you may have to fight your way in.

MAKAMAKA BEACH BURGER CAFÉ

Pg. de Joan de Borbó 76 Ⓜ Barceloneta ☎ 932 213 520. Sun–Thurs noon–2am, Fri & Sat noon–2.30am). MAP P.58–59, POCKET MAP H8

You really can't ask for more: creative cocktails and some of the city's finest burgers served on a large, beachside *terrassa*. It's Hawaii-meets-Barcelona – laidback, late night and lots of fun.

CAN PAIXANO

El Raval

The Old Town area west of the Ramblas is known as El Raval (from the Arabic word for suburb), and has always formed a world apart from the nobler Gothic quarter. Traditionally a red-light area, and once notorious for its sleazy Barri Xinès (China Town), it still has some very seedy corners (particularly south of Carrer de Sant Pau), though it's changing rapidly, notably in the "upper Raval" around Barcelona's contemporary art museum, MACBA. Cutting-edge galleries, designer restaurants and fashionable bars are all part of the scene these days, while an arty, affluent crowd rubs shoulders with the area's Asian and North African immigrants and the older, traditional residents. Metros Catalunya, Liceu, Drassanes and Paral.lel serve the neighbourhood.

MUSEU D'ART CONTEMPORANI DE BARCELONA (MACBA)

Pl. dels Àngels 1 ⓜ Catalunya ☎ 934 120 810, ⓦ www.macba.cat. Mon & Wed–Fri 11am–7.30pm, Sat 10am–9pm, Sun & hols 10am–3pm; closed Tues all year. €10. MAP P.64–65, POCKET MAP B10/11–C10/11

The iconic contemporary art museum – with a stark main facade constructed entirely of glass – anchors the regenerated upper Raval. The collection represents the main movements in art since 1945, mainly (but not exclusively) in Catalunya and Spain, and depending on the changing exhibitions you may catch works by major names such as Joan Miró, Antoni Tàpies or Eduardo Chillida. Joan Brossa, leading light of the Catalan Dau al Set group of the 1950s, also has work here. There are free guided tours of the permanent collection (tour times vary; check website for details), and a good museum shop.

MUSEU D'ART CONTEMPORANI DE BARCELONA

FILMOTECA DE CATALUNYA

Pl. Salvador Seguí 1–9 ⓂLiceu ⓦwww
.filmoteca.cat. Cinema Tues–Fri 5–10pm, Sat
& Sun 4.30–10pm. Exhibition Hall Tues–Sun
4–9pm. €4. MAP P.64–65, POCKET MAP B13

The Josep Lluís Mateo-designed
Filmoteca de Catalunya marks
yet another step in the
government's push to revitalize
El Raval. Opened in early 2012,
the building has two below-
ground cinemas, as well as a
film library, a bookshop and
spaces for permanent and
temporary cinema-related
exhibitions. All the films are
shown in their original
language with Spanish or
Catalan subtitles.

CENTRE DE CULTURA
CONTEMPORÀNIA DE
BARCELONA (CCCB)

C/Montalegre 5 ⓂCatalunya ☎ 933 064
100, ⓦwww.cccb.org. Tues–Sun 11am–8pm.
€6, free on Sun after 3pm. MAP P.64–65,
POCKET MAP B10–C10

There's a wide range of
city-related exhibitions on
show at the contemporary
culture centre (ranging from
photography to architecture),
as well as a varied cinema,
concert and festival
programme. The imaginatively
restored building was once
an infamous workhouse
and asylum, and the main
courtyard still retains its old
tile panels and presiding
statue of patron saint, Sant
Jordi. At the back, the C3

café-bar makes the most of its
terrassa overlooking the
modern square joining the
CCCB to MACBA.

PLAÇA DE VICENÇ MARTORELL

ⓂCatalunya. MAP P.64–65, POCKET MAP C11

The Raval's nicest traffic-free
square lies just a few minutes'
walk from MACBA. The small
playground here is well used by
local families, and the arcaded
square features a first-rate café,
the *Kasparo* – a real find if
you're looking for a break from
sightseeing. Meanwhile, around
the corner are several other
cafés, while the narrow **Carrer
del Bonsuccés**, **Carrer Sitges**
and **Carrer dels Tallers** house
a concentrated selection of the
city's best independent music
stores and urban and
streetwear shops.

The beat from the street

The Barcelona sound – *mestiza* – is a cross-cultural musical fusion
whose heartland is the immigrant melting-pot of the Raval.
Parisian-born Barcelona resident Manu Chao kick-started the whole
genre, but check out the Carrer dels Tallers music stores for the other
flag-bearers – Cheb Balowski (Algerian–Catalan fusion), Ojos de Brujo
(Catalan flamenco and rumba), GoLem System (dub/reggae) and Macaco
(rumba, raga, hip-hop).

CENTRE DE CULTURA CONTEMPORÀNIA DE BARCELONA

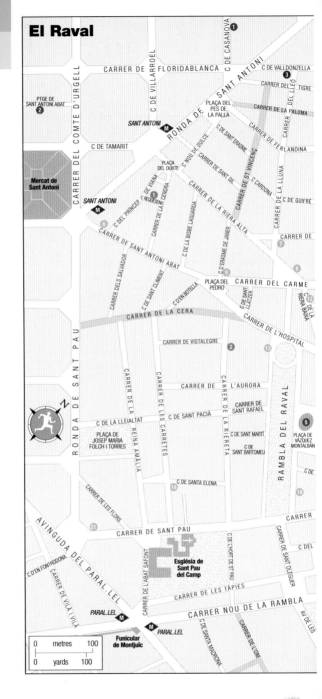

El Raval

ACCOMMODATION

Barceló Raval	5
Casa Camper	4
Hostal Cèntric	1
Hostal Grau	3
Hotel España	8
Hotel Onix Liceo	9
Hotel Peninsular	7
Hotel Sant Agustí	6
Market Hotel	2

CAFÉS

Cafè de les Delícies	19
Granja M. Viader	10
El Jardí	14
Kasparo	3
Mendizábal	15

RESTAURANTS AND TAPAS BARS

Biblioteca	16
Elisabets	4
Dos Palillos	5
Mam i Teca	7
Mesón David	18
Romesco	17
Sesamo	6
Teresa Carles	1
La Verònica	13

BARS

Almirall	2
La Confiteria	21
Marmalade	8
Marsella	20
Muy Buenas	11
Resolis	12
Zelig	9

SHOPPING

La Central del Raval	5
Discos Castelló	4
Fantastik	2
Gotham	3
Holala! Plaza	1
Lailo	6

CLUBS

Café Teatre Llantiol	2
La Concha	3
Jazz Sí Club	1
Moog	4

HOSPITAL DE LA SANTA CREU

Entrances on c/del Carme and c/de l'Hospital ⓂLiceu. Daily 10am–dusk. Free. La Capella exhibition information available on ⓦwww.lacapella.bcn.cat. ☎934 427 171. MAP P.64–65, POCKET MAP B12–C12

The neighbourhood's most historic relic is the Gothic hospital complex founded in 1402. After the hospital shifted location in 1930, the buildings were subsequently converted to cultural and educational use (including the Catalan national library), and visitors now wander freely through the charming medieval cloistered garden. Inside the c/del Carme entrance (on the right) you can see some superb seventeenth-century decorative tiles, while opposite is a remarkable eighteenth-century anatomical theatre inside the **Reial Acadèmia de Medicina** (open Wed only 10am–noon; free; ring the bell). There's also the rather nice open-air *El Jardí* café at the c/de l'Hospital side, while the hospital's former chapel, **La Capella** (entered separately from c/de l'Hospital), is an exhibition space for new contemporary artists.

CAT SCULPTURE ON THE RAMBLA DE RAVAL

RAMBLA DEL RAVAL

ⓂLiceu. MAP P.64–65, POCKET MAP B12/13

The most obvious manifestation of the changing character of El Raval is the palm-lined boulevard that was gouged through former tenements and alleys, providing a huge pedestrianized space between c/de l'Hospital and c/de Sant Pau. The *rambla* has a distinct character that's all its own, mixing kebab joints, phone shops and grocery stores with an increasing number of fashionable cafés and bars. Signature building, halfway down, is the glow-in-the-dark, designer *Barceló Raval* hotel, while kids find it hard to resist a clamber on the bulbous cat sculpture. A weekend street market (selling everything from samosas to hammocks) adds a bit more character.

Just off the top of the *rambla*, **Carrer de la Riera Baixa** is at the centre of the city's secondhand/vintage clothing scene. A dozen funky little independent clothes shops provide the scope for an hour's browsing.

PALAU GÜELL

C/Nou de la Rambla 3–5 ⓂLiceu ☎934 725 775, ⓦwww.palauguell.cat. Tues–Sun & hols 10am–8pm (Nov–March until 5.30pm), last admission 1hr before closing. €12, free first Sun of the month. MAP P.64–65, POCKET MAP C13

El Raval's outstanding building is the extraordinary townhouse designed (1886–90) by the young Antoni Gaudí for a wealthy industrialist. At a time when other architects sought to conceal the iron supports within buildings, Gaudí displayed them instead as decorative features. Columns, arches and ceilings are all shaped and twisted in an elaborate style that was to become the hallmark of Gaudí's

High society hotel

Some of the most influential names in Catalan *modernista* design came together to transform the dowdy nineteenth-century **Hotel España** (c/de Sant Pau 9–11, ⓦwww.hotelespanya.com; map p.64–65, pocket map C13) into one of the city's most lavish addresses. With a gloriously tiled dining room, an amazing marble fireplace and a mural-clad ballroom, the hotel was the fashionable sensation of its day. A contemporary restoration has done a wonderful job of showing off the classy interior – there are guided tours (€5) twice a day, Mon–Fri; ask at the reception.

later works, while the roof terrace culminates in a fantastical series of tiled chimneys. Visitor numbers are limited – expect to queue or to receive a time-specific ticket.

ESGLÉSIA DE SANT PAU DEL CAMP

C/de Sant Pau 101 ⓜ Paral.lel ☎ 934 410 001. Mon–Sat 10am–1.30pm & 4–7.30pm. Admission to cloister €3. MAP P.64–65, POCKET MAP A13

The unusual name of the church of Sant Pau del Camp (St Paul of the Field) is a graphic reminder that it once stood in open countryside beyond the city walls. Sant Pau was a Benedictine foundation of the tenth century, and above the main entrance are primitive thirteenth-century carvings of fish, birds and faces, while others adorn the charming cloister.

MERCAT DE SANT ANTONI

C/del Comte d'Urgell 1 ⓜ Sant Antoni ⓦ www.mercatsbcn.cat. Mon–Thurs 7am–2.30pm & 5–8.30pm, Fri & Sat 7am–8.30pm. MAP P.64–65, POCKET MAP E5

The neighbourhood's impressive nineteenth-century produce market is another that's being entirely remodelled but a provisional market building continues in operation in the meantime (on Ronda Sant Antoni). Come on Sunday and there's a **book and coin market** (9am–2pm) here instead, with collectors and enthusiasts arriving early to pick through the best bargains. The traditional bolt hole is *Els Tres Tombs*, the restaurant-bar on the corner of Ronda de Sant Antoni, open from 6am until late for a good-natured mix of locals, market traders and tourists.

PALAU GÜELL

Shops

LA CENTRAL DEL RAVAL

C/d'Elisabets 6 Ⓜ Catalunya Ⓦ www
.lacentral.com. Mon–Fri 9.30am–9pm, Sat
10am–9pm. MAP P.64–65, POCKET MAP C11
Occupying a unique space in
the former Misericordia chapel,
this is a fantastically stocked
arts and humanities treasure-
trove, with books piled high in
every nook and cranny and a
big English-language section.
There are further outlets in
MACBA (contemporary art
museum) and MUHBA
(Barcelona History Museum).

DISCOS CASTELLÓ

C/Tallers 7 Ⓜ Catalunya Ⓦ www
.castellodiscos.es. Mon–Sat 10am–8.30pm.
MAP P.64–65, POCKET MAP C11–D11
You can track down pretty
much anything in this
well-stocked shop (it has been
around since 1928), including
classical recordings and pop,
rock, *mestiza*, electronica,
hardcore and Spanish and
Catalan sounds – and if not,
other nearby specialists should
do the job.

FANTASTIK

C/Joaquin Costa 62 Ⓜ Universitat Ⓦ www
.fantastik.es. Mon–Fri 11am–2pm & 4–8.30pm,
Sat noon–9pm. MAP P.64–65, POCKET MAP B10
Beguiling gifts, crafts and
covetable objects from four
continents. You'll never know
how you lived without them,
whether it's Chinese robots,
African baskets, Russian
domino sets or Vietnamese
kitchen scales.

GOTHAM

C/Lleó 28 Ⓜ Universitat ☏ 934 124 647,
Ⓦ gotham-bcn.com. Mon–Fri 5–8pm, other
times by appointment only. MAP P.64–65,
POCKET MAP B10
This stylish shop is the place
to come for retro (1950s to

1980s) furniture, lighting,
homeware and accessories,
plus original designs.

HOLALA! PLAZA

Pl. Castella 2 Ⓜ Universitat Ⓦ www
.holala-ibiza.com. Mon–Sat 11am–9pm.
MAP P.64–65, POCKET MAP C10
Vintage heaven in a
warehouse setting (up past
CCCB), for denim, flying
jackets, Hawaiian shirts,
baseball gear and much, much
more. Also check out the
other Raval stores at c/Riera
Baixa 11 and c/Tallers 73.

LAILO

C/de la Riera Baixa 20 Ⓜ Liceu Ⓦ www
.lailovintage.es. Mon–Fri 10.30am–2pm &
5–8pm, Sat 10.30am–2.30pm & 5–8.30pm.
MAP P.64–65, POCKET MAP B12
Secondhand and vintage
clothes shop with a
massively wide-ranging stock.
If you're serious about the
vintage scene, this is your
first stop – and if you don't
find what you want just move
on down the street to the
neighbouring outlets.

Cafés

CAFÈ DE LES DELÍCIES

Rambla de Raval 47 Ⓜ Liceu ☎ 934 415 714.
Mon–Thurs 8.30am–11pm, Fri 8.30am–2am,
Sat 11am–2am, Sun 11am–midnight.
MAP P.64–65, POCKET MAP B13

One of the first off the blocks
in this revamped part of the
neighbourhood, and still
perhaps the best, plonking
thrift-shop chairs and tables
beneath exposed pipes and
girders and coming up with
something cute, cosy, mellow
and arty. Locals love to linger
here, meeting for breakfast,
sandwiches and tapas to share.

GRANJA M. VIADER

C/Xuclà 4–6 Ⓜ Catalunya ☎ 933 183 486,
Ⓦ www.granjaviader.cat. Mon–Sat
9am–1.15pm & 5–9.15pm. MAP P.64–65,
POCKET MAP C11

The oldest traditional *granja*
(milk bar) in town is a real
historical survivor – it even has
a pavement plaque outside for
services to the city. The original
owner was the inventor of
"Cacaolat" (a popular chocolate
drink), but for a taste of the
old days you could also try
mel i mató (curd cheese and
honey) or *llet Mallorquina*
(fresh milk with cinnamon and
lemon rind).

EL JARDÍ

C/de l'Hospital 56 Ⓜ Liceu ☎ 933 291 550,
Ⓦ www.eljardibarcelona.es. Mon–Fri
9am–midnight, Sat noon–midnight, Sun
11am–midnight. MAP P.64–65, POCKET MAP B12

The "garden bar", hidden in
the elegant courtyard of the
Gothic Hospital de la Santa
Creu, is a real away-from-the-
bustle find – a year-round
covered deck offering drinks,
snacks, salads and sandwiches
during the day, plus a decent
lunch menu and a changing list
of market-fresh tapas.

KASPARO

Pl. Vicenç Martorell 4 Ⓜ Catalunya ☎ 933 022
072. Daily 9am–midnight; closed four weeks
over Dec & Jan. MAP P.64–65, POCKET MAP C11

A place to relax, in the arcaded
corner of a quiet square, with
outdoor seating year-round.
There's muesli, Greek yoghurt
and toast and jam for early
birds. Later, sandwiches, tapas
and assorted *platos del dia*
(dishes of the day) are on offer
– things like hummus and
bread, vegetable quiche,
couscous or pasta.

MENDIZÁBAL

C/Junta de Comerç 2 Ⓜ Liceu.
Daily 10am–midnight, June–Sept until 1am.
MAP P.64–65, POCKET MAP C12

Don't look for a café because
there isn't one. Instead, this
cheery stand-up counter across
from the Hospital de la Santa
Creu dispenses juices, shakes,
beer and sandwiches to passing
punters. The lucky ones grab a
table over the road in the shady
little square.

GRANJA M. VIADER

Restaurants and tapas bars

BIBLIOTECA

C/Junta del Comerç 28 Ⓜ Liceu ☎ 934 126 261, Ⓦ labibliotecagourmande.com. Mon–Sat 1–4pm & 8–11.30pm; closed 2 weeks in Aug. MAP P.64–65, POCKET MAP B12

One of the finest places to sample what Barcelona tends to call "creative cuisine". It's a stylish operation, with an open kitchen turning out fish dishes that might be cooked Japanese- or Basque-style, lamb given the local treatment (with parsnip and turnip), or the signature dish of venison pie served with a zippy veg purée of the day. Meals cost from around €40, and clued-up English-speaking staff make it a hassle-free dining experience. Reservations advisable.

DOS PALILLOS

C/d'Elisabets 9 Ⓜ Catalunya ☎ 933 040 513, Ⓦ www.dospalillos.com. Tues & Wed 7.30–11.30pm, Thurs–Sat 1.30–3.30pm & 7.30–11.30pm; closed 2 weeks in Jan & 3 weeks in Aug. MAP P.64–65, POCKET MAP C11

DOS PALILLOS

Flag-waver for Asian fusion tapas is this hipster hang-out, which offers à la carte dim sum in the front galley bar (steamed dumplings to grilled oysters and stir-fried prawns; average spend €30) and a back-room, counter-style Asian bar where tasting menus (€60, €70 and €85, reservations required) wade their way through the highlights.

ELISABETS

C/d'Elisabets 2 Ⓜ Catalunya ☎ 933 175 826. Mon–Sat 8am–11pm; closed Aug. MAP P.64–65, POCKET MAP C11

Reliable Catalan home cooking served at cramped tables in a jovial brick-walled dining room. Everyone piles in early for breakfast, the hearty lunch (1–4pm) is hard to beat for price, or you can just have tapas, sandwiches and drinks at the bar.

MAM I TECA

C/de la Lluna 4 Ⓜ Sant Antoni ☎ 934 413 335. Mon, Wed–Fri & Sun 1–4pm & 8pm–midnight, Sat 8.30pm–midnight; closed 2 weeks in Aug. MAP P.64–65, POCKET MAP B11

An intimate (code for very small) place for superior tapas and fine wines, run by a wine-loving gourmet. All the meat is organic, the regional cheeses are well chosen, and market-fresh ingredients go to make up things like daily pasta dishes, a platter of grilled vegetables or a serving of lamb cutlets (most dishes €6–12, though some up to €20). Finish with chocolate truffles or home-made ice cream. There are only three or four tables, or you can perch at the bar.

MESÓN DAVID

C/de les Carretes 63 Ⓜ Paral.lel ☎ 934 415 934, Ⓦ www.mesondavid.com. Daily 1–4pm & 7.30–11.30pm. MAP P.64–65, POCKET MAP A13

This down-to-earth Galician bar-restaurant is a firm

grilled prawns from the market, scattered with parsley and chopped garlic. If you spend more than €15, you've probably eaten someone else's dinner as well.

SESAMO

C/Sant Antoni Abat 52 ⓜ Sant Antoni
☎ 934 416 411. Tues–Sun 7.30pm–midnight.
MAP P.64–65, POCKET MAP A11

A classy fusion tapas place offering up a vegetarian-orientated chalkboard menu of innovative dishes. Small and not-so-small plates roll out of the open kitchen – veggie-stuffed courgette rolls (a sort of Catalan sushi), slow-roast tomato tart, coconut curry or a daily risotto and pasta dish, all in the €7–15 range. The Catalan wines and cheeses are a high point too.

TERESA CARLES

C/Jovellanos 2 ⓜ Catalunya ☎ 933 171 829,
ⓦ www.teresacarles.com. Daily 9am–11.30pm.
MAP P.64–65, POCKET MAP C10

Stylish vegetarian and vegan cuisine served in a hip – but most certainly not "hippie" – space with soaring ceilings, exposed bricks walls and soft, white lighting. The lunch menu (€9.50) is a great bargain, while à la carte offerings like artisanal pastas, a hearty seitan burger and vegan ceviche cost €9–12. Brunch served until 2pm.

LA VERÒNICA

Rambla de Raval 2–4 ⓜ Liceu ☎ 933 293 303. Mon–Thurs 1pm–midnight, Fri & Sat noon–1am, Sun noon–12.30am; closed 2 weeks in Aug. MAP P.64–65, POCKET MAP B12

Funky, retro pizzeria *La Verònica* fits right into the new-look Rambla de Raval. Loads of crispy pizzas (mostly vegetarian, between €10 and €15) and inventive salads, enjoyed by a young crowd.

favourite with neighbourhood families, who bring their kids before they can even walk. The weekday *menú del dia* is a steal – maybe lentil broth followed by grilled trout – while traditional Galician dishes like octopus or the *combinado Gallego* ("ham, salami, ear") go down well with the regulars. Lunch is around €12, otherwise most dishes €7–15, and there's a good-natured bang on the clog gong for anyone who leaves a tip.

ROMESCO

C/Sant Pau 28 ⓜ Liceu ☎ 933 189 381.
Mon–Fri 1–11.30pm, Sat 1–4.30pm; closed Aug. MAP P.64–65, POCKET MAP C13

Old Barcelona hands talk lovingly of the *Romesco*, and as long as you accept its limitations (dining under strip-lights, gruff waiters) you can hardly go wrong, as the most expensive thing on the menu is a €10 grilled steak and most dishes go for €6 or less. It's basic but good, with big salads, country broths and grilled veg to start, followed by tuna steak, lamb chops or

Bars

ALMIRALL

C/de Joaquin Costa 33 Ⓜ Universitat ☎ 933 189 917. Ⓦ www.casaalmirall.com. Daily 6pm–2am (Fri & Sat until 3am). MAP P.64–65, POCKET MAP B11

Dating from 1860, Barcelona's oldest bar is a *modernista* classic – check out the ornate doors, counter and stupendous, glittering bar. It's long been a venerated leftist hangout and because it's not too young and not too loud, it's always good for a late-night drink away from the party crowd.

LA CONFITERÍA

C/de Sant Pau 128 Ⓜ Paral.lel. Mon–Fri 6pm–3am, Sat & Sun 2pm–3am. MAP P.64–65, POCKET MAP A13

This old bakery and confectioner's – carved wood bar, faded tile floor, murals, antique chandeliers and mirrored cabinets – is now a popular bar and meeting point. It's out on a limb in the Raval, but the glorious interior is certainly worth a detour, and it's a handy stop-off in any case on the way to a night out in Poble Sec.

MARMALADE

C/de Riera Alta 4–6 Ⓜ Sant Antoni ☎ 934 423 966. Ⓦ www.marmaladebarcelona.com. Mon–Wed 6.30pm–2am, Thurs–Sun 10am–2.30am. MAP P.64–65, POCKET MAP B11

A hugely glam facelift for the old Muebles Navarro furniture store goes for big, church-like spaces and a back-lit Art Deco bar that resembles a high altar. Cocktails, bistro meals and gourmet burgers pull in a relaxed dine-and-lounge crowd, and there's a popular weekend brunch too. If you like the style, give the more informal Barri Gòtic sister bar, *Milk*, a whirl.

MARSELLA

C/de Sant Pau 65 Ⓜ Liceu ☎ 934 427 263. Daily 10pm–2.30am. MAP P.64–65, POCKET MAP B13

Authentic, atmospheric, sleaze-period bar – named after the French port of Marseilles – where absinthe is the drink of choice. It's frequented by a spirited mix of oddball locals and young trendies, all looking for a slice of the old Barri Xines.

MUY BUENAS

C/del Carme 63 Ⓜ Liceu ☎ 645 309 671. Tues–Sat 9am–3am. MAP P.64–65, POCKET MAP B11

Arguably the Raval's nicest traditional watering hole, with a restored *modernista* interior and eager-to-please staff. A long marble trough does duty as the bar, and the beer's pulled from antique beer taps.

RESOLIS

C/Riera Baixa 22 Ⓜ Sant Antoni ☎ 934 412 948. Mon–Thurs 6pm–1am, Fri & Sat 6pm–3am. MAP P.64–65, POCKET MAP B11

A decayed, century-old bar turned into a cool hangout with decent tapas, from veggie bruschetta to steamed mussels. They didn't do much – a lick of paint, polish the panelling, patch up the brickwork – but now punters spill out of the door onto "secondhand

LA CONFITERIA

clothes street" and a good time is had by all.

ZELIG

C/del Carme 116 Ⓜ Sant Antoni Ⓦ www
.zelig-barcelona.com. Tues–Thurs & Sun
11am–2am, Fri & Sat 11am–3am. MAP P.64–65,
POCKET MAP A11

The photo-frieze on granite walls and a fully stocked cocktail bar make it very much of its *barri*, but *Zelig* stands out from the crowd. It offers a chatty welcome, a tendency towards 1980s sounds and a slight whiff of camp.

Clubs

CAFÉ TEATRE LLANTIOL

C/Riereta 7 Ⓜ Sant Antoni ☎ 933 299 009,
Ⓦ www.llantiol.com. Shows daily 9pm & 11pm
(Sun 6pm & 9pm); late show Sat. MAP P.64–65,
POCKET MAP A12

Local-language theatre isn't accessible to non-speakers, but you might want to give this idiosyncratic café-cabaret a try. As well as Catalan-language plays, there are shows featuring a mix of mime, song, clowning, magic and dance, and sometimes there's English-language stand-up comedy by local and visiting acts. Check the website to see what's on when. Tickets €10–15.

LA CONCHA

C/Guardia 14 Ⓜ Drassanes ☎ 933 024 118.
Daily 5pm–3am. MAP P.64–65, POCKET MAP B13

The Arab-flamenco fusion creates a great atmosphere, worth braving the slightly dodgy area for. It's a kitsch, gay-friendly joint, dedicated to the "incandescent presence" of Sara Montiel, Queen of Song and Cinema (a much-loved Spanish actress and singer), with uninhibited dancing by tourists and locals alike. Admission free.

RESOLIS

JAZZ SÍ CLUB

C/Requesens 2 Ⓜ Sant Antoni ☎ 933 290
020, Ⓦ www.tallerdemusics.com. MAP P.64–65,
POCKET MAP A11

This is a great place for inexpensive (€6–8) gigs in a tiny sweat-box of a club associated with the Taller de Musics (music school). Every night from around 7.45 or 8pm there's something different, from exuberant rock, blues, jazz and jam sessions to the popular weekly Cuban (Thursday) and flamenco (Friday) nights. There are usually a couple of sessions a night, with an interval in between – your first drink is included in the price, and the bar is as cheap as chips.

MOOG

C/Arc del Teatre 3 Ⓜ Drassanes ☎ 933 191
789, Ⓦ www.masimas.com. Daily midnight–5am.
MAP P.64–65, POCKET MAP C14

Influential club with a minimalist look, playing techno, electro, drum 'n' bass and trance to a cool but up-for-it crowd. There's a second, less manic dancefloor as well. Admission €10.

Sant Pere

Perhaps the least visited part of the Old Town is the medieval *barri* of Sant Pere, the area that lies immediately north of the Barri Gòtic and across Carrer de la Princesa from La Ribera. It has two remarkable buildings – the *modernista* concert hall, known as the Palau de la Música Catalana, and the stylishly designed neighbourhood market, Mercat Santa Caterina. There's been much regeneration in the *barri* over recent years, and it's well worth an afternoon's stroll or a night out, with new boulevards and community projects alongside DJ bars and designer shops. To walk through the neighbourhood, you can start at Metro Urquinaona, close to the Palau de la Música Catalana, with Metro Jaume I marking the southern end of Sant Pere.

PALAU DE LA MÚSICA CATALANA

C/Sant Pere Més Alt ⓜ Urquinaona
☎ 902 442 882, ⓦ www.palaumusica.org.
Guided tours daily 10am–3.30pm, plus Easter week & July 10am–6pm, in English every 30 mins. €18. MAP P.75, POCKET MAP E11

Barcelona's most extraordinary concert hall was built in 1908, to a design by visionary *modernista* architect Lluís Domènech i Montaner. The elaborate exterior is simply smothered in tiles and mosaics, while a mighty bulbous stained-glass skylight caps the second-storey auditorium (which contemporary critics claimed to be an engineering impossibility). The more recent Petit Palau offers a smaller auditorium space, while to the side a contemporary glass facade and courtyard provide the main public access. Concerts here

PALAU DE LA MÚSICA CATALANA

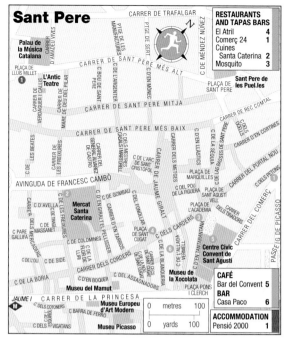

Sant Pere

(throughout the year) include performances by the Orfeo Català choral group and the Barcelona city orchestra, though you can also catch anything from flamenco to world music. Numbers are limited on the very popular fifty-minute guided tours, so it's best to buy a ticket a day or two in advance (by phone, online or at the box office).

L'ANTIC TEATRE

C/Verdaguer i Callis 12 Ⓜ Urquinaona
☎ 933 152 354, ⓦ www.anticteatre.com.
MAP P.75, POCKET MAP E11

An independent theatre with a wildly original programme, from video shows and offbeat cabaret to modern dance and left-field music. The best bit may just be the magical, light-strung garden-bar (daily 4pm–midnight), a real insiders' place but open to all.

PLAÇA DE SANT PERE

Ⓜ Arc de Triomf. MAP P.75, POCKET MAP G11

The neighbourhood extends around three parallel medieval streets, carrers de Sant Pere Més Alt (upper), Mitja (middle) and Baix (lower), which contain the bulk of the finest buildings and shops – a mixture of boutiques, textile shops, groceries and old family businesses. The streets all converge on the original neighbourhood square, Plaça de Sant Pere, whose foursquare church flanks one side, overlooking a flamboyant iron drinking fountain. Originally built in the shape of a Greek cross, the church, **Sant Pere de les Puel.les** (ⓦ www.parroquiasantpere .org), dates back to 945 AD and was the city's first convent of Benedictine nuns. It occasionally hosts concerts.

MERCAT SANTA CATERINA

Av. Francesc Cambò 16 Ⓜ Jaume I
☎ 933 195 740, Ⓦ www.mercatsantacaterina
.com. Mon 7.30am–2pm, Tues, Wed & Sat
7.30am–3.30pm, Thurs & Fri 7.30am–8.30pm;
July & Aug open mornings only. MAP P.75,
POCKET MAP F12

An eye-catching renovation of
the neighbourhood market
retained its original walls but
added slatted wooden doors
and windows and a dramatic
multicoloured wave roof. It's
one of the best places in the
city to shop for food, and its
market restaurant and bar are
definitely worth a visit in any
case. During renovation work,
the foundations of a medieval
convent were discovered here
and the excavations are visible
in the **Espai Santa Caterina**
(Mon–Sat 10am–2pm; free) at
the rear of the market.

PLAÇA DE SANT AGUSTI VELL

Ⓜ Jaume I. MAP P.75, POCKET MAP G12

The pretty, tree-shaded Plaça
de Sant Agusti Vell sits in the
middle of an ambitious urban
regeneration project, which has
transformed previously
crowded alleys. To the north,
locals tend organic allotments
in the middle of the landscaped
Pou de la Figuera *rambla*,
while south down **Carrer
d'Allada Vermell** are

overarching trees, a children's
playground and a series of
outdoor cafés and bars.
Meanwhile, running down
from Plaça de Sant Agusti Vell,
Carrer dels Carders – once
"ropemakers' street" – is now
a funky retail quarter mixing
grocery stores, cafés, boutiques
and craft shops.

CENTRE CÍVIC CONVENT DE SANT AGUSTI

C/del Comerç 36 Ⓜ Jaume I ☎ 932 565 000,
Ⓦ www.bcn.cat/centrecivicsantagusti. Mon–Fri
9am–10pm, Sat 10am–2pm & 4–9pm.
Admission charges vary, some events free.
MAP P.75, POCKET MAP F12–G12

Driving many of the
neighbourhood improvements
is the community centre
installed inside the revamped
Convent de Sant Agusti, whose
thirteenth-century cloister
provides a unique performance
space. There's a full cultural
programme here, from
workshops to concerts, with
a particular emphasis on
electronic and experimental
music and art, and don't miss
the excellent convent café.

MUSEU DE LA XOCOLATA

C/del Comerç 36 Ⓜ Jaume I ☎ 932 687
878, Ⓦ www.pastisseria.com. Mon–Sat
10am–7pm, Sun 10am–3pm. €5. MAP P.75,
POCKET MAP F12–G13

Part of the Convent de Sant
Agusti contains Barcelona's
chocolate museum, which is
a rather uninspiring plod
through the history of the stuff.
Whether you go in or not
depends on how keen you are
to see models of Gaudí
buildings or religious icons
sculpted in chocolate. There are
some very nice chocs to buy in
the shop though (free to enter),
while at the adjacent Escola de
Pastisseria, glass windows look
onto the students learning their
craft in the kitchens.

MERCAT SANTA CATERINA

Café

BAR DEL CONVENT

Pl. de l'Acadèmia, C/del Comerç 36
Ⓜ Jaume I ☎ 932 565 017, Ⓦ www
.bardelconvent.com. Tues–Thurs 10am–9pm,
Fri & Sat 10am–10pm, Sun 11am–5pm.
MAP P.75, POCKET MAP G12

The cloister café-bar is a bargain
for lunch and light meals, with
soups, stir-fries, lasagne and
couscous for €4–7. At night it's
more of a bar, with a range of
live shows, DJs and concerts.

Restaurants and tapas bars

EL ATRIL

C/dels Carders 23 Ⓜ Jaume I ☎ 933 101
220, Ⓦ www.atrilbarcelona.com. Mon
6pm–midnight, Tues–Sun noon–midnight.
MAP P.75, POCKET MAP F12

The "Music Stand" is a cosy
bar-restaurant complete with
summer *terrassa* and an
international menu, from Thai
red curry to *moules frites*
(mains €10–15). There's a
good-value lunch, and dinner
from 7pm, otherwise it's
modern tapas, drinks and a
decent Sunday brunch.

COMERÇ 24

C/Comerç 24 Ⓜ Jaume I ☎ 933 192 102,
Ⓦ carlesabellan.com. Tues–Sat 1.30–3.30pm
& 8.30–11pm; closed 2 weeks in Aug. MAP P.75,
POCKET MAP G12

Carles Abellan calls his cuisine
"glocal" (ie global + local) and
in the oh-so-cool interior you're
presented with tapas-style
dishes mixing flavours and
textures to calculated effect
(foie gras and truffle hamburger,
tuna sashimi on pizza). This is
pricey, cutting-edge Barcelona
dining (€80 or so a head);
reservations advised.

CASA PACO

CUINES SANTA CATERINA

Mercat Santa Caterina, Av. Francesc
Cambó 16 Ⓜ Jaume I ☎ 932 689 918,
Ⓦ grupotragaluz.com. Bar daily 9am–11.30pm
(Thurs–Sat until 12.30am), restaurant daily
1–4pm & 8pm–midnight (Thurs–Sat until
12.30am). MAP P.75, POCKET MAP F12

A ravishing open-plan tapas
bar and market restaurant with
tables under soaring rafters.
Food touches all bases – pasta
to sushi, Catalan rice to Thai
curry – with most things
costing €9–12.

MOSQUITO

C/dels Carders 46 Ⓜ Jaume I ☎ 932 687
569, Ⓦ www.mosquitotapas.com. Mon
7.30pm–1am, Tues–Sun 1pm–1am. MAP P.75,
POCKET MAP F12

Asian tapas bar with paper
lanterns, artisan beers and an
authentic, made-to-order dim
sum menu (dishes €3–5), from
shrimp dumplings to tofu rolls.

Bar

CASA PACO

C/d'Allada Vermell 10 Ⓜ Jaume I ☎ 933 149
320. Daily 9am–2am (Fri & Sat until 3am),
Oct–March opens 6pm. MAP P.75, POCKET MAP F12

This cool music joint is a hit on
the weekend DJ scene. There's a
great *terrassa* under the trees,
but if you can't get a table here
try one of several other alfresco
bars down the boulevard.

La Ribera

The traditional highlights of the old artisans' quarter of La Ribera are the Museu Picasso (Barcelona's single biggest tourist attraction) and the graceful church of Santa María del Mar. The cramped streets between the two were at the heart of medieval industry and commerce, and it's still the neighbourhood of choice for local designers, craftspeople and artists, whose boutiques and workshops lend La Ribera an air of creativity. Galleries and applied art museums occupy the medieval mansions of Carrer de Montcada – the neighbourhood's most handsome street – while the *barri* is at its most hip in the area around the Passeig del Born, whose cafés, restaurants and bars make it one of the city's premier nightlife centres. The most direct access point for La Ribera is Metro Jaume I.

MUSEU PICASSO

C/de Montcada 15–23 Ⓜ Jaume I ☎ 932 563 000, Ⓦ www.museupicasso.bcn.cat. Tues–Sun & hols 9am–7pm. €11, Sun after 3pm & first Sun of the month free. MAP P.80, POCKET MAP F13

The celebrated Museu Picasso is one of the most important collections of Picasso's work in the world, but even so some visitors are disappointed, since the museum contains none of his best-known pictures and few in the Cubist style. But there are almost 4000 works in the permanent collection – housed in five adjoining medieval palaces – which provide a fascinating opportunity to trace Picasso's development from his drawings as a young boy to the mature works of later years. Paintings

PASSEIG DEL BORN

from his art-school days in Barcelona (1895–97) show tantalizing glimpses of the city that the young Picasso was beginning to explore, while works in the style of Toulouse-Lautrec reflect his interest in Parisian art. Other selected works are from the famous Blue Period (1901–04) and Pink Period (1904–06), and from his Cubist (1907–20) and Neoclassical (1920–25) stages. The large gaps in the main collection only underline Picasso's extraordinary changes of style and mood, best illustrated by the jump to 1957, a year represented by his interpretations of Velázquez's masterpiece *Las Meninas*.

As well as showing changing selections of sketches, prints and drawings, the museum addresses Picasso's work as a ceramicist, highlighting the vibrantly decorated dishes and jugs donated by his wife Jacqueline.

A free guided tour is the best way to get to grips with the collection – in English currently on Sundays at 11am (book in advance by phone or via the website). There's a courtyard café, and, of course, a shop full of Picasso-related gifts.

Picasso in Barcelona

Although born in Málaga, **Pablo Picasso** (1881–1973) spent much of his youth – from the age of 14 to 23 – in Barcelona. This time encompassed the whole of his Blue Period (1901–04) and provided many of the formative influences on his art. Not far from the Museu Picasso you can see many of the buildings in which Picasso lived and worked, notably the Escola de Belles Arts de Llotja (c/Consolat del Mar, near Estació de França), where his father taught drawing and where Picasso himself absorbed an academic training. The apartments where the family lived when they first arrived in Barcelona were at Pg. d'Isabel II 4 and c/Reina Cristina 3, both near the Escola, while Picasso's first real studio (in 1896) was located over on c/de la Plata at no. 4. A few years later, many of his Blue Period works were finished at a studio at c/del Comerç 28. His first public exhibition was in 1901 at the extravagantly decorated *Els Quatre Gats* tavern (c/Montsió 3, Barri Gòtic; ⊛ www.4gats.com); you can still have a meal there today.

MUSEU EUROPEU D'ART MODERN

C/Barra de Ferro 5 Ⓜ Jaume I ☎ 933 195 693, Ⓦ meam.es. Tues–Sun 10am–8pm. €7, guided tour €2 (Sat & Sun noon). MAP P.80, POCKET MAP F13

There is not one photograph on display at the Museu Europeu d'Art Modern, a fact you may find hard to believe considering how photorealistic many of the paintings are. Located in a renovated eighteenth-century palace – and just metres from the Museu Picasso – the museum focuses primarily on modern and contemporary figurative art. Its three floors brim with haunting, humorous and sometimes disturbing works by the likes of Eduardo Naranjo, Paul Beel and Carlos Saura Riaza. It's also home to modern, Art Deco and Catalan sculptures.

MUSEO DEL MAMUT

C/Montcada 1 Ⓜ Jaume I ☎ 932 688 520, Ⓦ museomamut.com. Daily: April–Oct 10am–9pm; Nov–March 10am–8pm. €7.50. MAP P.80, POCKET MAP F13

Though by no means mammoth in size, the Museu del Mamut (Mammoth Museum) will appeal to Ice Age film fans and anyone with an interest in prehistoric animals. As well as a shaggy, life-sized mammoth reaching to within an inch of the ceiling, there's a sabre-toothed tiger and a musk buffalo along with plenty of authentic skeletons and several reproductions of cave paintings. The experience is refreshingly hands-on without the "no touching" signs seen at most of the city's museums. Displays are in Spanish and Catalan with English-language notes available at the ticket counter.

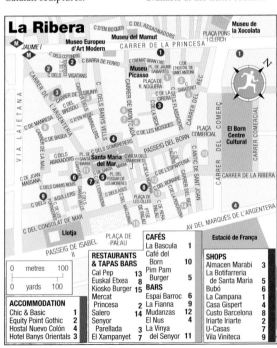

CAFÉS	
La Bascula	1
Café del Born	10
Pim Pam Burger	5

BARS	
Espai Barroc	6
La Fianna	9
Mudanzas	12
El Nus	4
La Vinya del Senyor	11

RESTAURANTS & TAPAS BARS	
Cal Pep	13
Euskal Etxea	8
Kiosko Burger Mercat	15
Princesa	2
Salero	14
Senyor Parellada	3
El Xampanyet	7

ACCOMMODATION	
Chic & Basic	1
Equity Point Gothic	2
Hostal Nuevo Colón	4
Hotel Banys Orientals	3

SHOPS	
Almacen Marabi	3
La Botifarreria de Santa Maria	5
Bubó	6
La Campana	1
Casa Gispert	4
Custo Barcelona	8
Iriarte Iriarte	2
U-Casas	7
Vila Viniteca	9

ESGLÉSIA DE SANTA MARÍA DEL MAR

Pl. de Santa Maria ⓜ Jaume I. ☎ 933 102 390. Daily 9am–1pm & 5–8pm. Free during general admission times, otherwise €5/10 guided tours 1–5pm. MAP P.80, POCKET MAP F13

The Ribera's flagship church was begun on the order of King Jaume II in 1324, and finished in only five years. Built on what was the seashore in the fourteenth century, Santa María was at the centre of the medieval city's trading district (nearby c/Argentería, for example, is named after the silversmiths who once worked there), and it came to embody the commercial supremacy of the Crown of Aragon, of which Barcelona was capital. It's an exquisite example of Catalan-Gothic architecture – as all the later Baroque trappings were destroyed during the Civil War, eyes instead are concentrated on the simple spaces of the interior, especially the beautiful stained glass.

PASSEIG DEL BORN

ⓜ Jaume I. MAP P.80, POCKET MAP F13

Fronting the church of Santa María del Mar is the fashionable Passeig del Born, once the site of medieval fairs and entertainments ("born" means tournament) and now an avenue lined with a parade of plane trees shading a host of classy bars, delis and shops. At night the Born becomes one of Barcelona's biggest bar zones, as spirited locals frequent a panoply of drinking haunts – from old-style cocktail lounges to thumping music bars. Shoppers and browsers, meanwhile, scour the narrow medieval alleys on either side of the *passeig* for boutiques and craft workshops – carrers Flassaders, Vidreria and Rec, in particular, are noted for clothes, shoes, jewellery and design galleries.

EL BORN CENTRE CULTURAL

Pl. Comercial 12 ⓜ Jaume I/Barceloneta ☎ 932 564 190, ⓦ elborncentrecultural.cat. Tues–Sun 10am–8pm. Free access to the centre, €5.50 guided tours. MAP P.80, POCKET MAP G13

The Antic Mercat del Born (1873–76) was the biggest of Barcelona's nineteenth-century market halls. It was the city's main wholesale fruit and veg market in 1971, and was then due to be demolished, but was saved thanks to local protests. It lay empty for decades, but in 2013 reopened as El Born Centre Cultural, where the extensive archeological remains of eighteenth-century shops, factories, houses and taverns are showcased inside the building's restored glass-and-cast iron frame.

Shops

ALMACEN MARABI

C/Cirera 6 ⓜ Jaume I ⓦ www.almacenmarabi
.blogspot.com. Mon–Sat noon–2.30pm &
5–8.30pm. MAP P.80, POCKET MAP F13

Mariela Marabi, originally
from Argentina, makes
handmade felt finger dolls,
mobiles, puppets and
animals of extraordinary
invention. She's often at
work at the back, while her
eye-popping showroom
also has limited-edition
pieces by other selected artists
and designers.

LA BOTIFARRERIA DE SANTA MARIA

C/Santa Maria 4 ⓜ Jaume I ⓦ labotifarreria
.com. Mon–Fri 8.30am–2.30pm & 5–8.30pm,
Sat 8.30am–2.30pm. MAP P.80, POCKET MAP F14

If you ever doubted the power
of the humble Catalan pork
sausage, drop by this designer
temple-deli where otherwise
beautifully behaved locals
jostle at the counter for the
day's home-made *botifarra*,
plus rigorously sourced hams,
cheese, pâtés and salamis.
True disciples can even buy
the T-shirt.

CASA GISPERT

BUBÓ

C/Caputxes 10 ⓜ Jaume I ⓦ www.bubo.es.
Daily 10am–10pm (Fri & Sat until 1am).
MAP P.80, POCKET MAP E14

There are chocolates and then
there are Bubó chocolates –
jewel-like creations and playful
desserts by pastry maestro
Carles Mampel. This very classy
shop is complemented by their
minimalist new-wave tapas
place, *Bubóbar*, a couple of
doors down at no.6.

LA CAMPANA

C/Princesa 36 ⓜ Jaume I. ⓦ turronels
lacampana.com. Daily 9am–11pm; closed Feb.
MAP P.80, POCKET MAP F13

This lovely old shop from 1890
presents handmade pralines
and truffles, but is best known
for its beautifully packaged
squares and slabs of *turrón*,
traditional Catalan nougat.

CASA GISPERT

C/Sombrerers 23 ⓜ Jaume I ⓦ www.casa
gispert.com. Tues–Fri 9.30am–2pm & 4–8.30pm
(also Mon in Oct, Nov & Dec), Sat 10am–2pm &
5–8.30pm. MAP P.80, POCKET MAP F13

Roasters of nuts, coffee and
spices for over 150 years. It's
a truly delectable store of
wooden boxes, baskets, stacked
shelves and tantalizing smells,
and there are organic nuts and
dried fruit, teas and gourmet
deli items available too.

CUSTO BARCELONA

Pl. de les Olles 7 ⓜ Barceloneta ⓦ www
.custo-barcelona.com. Mon–Sat 10am–9pm,
Sun noon–8pm. MAP P.80, POCKET MAP F14

Where the stars get their
T-shirts – hugely colourful
(highly priced) designer tops
and sweaters for men and
women. There are other
branches around town (at
Ramblas 109, c/de Ferran 36,
and at L'Illa shopping), while
last season's gear gets another
whirl at Pl. del Pi in the
Barri Gòtic.

IRIARTE IRIARTE

C/Cotoners 12 Ⓜ Jaume I Ⓦ www
.iriarteiriarte.com. Tues–Sat 4.30–8.30pm.
MAP P.80, POCKET MAP E13

Atelier-showroom for
sumptuous handmade leather
bags and belts. The alley (off
c/Cotoners) has several other
interesting craft workshops and
galleries to browse.

U-CASAS

C/Espaseria 4 Ⓜ Jaume I Ⓦ www.casasclub
.com. Mon–Sat 10.30am–8.30pm (Fri & Sat
until 9pm). MAP P.80, POCKET MAP F14

Casas has four lines of shoe
stores across Spain, with the
U-Casas brand at the young
and funky end of the market.
Never mind the shoes, the
stores are pretty spectacular,
especially here in the Born
where an enormous shoe-
shaped bench-cum-sofa takes
centre-stage. Other branches
are at c/Tallers 2 (Raval),
c/Portaferrissa 25 (Barri Gòtic)
and L'Illa and Maremàgnum
shopping centres.

VILA VINITECA

C/Agullers 7 & 9 Ⓜ Jaume I Ⓦ www
.vilaviniteca.es. Mon–Sat 8.30am–8.30pm
(closes Sat at 2.30pm in July & Aug). MAP P.80,
POCKET MAP E14

A very knowledgeable
specialist in Catalan and
Spanish wines. Pick your
vintage and then nip over the
road for the gourmet deli part
of the operation.

Cafés

LA BASCULA

C/Flassaders 30 Ⓜ Jaume I ☎ 933 199 866.
Wed–Sat 1pm–midnight, Sun 1–8pm. MAP P.80,
POCKET MAP F13

A hippy-chic makeover for
an old backstreet chocolate
factory. It's a welcoming
veggie place, serving pastas,

CUSTO BARCELONA

sandwiches, turnovers, crepes,
dipping platters and salads
(dishes €9), and there are
dozens of organic teas, coffees,
wines, juices and shakes.

CAFÉ DEL BORN

Pl. Comercial 10 Ⓜ Barceloneta ☎ 932 683
272. Mon–Thurs 8am–1am, Fri 8am–3am,
Sat 9am–3am, Sun 9am–1am. MAP P.80,
POCKET MAP F13

No gimmicks, no fusion food,
and dodgy local art kept to a
bare minimum – the recipe
for success at this ever-
popular neighbourhood
café-bar. There's a simple
Mediterranean menu on offer,
while Sunday brunch is the
big weekend draw.

PIM PAM BURGER

C/Sabateret 4 Ⓜ Jaume I ☎ 933 152 093,
Ⓦ pimpamburger.com. Daily 1pm–midnight
(Fri & Sat until 12.30am). MAP P.80,
POCKET MAP F13

The go-to choice for a quick
burger and fries, or franks or
sandwiches (€2.50–6). There
are a few stools and tables if
you'd rather not eat on the
hoof, while Pim Pam Plats,
around the corner on c/del Rec,
is their outlet for budget-
beating take-home meals.

Restaurants and tapas bars

SENYOR PARELLADA

CAL PEP

Pl. de les Olles 8 Ⓜ Barceloneta ☎ 933 107
961, Ⓦ www.calpep.com. Mon 7.30–11.30pm,
Tues–Fri 1–3.45pm & 7.30–11.30pm, Sat
1.15–3.45pm; closed Easter week & Aug.
MAP P.80, POCKET MAP F14

There's no equal in town for
off-the-boat and out-of-the-
market tapas. You may have to
queue, and prices are high for
what's effectively a bar meal
(up to €60), but it's definitely
worth it for the likes of
impeccably fried shrimp,
grilled sea bass, Catalan
sausage, or squid and
chickpeas – all overseen by
Pep himself, bustling up and
down the counter.

EUSKAL ETXEA

Pl. de Montcada 1–3 Ⓜ Jaume I ☎ 933 102
185, Ⓦ www.euskaletxea.cat. Daily
10am–12.30am (Fri & Sat until 1am). MAP P.80,
POCKET MAP F13

The bar at the front of the local
Basque community centre is
great for sampling *pintxos*
– elaborately fashioned
pint-sized tapas, held together
by a stick. Just point to what
you want (and keep the sticks
so the bill can be tallied).

KIOSKO BURGER

Av. del Marquès de l'Argentera 1
Ⓜ Barceloneta ☎ 933 107 313,
Ⓦ kioskoburger.com. Daily 1pm–1.30am.
MAP P.80, POCKET MAP F14

In Barcelona's best gourmet
burger outlet, great-tasting
artisan bread rolls and
homemade sauces set the
tone, while a dozen superb
types of burger (€6–9) come
any way you like, from
Catalan (with a roast garlic
alioli) to Japanese (with
teriyaki sauce).

MERCAT PRINCESA

C/Flassaders 21 Ⓜ Jaume I ☎ 932 681 518,
Ⓦ mercatprincesa.com. Daily 9am–midnight
(Thurs–Sat until 1am). MAP P.80, POCKET MAP F13

Enjoy food from more than a
dozen gourmet stalls (think
plump Chinese dumplings,
grilled artisan sausages and
artfully mounded *montaditos*) at
communal tables in a restored
fourteenth-century palace's
interior courtyard. It's a great
option, especially if your taste
buds are pulling you in multiple
directions. From €2.50 a dish.

SALERO

C/Rec 60 Ⓜ Barceloneta ☎ 933 198 022,
Ⓦ www.restaurantesalero.com. Mon–Sat
1.30–4pm & 8.30pm–midnight, Sun
8.30pm–midnight; closed 2 weeks in Aug.
MAP P.80, POCKET MAP F14

A crisp, modern space fashioned
from a former salt-cod
warehouse – if white is your
colour, you'll enjoy the space.
The food's Mediterranean-Asian,
presenting delights like vegetable
tempura or a *mee goreng*
(fried noodle) of the day (most
dishes €12–18).

SENYOR PARELLADA

C/Argenteria 37 Ⓜ Jaume I ☎ 933 105 094,
Ⓦ www.senyorparellada.com. Daily 1–3.45pm
& 8.30–11.30pm. MAP P.80, POCKET MAP E13

A gorgeous renovation of an eighteenth-century building is the mellow background for genuine Catalan food – home-style cabbage rolls, duck with figs, a papillote of beans with herbs – served from a long menu that doesn't bother dividing starters from mains. Most mains cost €8–19.

EL XAMPANYET

C/de Montcada 22 Ⓜ Jaume I ☎ 933 197 003.
Tues–Sun noon–3.30pm & 7–11.30pm; closed
two weeks in Aug. MAP P.80, POCKET MAP F13

Traditional blue-tiled bar doing a roaring trade in sparkling *cava*, cider and traditional tapas (anchovies are the speciality). The drinks are cheap and the tapas turn out to be rather pricey, but there's usually a good buzz about the place.

Bars

ESPAI BARROC

Palau Dalmases, c/de Montcada 20
Ⓜ Jaume I ☎ 933 100 673, Ⓦ www.palau
dalmases.com. Daily 7pm–2am. MAP P.80,
POCKET MAP F13

The handsome Baroque mansion of Palau Dalmases is open in the evenings for wine, champagne or cognac in refined surroundings or, once a week, the billowing strains of live opera (Thurs at 11pm; €20, first drink included).

LA FIANNA

C/Manresa 4 Ⓜ Jaume I ☎ 933 151 810,
Ⓦ www.lafianna.com. Daily 6pm–2am.
MAP P.80, POCKET MAP F13

Flickering candelabras, rough plaster walls and deep colours set the Gothic mood in this stylish lounge-bar. Relax on the chill-out beds and velvet sofas, or book ahead to eat – the fusion-food restaurant is open from 8.30pm.

MUDANZAS

C/Vidrería 15 Ⓜ Barceloneta ☎ 933 191
137. Daily 10am–2.30am, Aug opens at 6pm.
MAP P.80, POCKET MAP F14

Locals like the relaxed atmosphere, while those in the know come for the wide selection of rums, whiskies and vodkas from around the world.

EL NUS

C/Mirallers 5 Ⓜ Jaume I ☎ 933 195 355.
Mon–Thurs 7.30pm–2.30am, Fri & Sat
7.30pm–3am. MAP P.80, POCKET MAP F13

Still has the feel of the shop it once was, down to the antique cash register, though now it's a kind of jazz-bar-cum-gallery – a quiet, faintly old-fashioned, late-night place.

LA VINYA DEL SENYOR

Pl. Santa Maria 5 Ⓜ Jaume I ☎ 933 103 379.
Mon–Thurs noon–1am, Fri & Sat noon–2am,
Sun noon–midnight. MAP P.80, POCKET MAP F14

A great wine bar with front-row seats onto the lovely church of Santa María del Mar. The wine list is really good – with a score available by the glass – and there are oysters, smoked salmon and other classy tapas available.

EL XAMPANYET

Parc de la Ciutadella

While you might escape to Montjuïc or the Collserola hills for the air, there's no beating the city's green lung, Parc de la Ciutadella (open daily 10am until dusk), for a break from the downtown bustle. Though the park holds a full set of attractions, on lazy summer days you may simply want to stroll along the garden paths and row lazily across the ornamental lake. The name of the park recalls a Bourbon citadel which used to occupy the site, the building of which caused the brutal destruction of a great part of La Ribera neighbourhood. This symbol of authority survived uneasily until 1869; after this the area was made into a park. It was subsequently chosen as the site of the 1888 Universal Exhibition, from which period dates a series of eye-catching buildings and monuments by the city's pioneering *modernista* architects.

ARC DE TRIOMF

Pg. Lluís Companys Ⓜ Arc de Triomf.
MAP P.87, POCKET MAP G11

A giant brick arch announces the architectural splendours to come in the park itself. Conceived as a bold statement of Catalan intent, it's studded with ceramic figures and motifs and topped by two pairs of bulbous domes. The reliefs on the main facade show the city of Barcelona welcoming visitors to the 1888 Universal Exhibition, held in the park to the south. Connecting the arch to the park is a gorgeous promenade flanked by linden and palm trees and ornate lamp posts. Just before the park's entrance on Passeig de Pujades stands the monument to Francisco de Paula Rius i Taulet, the four-time mayor of Barcelona credited with helping bring the Universal Exhibition to the city.

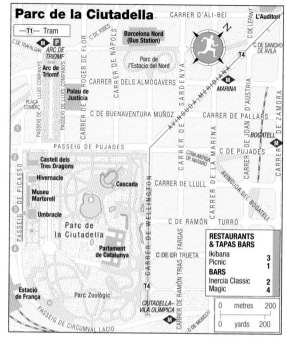

Parc de la Ciutadella

0	metres	200
0	yards	200

CASCADA

Parc de la Ciutadella Ⓜ Arc de Triomf.
MAP P.87, POCKET MAP K6

The first of the major projects undertaken inside the park was the Cascada, the monumental fountain in the northeast corner. It was designed by Josep Fontseré i Mestrès, the architect chosen to oversee the conversion of the former citadel grounds into a park, and his assistant was the young Antoni Gaudí, then a student. The Baroque extravagance of the Cascada is suggestive of the flamboyant decoration that was later to become Gaudí's trademark. The best place to contemplate the fountain is from the small open-air café-kiosk. Near here you'll also find a small lake, where you can rent a rowing boat and paddle about among the ducks.

HIVERNACLE AND UMBRACLE

Pg. de Picasso Ⓜ Arc de Triomf. Under renovation at the time of writing. Free.
MAP P.87, POCKET MAP G13

The two unsung glories of Ciutadella are its plant houses, arranged either side of the Museu Martorell. The larger Hivernacle (conservatory) features enclosed greenhouses separated by a soaring glass-roofed terrace. If anything, the Umbracle (palm-house) is even more imposing, with a vaulted wood-slat roof supported by cast-iron pillars, which allows shafts of light to play across the assembled palms and ferns. Traditionally, there's always been a café-bar in the Hivernacle, set among the plants and trees, though it was closed at the time of writing while restoration work continued on the building.

MUSEU DE CIÈNCIES NATURALS

Pg. de Picasso ⓜ Arc de Triomf ⓜ museu ciencies.bcn.cat. MAP P.87, POCKET MAP G12 & G13

The city's Natural Science Museum has its public showcase, the Museu Blau, over at the Diagonal Mar Fòrum site, but its genesis lies in two interesting buildings in Ciutadella park that are currently undergoing major renovation (and will be for some time). The Neoclassical **Museu Martorell**, which opened in 1882, was actually the first public museum to be built in the city, designed by leading architect of the day Antoni Rovira i Trias. For decades this housed the city's geological collections; the new permanent exhibition here will concentrate on the development of the natural sciences in Barcelona. The other building has always been a city favourite, a whimsical red-brick confection that was long the zoology museum. It's universally known as the

Castell dels Tres Dragons (Three Dragons Castle), designed by *modernista* architect Lluís Domènech i Montaner and originally intended for use as the café-restaurant for the 1888 Universal Exhibition. It's going to become the research, study and conservation centre for the Natural Science Museum's geology and zoology collections, and will be known as the Laboratori de Natura (Laboratory of Nature).

PARC ZOOLÒGIC

C/de Wellington ⓜ Ciutadella-Vila Olímpica ☎ 902 457 545. ⓦ www.zoobarcelona.com. Daily: Jan–March & late Oct–Dec 10am–5pm; April–mid-May & mid-Sept–late late Oct 10am–6pm; mid-May–mid-Sept 10am–7pm. €17.90. MAP P.87, POCKET MAP J7–K7

Ciutadella's most popular attraction by far is the city zoo, which takes up most of the southeastern part of the park (main entrance on c/Wellington, signposted from ⓜ Ciutadella-Vila Olímpica). It boasts more than 2000 animals from over 400 different species – which is seen by some as too many for a zoo that is still essentially nineteenth century in character, confined to the formal grounds of a public park. Nonetheless it's hugely popular with families, as there are mini-train and pony rides, a petting zoo and daily dolphin shows alongside the main animal attractions. The many endangered species on show include the Iberian wolf, and big cats such as the Sri Lankan leopard, snow leopard and the Sumatran tiger. The zoo's days in its current form are numbered: over the next few years parts of it will be completely remodelled as it attempts to expand its facilities and modernize.

PARC ZOOLÒGIC

PICNIC

Restaurants and tapas bars

IKIBANA

Pg. Picasso 32 Ⓜ Barceloneta ☎ 932 956 732, Ⓦ www.ikibana.es. Daily: June–Sept 1pm–1am; Oct–May 1–4pm & 8.30pm–12.30am (Fri & Sat until 1am). MAP P.87, POCKET MAP G13

Riding the fusion wave is this glam Japanese-Brazilian with a lounge-bar setting, just a step or two out of the park, which offers a great weekday lunch deal. A series of dainty little dishes presents a mix of zingy rice- and seaweed-roll combos and exotic tempuras, with the full menu extending to ceviches and Kobe beef burgers (dishes €6–13, tasting menu €33).

PICNIC

C/Comerç 1 Ⓜ Arc de Triomf ☎ 935 116 661, Ⓦ www.picnic-restaurant.com. Mon 1–4pm, Tues–Fri 1–4pm & 8pm–12.30am (cocktails until 2am), Sat & Sun 11.30am–5pm. MAP P.87, POCKET MAP G12

Just a short stroll from the park, this lovely little spot serves classic brunch food such as eggs Benedict, pancakes and French toast, plus more creative dishes like duck hash and fried green tomatoes (brunch Fri–Sun; €5.50–14). The dinner menu focuses on tapas, with offerings that include oysters in tempura, grilled kangaroo and Myanmar pickled tealeaf salad. There's also a weekday lunch menu (Tues–Thurs; from €12), as well as thirst-quenching drinks such as the refreshingly tart pink lemonade.

Bar

INERCIA CLASSIC

Pg. Picasso 20 Ⓜ Barceloneta ☎ 933 107 207, Ⓦ www.inerciagroup.com. Daily 8am–3am. MAP P.87, POCKET MAP G12

During the summer heat, a cold drink on the shaded *terrassa* – which sits under the arcaded walkway of Passeig de Picasso across from the park – is just the ticket. It's a great spot to start the evening before diving into Born's vibrant nightlife.

Club

MAGIC

Pg. Picasso 40 Ⓜ Barceloneta ☎ 933 107 267, Ⓦ www.magic-club.net. Thurs–Sat 11pm–6am. MAP P.87, POCKET MAP G13

A Barcelona classic that's been rocking out since the mid-1970s. While first and foremost a rock 'n' roll club, *Magic* doesn't take itself too seriously. The usual suspects (Ramones, AC/DC and Iggy Pop) are played alongside hits from the likes of the Beastie Boys, the Violent Femmes and more.

Montjuïc

For art and gardens you need to head across the city to the verdant park area of Montjuïc, site of the 1992 Olympics. The hill is topped by a sturdy castle and anchored around the heavyweight art collections in the Museu Nacional d'Art de Catalunya (MNAC). Two other superb galleries also draw visitors, namely Caixa Forum and the celebrated Fundació Joan Miró, not to mention a whole host of family-oriented attractions, from the open-air Poble Espanyol (Spanish Village) to the cable-car ride to the castle. Meanwhile, the various gardens that spill down the hillsides culminate in Barcelona's excellent botanical gardens. For Caixa Forum, Poble Espanyol and MNAC use Metro Espanya; the Trasbordador Aeri (cable car from Barceloneta) and Funicular de Montjuïc (from Metro Paral. lel) drop you near the Fundació Joan Miró.

PLAÇA D'ESPANYA

Ⓜ Espanya. MAP P.92, POCKET MAP C4

Montjuïc's characteristic gardens, terraces, fountains and monumental buildings were established for the International Exhibition of 1929. Gateway to the Exhibition was the vast Plaça d'Espanya and its huge Neoclassical fountain, with striking twin towers, 47m high, standing at the foot of the imposing Avinguda de la Reina Maria Cristina. This avenue heads up towards Montjuïc, and is lined by exhibition halls used for trade fairs. At the end, monumental steps (and modern escalators) ascend the hill to the Palau Nacional (home of MNAC), past water cascades and under the flanking walls of two grand Viennese-style pavilions. The higher you climb, the better the views, while a few café-kiosks put out seats on the way up to MNAC.

MONUMENT DE LES QUATRE COLUMNES

Ⓜ Espanya. MAP P.92, POCKET MAP C4

Simplest of architect Josep Puig i Cadafalch's ideas for the ceremonial gateway to Montjuïc at Plaça d'Espanya were four 20m-high columns, erected in 1919 on a raised site below the future Palau Nacional. Who could possibly object? The authoritarian

government of General Primo de Rivera, as it happened, knowing perfectly well that the architect, a Catalan nationalist, meant the four columns to represent the four stripes of the Catalan flag. Down they came in 1928, to be replaced by the Magic Fountain, and not until 2010 were the columns (reconstructed using the original plans) to be seen again in public – erected across from the fountain by the city government as "an act of memory" and symbol of freedom and democracy.

CAIXA FORUM

Av. Francesc Ferrer i Guàrdia 6–8 ⓜ Espanya ☎ 934 768 600, ⓦ www.fundacio.lacaixa.es. Sept–June daily 10am–8pm; July & Aug Thurs–Tues 10am–8pm, Wed 10am–11pm. €4. MAP P.92, POCKET MAP C4

The former Casaramona textile factory (1911) at the foot of Montjuïc conceals a terrific arts and cultural centre. The exhibition halls were fashioned from the former factory buildings, whose external structure was left untouched – girders, pillars, brickwork and crenellated walls appear at

every turn. The undulating roof (signposted "terrats") offers unique views, while the high Casaramona tower, etched in blue and yellow tiling, is as readily recognizable as the huge Miró starfish logos emblazoned across the building. The contemporary art collection focuses on the period from the 1980s to the present, and works are shown in partial rotation alongside an excellent programme of changing exhibitions across all aspects of the arts. There's also the Mediateca multimedia space, plus an arts bookshop, children's activities and a 400-seat auditorium for music, art and literary events.

FONT MÀGICA

Pl. de Carles Buigas ⓜ Espanya. April–Oct Thurs–Sun 9–11.30pm; Nov–March Fri, Sat & hols 7–8.30pm. Free. MAP P.92, POCKET MAP C5

On selected evenings, the "Magic Fountain" at the foot of the Montjuïc steps becomes the centrepiece of an impressive, if slightly kitsch, sound-and-light show, as the sprays and sheets of brightly coloured water dance to the music.

PAVELLÓ MIES VAN DER ROHE

Av. Francesc Ferrer i Guàrdia 7 Ⓜ Espanya
🕾 934 234 016, Ⓦ www.miesbcn.com. Daily
10am–8pm; guided visits in English on Sat at
10am. €5. MAP P.92, POCKET MAP C5

The German contribution to
the 1929 International
Exhibition was a pavilion
designed by Mies van der Rohe
(and reconstructed in 1986 by
Catalan architects). It's
considered a major example of
modern rationalist architecture
– a startling conjunction of
dark-green polished onyx,
shining glass and watery
surfaces. Unless there's an
exhibition in place (a fairly
regular occurrence) there is
little to see inside, though you
can buy postcards and books
from the small shop and debate
quite how much you want a
Mies mousepad or a "Less is
More" T-shirt.

POBLE ESPANYOL

Av. Francesc Ferrer i Guàrdia 13 Ⓜ Espanya
🕾 935 086 300, Ⓦ www.poble-espanyol.com.
Mon 9am–8pm, Tues–Thurs 9am–midnight, Fri
9am–3am, Sat & Sun 9am–4am. €9.50, family
ticket €30, night ticket €6.50, combined
ticket with MNAC €18. MAP P.92, POCKET MAP B5

"Get to know Spain in one
hour" is what's promised at the
Spanish Village – an open-air
park of reconstructed Spanish
buildings, such as the medieval
walls of Ávila, through which
you enter. The echoing main
square is lined with cafés, while
the surrounding streets and
alleys contain around forty
workshops, where you can
witness crafts like engraving,
weaving and pottery. Inevitably,
it's one huge shopping
experience, and prices are
inflated, but children will love
it (they can run free as there's
no traffic) and there are plenty

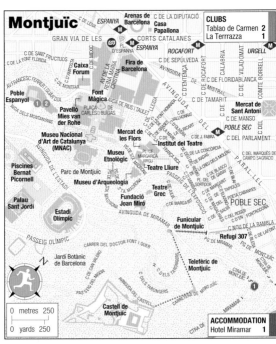

of family activities. Get to the village early to enjoy it in relatively crowd-free circumstances – once the tour groups arrive, it becomes a bit of a scrum. You could always come instead at the other end of the day, to venues like *Tablao de Carmen* or *La Terrrazza*, when the village transforms into a vibrant centre of Barcelona nightlife.

MUSEU DE CARROSSES FÚNEBRES

C/Mare de Déu de Port 56–58. Bus #21 from Ⓜ Paral.lel ☎ 934 841 999, ⓦ cbsa.cat. Wed–Sun 10am–2pm. Free. POCKET MAP A8

One of the city's more esoteric attractions, the Funerary Carriage Museum is fittingly located at the entrance to Montjuïc Cemetery. The horse-drawn carriages on display were used for city funeral processions from the 1830s until the service was mechanized in the 1950s, when the silver Buick (also on display) came into use. Most of the carriages and hearses are extravagantly decorated, and some carried dignitaries, politicians and big-name bullfighters to their final resting places. There are also plenty of old photographs of them in use in the city's streets, alongside antique uniforms, mourning wear and formal riding gear.

MUSEU NACIONAL D'ART DE CATALUNYA (MNAC)

Palau Nacional Ⓜ Espanya ☎ 936 220 376, ⓦ www.mnac.cat. Tues–Sat 10am–8pm (Oct–April until 6pm), Sun & hols 10am–3pm. €12, ticket valid 48hr, first Sun of the month free; special exhibitions, varied charges apply. MAP P.92, POCKET MAP C5/6

Catalunya's national art gallery is one of Barcelona's essential visits, showcasing a thousand years of Catalan art in stupendous surroundings. For first-time visitors it can be difficult to

MUSEU NACIONAL D'ART DE CATALUNYA

know where to start, but if time is limited it's recommended you concentrate on the medieval collection. It's split into two main sections, one dedicated to Romanesque art and the other to Gothic – periods in which Catalunya's artists were pre-eminent in Spain.

The collection of Romanesque frescoes in particular is the museum's pride and joy – removed from churches in the Catalan Pyrenees, and presented in a reconstruction of their original setting. MNAC also boasts an unsurpassed nineteenth- and twentieth-century Catalan art collection (until the 1940s – everything from the 1950s onwards is covered by MACBA in the Raval). It's particularly strong on *modernista* and *noucentista* painting and sculpture, the two dominant schools of the period, while there are some fascinating diversions into subjects like *modernista* interior design, avant-garde sculpture and historical photography.

Blockbuster exhibitions, and special shows based on the museum's archives are popular (separate charges may apply).

MUSEU ETNOLÒGIC

Pg. Santa Madrona 16–22 Ⓜ Espanya Ⓦ www
.museuetnologic.bcn.cat. The museum is
currently closed for renovation, expected to be
completed in late 2014. MAP P.92, POCKET MAP C6

The Ethnological Museum
boasts extensive global cultural
collections and puts on
excellent exhibitions, which
usually last for a year or two
and focus on a particular
subject or geographical area.
Refreshingly, pieces close to
home aren't neglected, which
means that there's also often a
focus on local and national
themes, like rural life and
work or Spanish carnival
celebrations.

MUSEU D'ARQUEOLOGIA

Pg. Santa Madrona 39–41 Ⓜ Espanya
☎ 934 232 129, Ⓦ www.mac.cat. Tues–Sat
9.30am–7pm, Sun & hols 10am–2.30pm.
€4.50, free last Tues of each month Oct–June.
MAP P.92, POCKET MAP C6

The city's main archeological
collection spans the centuries
from the Stone Age to the time
of the Visigoths, with the
Roman and Greek periods
particularly well represented.
Finds from Catalunya's
best-preserved archeological
site – the Greek remains at
Empúries on the Costa Brava
– are notable, while on an
upper floor life in Barcino
(Roman Barcelona) is
interpreted through a vivid
array of tombstones, statues,
inscriptions and friezes.

PERFORMANCE AT THE BARCELONA FESTIVAL

LA CIUTAT DEL TEATRE

Mercat de les Flors Ⓜ Poble Sec ☎ 932 562
600, Ⓦ www.mercatflors.org; Teatre Lliure
☎ 932 289 747, Ⓦ www.teatrelliure.cat;
Institut del Teatre ☎ 932 273 900,
Ⓦ teatrelliure.cat. MAP P.92, POCKET MAP C5–D6

At the foot of Montjuïc the
theatre area known as La Ciutat
del Teatre ("Theatre City")
occupies a corner of the old
working-class neighbourhood
of Poble Sec. Here, off c/de
Lleida, you'll find the **Mercat
de les Flors** – once a flower
market, now a centre for dance
and the "movement arts" – and
the progressive **Teatre Lliure**
("Free Theatre"), while the
sleek **Institut del Teatre** brings
together the city's major drama
and dance schools.

Teatre Grec and the Barcelona Festival

Centrepiece of Barcelona's annual summer cultural festival (Ⓦ grec.bcn
.cat) is the **Teatre Grec** (Greek theatre), cut into a former quarry on
the Montjuïc hillside. Starting in late June (and running throughout
July and sometimes early Aug), the festival incorporates drama, music and
dance, with some of the most atmospheric events staged in the Greek
theatre, from Shakespearean productions to shows by avant-garde
performance artists.

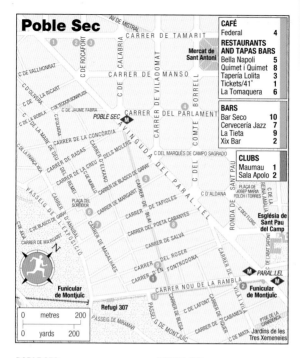

CAFÉ	
Federal	4
RESTAURANTS	
AND TAPAS BARS	
Bella Napoli	5
Quimet i Quimet	8
Tapería Lolita	3
Tickets/41°	1
La Tomaquera	6

BARS	
Bar Seco	10
Cervecería Jazz	7
La Tieta	9
Xix Bar	2

CLUBS	
Maumau	1
Sala Apolo	2

POBLE SEC

Ⓜ Poble Sec. MAP P.95, POCKET MAP D5–E6

The Poble Sec neighbourhood provides a complete contrast to the landscaped slopes of Montjuïc. The name ("Dry Village") is derived from the fact that this working-class neighbourhood originally had no water supply. Today, the hillside grid of streets is lined with down-to-earth grocery stores and good-value restaurants, while Poble Sec is also emerging as an "off-Raval" nightlife destination, with its fashionable bars and music clubs – pedestrianized Carrer de Blai is the epicentre of the scene. It has its own metro station, or it's an easy walk from El Raval, while the Montjuïc funicular has its lower station at nearby Ⓜ Paral.lel.

REFUGI 307

C/Nou de la Rambla 175 Ⓜ Paral.lel ☎ 932 562 100, Ⓦ www.museuhistoria.bcn.cat. Guided tours Sun at 10.30am, 11.30am & 12.30pm. €3.40. MAP P.92, POCKET MAP D7/8

For a fascinating look at one of the city's hidden corners, visit Poble Sec's old Civil War air-raid shelter, dug into the hillside by local people in 1936. The tunnels could shelter up to 2000 people from Franco's bombs – you follow your guide into the labyrinth to the sound of screaming sirens, which at the time gave the locals just two minutes to get safely underground. Storyboards and photographs by the entrance explain the gripping history of the Civil War in Barcelona. Tours are in Spanish or Catalan, though someone usually speaks English, and you can just turn up on the day.

ESTADI OLÍMPIC

Museu Olímpic i de l'Esport, Av. de l'Estadi 60 ⓜ Espanya ☎ 932 925 379, ⓦ www .museuolimpicbcn.cat. Tues–Sat 10am–6pm (April–Sept until 8pm), Sun & hols 10am–2.30pm. €5.10. MAP P.92, POCKET MAP B6

The 65,000-seater Olympic Stadium was the ceremonial venue for the 1992 Barcelona Olympics. From the front, a vast *terrassa* provides one of the finest vantage points in the city, while the space-age curve of Santiago Calatrava's communications tower dominates the skyline.

Around the other side, across the road from the stadium, the history of the Games – and Barcelona's successful hosting – are covered in the Olympic and Sports Museum. It's a fully interactive experience, with lots of sports gear and memorabilia displayed, but even so it's probably one for hardcore Olympics fans only.

FUNDACIÓ JOAN MIRÓ

Parc de Montjuïc ⓜ Espanya ☎ 934 439 470, ⓦ www.fundaciomiro-bcn.org. Tues–Sat 10am–7pm (July–Sept until 8pm), Thurs until 9.30pm, Sun & hols 10am–2.30pm. €11, exhibitions from €7. MAP P.92, POCKET MAP C6

Barcelona's most adventurous art museum houses the life's work of the great Catalan artist Joan Miró (1893–1983). Inside the stark white building is a permanent collection of works largely donated by Miró himself and covering the period from 1914 to 1978. The paintings and drawings in particular are instantly recognizable, being among the chief links between Surrealism and abstract art, while there's also a selection of fascinating original sketches – Miró's enormous tapestries and outdoor sculptures, for example, often started life as a doodle on a scrap of notepaper.

The museum's Sala K provides a rapid appraisal of Miró's entire *oeuvre* in a representative selection of works. Elsewhere are pieces by other artists in homage to Miró, and exhibitions by young experimental artists in the Espai 13 gallery.

The museum sponsors temporary exhibitions, film shows, lectures and children's theatre. There's also a café-restaurant with outdoor tables on a sunny patio – and you don't need a museum ticket to go in.

FUNICULAR DE MONTJUÏC

Av. del Paral.lel ⓜ Paral.lel ⓦ www.tmb.cat. Every 10min, Mon–Fri 7.30am–8pm, Sat, Sun & hols 9am–8pm (April–Oct daily until 10pm). €2.15, transport tickets and passes valid. MAP P.92, POCKET MAP D6

The quickest way to reach the lower heights of Montjuïc is to take the funicular, from inside the station at ⓜ Paral.lel. At the upper station you can switch to the Montjuïc cable car, or you're only a few minutes' walk from the Fundació Joan Miró.

HANGING TAPESTRY AT THE FUNDACIÓ JOAN MIRÓ

JARDÍ BOTÀNIC DE BARCELONA

TELEFÈRIC DE MONTJUÏC

Av. de Miramar Ⓜ Paral.lel, then Funicular
Ⓦ www.tmb.cat. Daily: April, May & Oct
10am–7pm; June–Sept 10am–9pm; Nov–March
10am–6pm. €7.50 one-way, €10.80 return.
MAP P.92, POCKET MAP D7

The cable car up to the castle and back is an exciting ride, and the views, of course, are stupendous. There's an intermediate station, called Mirador, where you can get out and enjoy more sweeping vistas.

CASTELL DE MONTJUÏC

Carretera de Montjuïc ☎ 932 564 445,
Ⓦ www.bcn.cat/castelldemontjuic. Daily:
April–Sept 10am–8pm; Oct–March
10am–6pm. €5, free Sun after 3pm. MAP P.92,
POCKET MAP C7/8

Barcelona's fortress served as a military base and prison for decades, and was where the last president of the prewar Catalan government, Lluís Companys, was executed on Franco's orders on October 15, 1940. However, in 2008 the castle was symbolically handed over to the city and restoration work is transforming the site into a combined peace museum, memorial space and Montjuïc interpretation centre. Exhibitions may take place here in the meantime, though

the cable-car ride and dramatic location merit a visit in any case. The rampart views are magnificent, while below the walls the panoramic **Camí del Mar** pathway looks out over port and ocean. It runs for 1km to the Mirador del Migdia viewpoint, where there's a great open-air bar called *La Caseta* (weekends from noon, plus summer weekend DJ nights).

JARDÍ BOTÀNIC DE BARCELONA

C/Dr Font i Quer 2 Ⓜ Espanya ☎ 932 564
160, Ⓦ www.museuciencies.bcn.cat. Daily:
April–Sept 10am–7pm; Oct–March
10am–5pm. €3.50, or combined ticket with
Museu Blau €7; free Sun after 3pm & first
Sun of month. MAP P.92, POCKET MAP B7

Principal among Montjuïc's many gardens is the city's Botanical Garden, laid out on terraced slopes offering fine views of the city. The Montjuïc buses run here directly, or it's a five-minute walk around the back of the Olympic Stadium. The beautifully kept contemporary garden has landscaped zones representing the flora of the Mediterranean, Canary Islands, California, Chile, South Africa and Australia. Just don't come in the full heat of the summer day, as there's very little shade.

Café

FEDERAL

C/del Parlament 39 Ⓜ Sant Antoni
🕾 931 873 607, 🌐 federalcafe.es. Mon–Thurs
8am–11pm, Fri 8am–1am, Sat 9am–1am, Sun
9am–5.30pm. MAP P.95, POCKET MAP E5

Sunday brunch is the hottest
ticket in town at this effortlessly
cool Aussie-owned café with a
great little roof garden, squished
into a corner townhouse.
Whether you're looking for a
flat white and French toast, or a
bacon butty and a glass of Kiwi
Sauv Blanc, there's nowhere else
quite like this in Barcelona.

Restaurants and tapas bars

BELLA NAPOLI

C/Margarit 14 Ⓜ Poble Sec 🕾 934 425 056.
Daily 1.30–4pm & 8.30pm–midnight. MAP P.95,
POCKET MAP E6

Authentic Neapolitan pizzeria
serving the city's finest pizzas
straight from a beehive-shaped
oven. Or there's a huge range
of pastas, risottos and veal
scaloppine (most dishes
between €9 and €15).

QUIMET I QUIMET

C/Poeta Cabanyes 25 Ⓜ Paral.lel 🕾 934 423
142. Tues–Sat noon–4pm & 7–10.30pm, Sun
noon–4pm; closed Aug. MAP P.95, POCKET MAP E6

Poble Sec's cosiest tapas bar is
a place of pilgrimage where
classy finger food (dishes
€3–10) is served from a
minuscule counter.

TAPERÍA LOLITA

C/Tamarit 104 Ⓜ Poble Sec 🕾 934 245 231,
🌐 www.lolitataperia.com. Tues & Wed 7pm–
midnight, Thurs 7pm–2am, Fri 7pm–2.30am, Sat
1–4pm & 7pm–2.30am. MAP P.95, POCKET MAP D5

A hip bar which serves classic
tapas to tuned-in city folk and

in-the-know tourists. You'll eat
for around €25 – don't miss the
signature-dish *patatas bravas*
or the deep-fried *bombas*
(meatballs) and *croquetas*.

TICKETS/41°

Av. Paral.lel 164 Ⓜ Poble Sec 🌐 ticketsbar.es,
🌐 41grados.es. Online reservations only.
Tickets Tues–Fri 7–11pm, Sat 1–3.30pm &
7–11.30pm. *41°* Daily opens to non-reservation-
holders at midnight; closed 2 weeks in Aug.
MAP P.95, POCKET MAP D5

Star-studded tapas bar by *El
Bulli*-famed chef Ferran Adrià,
where amazingly inventive
dishes (€5–20 each, expect to
spend €70) mix impeccably
sourced ingredients with sheer
flights of fancy. At the adjacent
and very sleek cocktail and
oyster bar *41°*, even more outré
snacks and canapés are served.
Reservations are hard to get,
and are taken up to two
months in advance.

LA TOMAQUERA

C/Margarit 58 Ⓜ Poble Sec. 🕾 675 902 389.
Tues–Sat 1–3.45pm & 8–11pm, Sun
1–3.45pm; closed Sun in June & July; closed
Aug. MAP P.95, POCKET MAP D6

Chatter-filled traditional tavern
where the chefs set to hacking
steaks and chops from great
hunks of meat. It's not for the
faint-hearted, but the grilled
chicken is sensational and the
entrecôtes enormous (most
mains €8–15).

Bars

BAR SECO

Pg. Montjuïc 74 Ⓜ Paral.lel ☎ 933 296 374, Ⓦ bar-seco.com. Mon–Wed 9am–5.30pm, Thurs 9am–1am, Fri 9am–2am, Sat 10am–2am, Sun 10am–6pm. MAP P.95, POCKET MAP E6

The "Dry Bar" is a local hit, with its mellow vibe, fresh juices and artisan beers.

CERVECERÍA JAZZ

C/Margarit 43 Ⓜ Poble Sec ☎ 934 433 259, Ⓦ cerveceriajazz.com. Tues–Sat 7pm–3am. MAP P.95, POCKET MAP D6

Grab a stool at the carved bar and shoot the breeze over a Catalan craft beer. It's an amiable joint with great music, jazz to reggae, and locals swear that the burgers are the best in town.

LA TIETA

C/de Blai 1 Ⓜ Paral.lel ☎ 600 742 532. May–Nov Mon 6pm–midnight, Tues–Thurs noon–midnight, Fri & Sat noon–1am; Dec–April Tues–Thurs noon–midnight, Fri & Sat noon–2am, Sun noon–4pm. MAP P.95, POCKET MAP E6

Small but perfectly formed, "The Aunt" is a cool drinks and tapas place with an open window onto the street and just enough room for a dozen or so good friends.

XIX BAR

C/Rocafort 19 Ⓜ Poble Sec ☎ 934 234 314, Ⓦ www.xixbar.com. Mon 6.30pm–2.30am, Tues–Sat 5pm–3am. MAP P.95, POCKET MAP D5

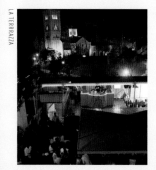

LA TERRAZZA

An old *granja* (milk bar) turned candlelit cocktail bar. It's big on gin, boasting over a hundred varieties.

Clubs

MAUMAU

C/Fontrodona 33 Ⓜ Paral.lel ☎ 934 418 015, Ⓦ www.maumaunderground.com. Thurs–Sat 9pm–2.30am. MAP P.95, POCKET MAP E6

Underground lounge-club, cultural centre and chill-out space, with nightly video projections, all sorts of exhibitions and guest DJs playing deep, soulful grooves.

SALA APOLO

C/Nou de la Rambla 113 Ⓜ Paral.lel ☎ 934 414 001, Ⓦ www.sala-apolo.com. Daily midnight–5am. MAP P.95, POCKET MAP A13

Old-time ballroom turned hip concert venue with gigs on two stages (local acts to big names) and an eclectic series of club nights, from punk to Catalan rumba sounds to the weekend's long-running *Nitsa Club* (Ⓦ www.nitsa.com). Gigs €10–35, club nights €10–15.

TABLAO DE CARMEN

Poble Espanyol Ⓜ Espanya ☎ 933 256 895, Ⓦ www.tablaodecarmen.com. Tues–Sun, shows at 7pm & 9.30pm. MAP P.92, POCKET MAP B5

Poble Espanyol's famous flamenco club features a variety of shows from seasoned performers and new talent. From €41, rising to €70 for the show plus dinner. Reservations required.

LA TERRRAZZA

Poble Espanyol Ⓜ Espanya ☎ 932 724 980, Ⓦ laterrrazza.com. May–Oct Thurs–Sat 11.45pm–6am. MAP P.92, POCKET MAP B5

Open-air summer club for nonstop dance, house and techno. Don't get there until 3am and be prepared for the style police. Admission €15–20.

Port Olímpic and Poble Nou

The main waterfront legacy of the 1992 Olympics was the Port Olímpic, the marina development which lies fifteen minutes' walk along the promenade from Barceloneta. Locals make full use of the beach and boardwalks, descending in force at the weekends for a leisurely lunch or late drink in one of the scores of restaurants and bars. There are also fine beaches further north near the old working-class neighbourhood of Poble Nou, while the impressive Museu Blau anchors the waterside zone known as the Parc del Fòrum. Access to the area is by metro to Ciutadella-Vila Olímpica or Poble Nou, or bus #59 runs from the Ramblas through Barceloneta and out to Port Olímpic.

PORT OLÍMPIC

Ⓜ Ciutadella-Vila Olímpica.
MAP P.101, POCKET MAP K8–M8

Approaching the Olympic port, the golden mirage above the promenade slowly reveals itself to be a huge **copper fish** (courtesy of Frank Gehry, architect of the Bilbao Guggenheim). It's the emblem of the seafront development constructed for the 1992 Olympics, incorporating the port itself – site of many of the Olympic watersports events – which is backed by the city's two tallest buildings, the **Torre Mapfre** and the steel-framed **Hotel Arts Barcelona**, both 154m tall. Two wharves contain the bulk of the action: the Moll de Mestral has a lower deck by the marina lined with bars, while the Moll de Gregal sports a double-decker tier of seafood restaurants. The beach, meanwhile, turns into a full-on summer resort, backed by class-conscious clubs along Passeig Marítim appealing to local rich kids and A-list celebs.

PORT OLÍMPIC

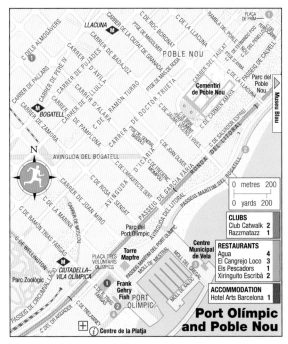

Port Olímpic and Poble Nou

CITY BEACHES

From Ⓜ Ciutadella-Vila Olímpica it's a 15min walk along the promenade to Bogatell beach. MAP P.101, POCKET MAP L6–M8

A series of sandy beaches stretches for 5km north of Port Olímpic. Split into different named sections (Nova Icària, Bogatell etc), which boast showers, playgrounds and open-air café-bars, it's a pretty extraordinary facility to find so close to a city centre. A sunny day, even in winter, brings the locals out in force, and the sands are regularly swept and replenished.

CENTRE DE LA PLATJA

Pg. Marítim Ⓜ Ciutadella-Vila Olímpica ☎ 932 210 348, Ⓦ www.bcn.cat/platges. June–Sept Tues–Sun 10am–7pm, plus March–May weekends only. MAP P.101, POCKET MAP K8

On the boardwalk arcade, in front of the Hospital del Mar,

the city council has opened a beach visitor centre. There's a full programme of walks, talks and sports, as well as buckets and spades for kids, and frisbees, volleyball and beach tennis gear available for pick-up games on the sands.

RAMBLA DEL POBLE NOU

Ⓜ Poble Nou. MAP P.101

A twenty-minute walk up the beach from Port Olímpic, the Rambla de Poble Nou runs through the most attractive part of **Poble Nou** ("New Village"). The old industrial neighbourhood is at the heart of a huge city regeneration scheme, but the local avenue remains unchanged – a run of modest shops, cafés and restaurants, including the classic juice and milk bar of *El Tio Che* (Rambla de Poble Nou 44–46).

101

THE EDIFICI FÒRUM

CEMENTIRI DE POBLENOU

Av. d'Icaria Ⓜ Bogatell. Daily 8am–6pm.
MAP P.101, POCKET MAP M7

This vast nineteenth-century mausoleum has its tombs set in walls 7m high. With birdsong accompanying a stroll around the flower-lined pavements, quiet courtyards and chapels, this village of the dead is a rare haven of peace in the city.

MUSEU BLAU

Pl. Leonardo da Vinci 4–5, Parc del Fòrum
Ⓜ El Maresme Fòrum, or tram T4 ☎ 932 566
002, Ⓦ www.museuciencies.bcn.cat. Tues–Sat
10am–7pm, Sun 10am–8pm. €7, includes
entrance to Montjuïc botanical garden; free
first Sun of the month & every Sun after 3pm.

The Natural Science Museum's million-strong collection of rocks, fossils, plants and animals has a state-of-the-art home in the visually stunning Blue Museum, housed in the Fòrum building, whose permanent exhibition – Planeta Vida (Planet Life) – plots a journey through the history of life on earth. It's heavily focused on evolutionary, whole-earth, Gaia principles, with plenty of entertaining, interactive bells and whistles to guide you through topics as diverse as sex and reproduction and conservation of the environment.

Diagonal Mar

The waterfront district north of Poble Nou was developed in the wake of the Universal Forum of Cultures Expo (held in 2004). It's promoted as **Diagonal Mar**, anchored by the Diagonal Mar shopping mall (Ⓜ El Maresme Fòrum or tram T4) and with several classy hotels, convention centres and exhibition halls grouped nearby. The dazzling **Edifici Fòrum** building is the work of Jacques Herzog (architect of London's Tate Modern), while the main open space is claimed to be the second-largest square in the world after Beijing's Tiananmen Square. This immense expanse spreads towards the sea, culminating in a giant solar-panelled canopy that overlooks the marina, beach and park areas. In summer, temporary bars, dancefloors and chill-out zones are established at the **Parc del Fòrum**, and the city authorities have shifted some of the bigger annual music festivals and events down here to inject a bit of life outside convention time. At other times it can be a bit soulless, but it's definitely worth the metro or tram ride if you're interested in heroic-scale public projects.

Restaurants

AGUA

Pg. Marítim 30 Ⓜ Ciutadella-Vila Olímpica ☎ 932 251 272, ⓦ grupotragaluz.com. Daily 1–3.45pm & 8–11.30pm (Fri & Sat until 4.30pm & 12.30am). MAP P.101, POCKET MAP K8

Nicest boardwalk restaurant on the strip, with a contemporary Mediterranean menu, from salads to grills. Prices are pretty fair (most dishes €10–25), so it's usually busy.

EL CANGREJO LOCO

Moll de Gregal 29–30 Ⓜ Ciutadella-Vila Olímpica ☎ 932 210 533, ⓦ www.elcangrejo loco.com. Daily 1pm–midnight. MAP P.101, POCKET MAP L8

The terrace at the "Crazy Crab" offers ocean views, and the food is first rate. A mixed fried-fish plate is a typically Catalan starter, and the rice dishes are thoroughly recommended. From around €40.

ELS PESCADORS

Pl. Prim 1 Ⓜ Poble Nou ☎ 932 252 018, ⓦ www.elspescadors.com. Daily 1–3.45pm & 8–11.30pm; closed two weeks in Dec. MAP P.101

The best top-class fish restaurant in Barcelona? It's a tough call, but many would choose this hideaway place in a pretty Poble Nou square. The menu offers daily fresh fish dishes, and plenty more involving rice, noodles or salt-cod. Don't go mad and you'll escape for around €60.

XIRINGUITO ESCRIBÀ

Ronda del Litoral 42, Platja Bogatell Ⓜ Ciutadella-Vila Olímpica ☎ 932 210 729, ⓦ xiringuitoescriba.com. Daily: Mon–Fri 1–4.30pm & 8–11pm, Sat & Sun 1–5pm & 8–11pm. MAP P.101, POCKET MAP M8

Beachfront restaurant (really a glorified beach shack) that's enough off the beaten track (a 15min walk from Port Olímpic)

to mark you out as in the know. High points are paellas and daily fish specials (around €20), followed by sensational cakes and pastries from the Escribà family patisserie.

Clubs

CLUB CATWALK

C/Ramon Trias Fargas 2–4 Ⓜ Ciutadella-Vila Olímpica ☎ 932 216 161, ⓦ www.club catwalk.net. Tues–Sun midnight–5am. MAP P.101, POCKET MAP K8

Portside club of choice playing house, funk, soul and r'n'b for well-heeled locals and visitors. It's under the *Hotel Arts*; admission €12–15.

RAZZMATAZZ

C/Pamplona 88 Ⓜ Bogatell ☎ 933 208 200, ⓦ www.salarazzmatazz.com. Thurs (Razz club only), Fri & Sat 1–6am. MAP P.101, POCKET MAP L5

Razzmatazz hosts the biggest in-town rock gigs, and at weekends turns into "five clubs in one", spinning mixed sounds in variously named bars. Admission €17.

CLUB CATWALK

Dreta de l'Eixample

The nineteenth-century street grid north of Plaça de Catalunya is the city's main shopping and business district. It was designed as part of a revolutionary urban plan – the Eixample in Catalan ("Extension" or "Widening") – that divided districts into regular blocks, whose characteristic wide streets and shaved corners survive today. Two parallel avenues, Passeig de Gràcia and Rambla de Catalunya, are the backbone of the Eixample, with everything to the east known as the Dreta de l'Eixample (the right-hand side). It's here that the bulk of the city's famous *modernista* (Catalan Art Nouveau) buildings are found, along with an array of classy galleries and some of the city's most stylish shops. Start your exploration from either Metro Passeig de Gràcia or Metro Diagonal.

PASSEIG DE GRÀCIA

🚇 Passeig de Gràcia. MAP P.105, POCKET MAP H1/4

The prominent avenue, which runs northwest from Plaça de Catalunya, was laid out in its present form in 1827. It later developed as a showcase for *modernista* architects, eagerly commissioned by status-conscious merchants and businessmen. Walk the length of Passeig de Gràcia from Plaça de Catalunya to Avinguda Diagonal (a 25min stroll) and you'll pass some of the city's most extraordinary architecture, notably the famous group of buildings (including casas Amatller and Batlló) known as the Mansana de la Discòrdia, or "Block of Discord", as they show off wildly varying manifestations of the *modernista* style and spirit. Further up is Antoni Gaudí's iconic apartment building La Pedrera, while, in between, wrought-iron Art Nouveau street lamps, fashion stores and designer hotels set the tone for this resolutely upscale avenue.

Dreta de l'Eixample

RESTAURANTS AND TAPAS BARS

La Bodegueta	3
Casa Calvet	11
Ciudad Condal	8
Elj Apo Nés	1
El Mussol	4, 10
Tapas, 24	7
Tragaluz	2

CAFÉS

Café del Centre	6
Forn de Sant Jaume	5
Laie Llibreria Café	9

SHOPS

Antonio Miró	1
Bulevard dels Antiquarius	5
Casa del Llibre	4
Colmado Quilez	6
Cubiñá	3
Mango	8
Purificacion Garcia	2
Reserva Ibérica	7

ACCOMMODATION

Equity Point Centric	4
Hostal L'Antic Espai	6
Hostal Girona	8
Hostal Goya	7
Hotel Condes de Barcelona	3
Hotel Majestic	2
Hotel Omm	1
Mandarin Oriental	5
the5rooms	9

0	metres	200
0	yards	200

CASA AMATLLER

MUSEU DEL PERFUM

Pg. de Gràcia 39 Ⓜ Passeig de Gràcia
☎ 932 160 121, Ⓦ www.museodelperfume
.com. Mon–Fri 10.30am–8pm, Sat 11am–2pm.
€5. MAP P.105, POCKET MAP H3

At the back of the Regia perfume store is a private collection of over five thousand perfume and essence bottles from Egyptian times onwards. There are some exquisite pieces, including Turkish filigree-and-crystal ware and bronze and silver Indian elephant flasks, while more modern times are represented by scents made for Brigitte Bardot, Grace Kelly and Elizabeth Taylor.

CASA AMATLLER

Fundació Amatller, Pg. de Gràcia 41
Ⓜ Passeig de Gràcia Ⓦ www.amatller.org.
MAP P.105, POCKET MAP G3

Josep Puig i Cadafalch's striking Casa Amatller (1900) was designed for Antoni Amatller, a Catalan chocolate manufacturer, art collector, photographer and traveller. It's awash with coloured ceramic decoration, while inside the hallway twisted stone columns are interspersed with dragon lamps. Guided tours are occasionally available (check website for details) while renovation works continue and usually include a visit to Amatller's photographic studio as well as chocolate-tasting in the original kitchen. The house also displays temporary exhibitions under the auspices of the Amatller Institute of Hispanic Art.

CASA BATLLÓ

Pg. de Gràcia 43 Ⓜ Passeig de Gràcia
☎ 932 160 306, Ⓦ www.casabatllo.es. Daily
9am–9pm, access occasionally restricted.
€18.50. Advance-purhase tickets advised, in
person, by phone or online. MAP P.105,
POCKET MAP G3

The most extraordinary creation on the "Block of Discord" is the Casa Batlló,

Modernisme

The Catalan offshoot of Art Nouveau, **modernisme**, was the expression of a renewed upsurge in Catalan nationalism in the 1870s. Its most famous exponent was **Antoni Gaudí i Cornet** (1852–1926), whose buildings are apparently lunatic flights of fantasy, which at the same time are perfectly functional. His architectural influences were Moorish and Gothic, while he embellished his work with elements from the natural world. The imaginative impetus he provided inspired others like **Lluís Domènech i Montaner** (1850–1923) – perhaps the greatest *modernista* architect – and **Josep Puig i Cadafalch** (1867–1957), both of whom also experimented with the use of ceramic tiles, ironwork, stained glass and stone carving. This combination of traditional methods with modern technology became the hallmark of *modernisme* – producing some of the most exciting architecture to be found anywhere in the world.

designed for the industrialist Josep Batlló and finished in 1907. Antoni Gaudí created an undulating facade that Salvador Dalí later compared to "the tranquil waters of a lake". The sinuous interior, meanwhile, resembles the inside of some great organism, complete with meandering, snakeskin-patterned walls. Self-guided audio tours show you the main floor, the patio and rear facade, the ribbed attic and celebrated mosaic roof-top chimneys. Advance tickets are recommended (by phone, in person or online); the scrum of visitors can be a frustrating business at peak times.

FUNDACIÓ ANTONI TÀPIES

C/Aragó 255 Ⓜ Passeig de Gràcia ☎ 934 870 315, 🖥 www.fundaciotapies.org. Tues–Sun 10am–7pm. €7. MAP P.105, POCKET MAP G3

The definitive collection of the work of Catalan abstract artist Antoni Tàpies i Puig (who died in 2012) is housed in *modernista* architect Lluís Domènech i Montaner's first important building, the Casa Montaner i Simon (1880). You can't miss it – the foundation building is capped by Tàpies's own striking sculpture, *Núvol i Cadira* ("Cloud and Chair", 1990), a tangle of glass, wire and aluminium. The artist was

born in Barcelona in 1923 and was a founding member (1948) of the influential avant-garde Dau al Set ("Die at Seven") artists' group. Tàpies's abstract style matured in the 1950s, with underlying messages and themes signalled by the inclusion of everyday objects and symbols on the canvas. Changing exhibitions focus on selections of Tàpies's work, while other shows highlight works by other contemporary artists.

MUSEU EGIPCI DE BARCELONA

C/de València 284 Ⓜ Passeig de Gràcia ☎ 934 880 188, 🖥 www.museuegipci.com. Mon–Sat 10am–8pm, Sun 10am–2pm. €11. MAP P.105, POCKET MAP H3

Barcelona's Egyptian Museum is an exceptional private collection of over a thousand ancient artefacts, from amulets to sarcophagi – there's nothing else in Spain quite like it. Visitors are given a detailed English-language guidebook, but the real pleasure is a serendipitous wander, turning up items like cat mummies or the rare figurine of a spoonbill (ibis) representing an Egyptian god. There are temporary exhibitions, plus a good shop and terrace café, while the museum also hosts children's activities and themed events.

CASA BATLLÓ

JARDINS DE LES TORRES DE LES AIGÜES

C/Roger de Llúria 56, between c/Consell de Cent and c/Diputació Ⓜ Girona. Daily 10am–dusk. Free. MAP P.105, POCKET MAP H3

The original nineteenth-century Eixample urban plan – by utopian architect Ildefons Cerdà – was drawn up with local inhabitants very much in mind. Space, light and social community projects were part of the grand design, and something of the original municipal spirit can be seen in the Jardins de les Torres de les Aigües, an enclosed square (reached down a herringbone-brick tunnel) centred on a Moorish-style water tower. It has been handsomely restored by the city council, who turn it into a backyard family beach every summer, complete with sand and paddling pool. Another example of the old Eixample lies directly opposite, across c/Roger de Llúria, where the cobbled **Passatge del Permanyer** cuts across an Eixample block, lined by candy-coloured single-storey townhouses.

MERCAT DE LA CONCEPCIÓ

Between c/de Valencia and c/d'Aragó Ⓜ Girona Ⓦ www.laconcepcio.com. Mon & Sat 8am–3pm, Tues–Fri 8am–8pm. MAP P.105, POCKET MAP J3

Flowers, shrubs and plants are a Concepció speciality (the florists on c/Valencia are open 24 hours a day), and there are some good snack bars inside the market and a few outdoor cafés to the side. The market takes its name from the nearby church of **La Concepció** (entrance on c/Roger de Llúria), whose quiet cloister is a surprising haven of slender columns and orange trees.

PALAU MONTANER

C/de Mallorca 278 Ⓜ Passeig de Gràcia Ⓣ 933 177 652, Ⓦ www.rutadelmodernisme. com. Guided visits: for groups only; reservations required. €6. MAP P.105, POCKET MAP H3

The Palau Montaner (1896) has a curious history – after the original architect quit, Lluís Domènech i Montaner took over halfway through construction, and the top half of the facade is clearly more elaborate than the lower part. Meanwhile, the period's most celebrated craftsmen were set to work on the interior, which sports rich mosaic floors, painted glass, carved woodwork and a monumental staircase.

The building is now the seat of the Madrid government's delegation to Catalunya, but it is possible to arrange **guided tours** that explain something of the house's history and show you the lavish public rooms, grand dining room and courtyard. It's unusual to be

FLOWERS AT THE MERCAT DE LA CONCEPCIÓ

LA PEDRERA

able to get inside a private *modernista* house of the period, so it's definitely worth the effort.

LA PEDRERA

Pg. de Gràcia 92, entrance on c/Provença
Ⓜ Diagonal ☏ 902 400 973, Ⓦ www
.lapedrera.cat. March–Nov daily 9am–8pm;
Dec–Feb daily 9am–6.30pm. €16.50. Nits
d'estiu: last week June to first week Sept
Thurs–Sat 9–11.30pm; €25, advance sales
online. MAP P.105, POCKET MAP H2

Antoni Gaudí's weird apartment building at the top of Passeig de Gràcia is simply not to be missed – though you can expect queues whenever you visit. Popularly known as La Pedrera, "the stone quarry", its rippled facade, curving around the street corner in one smooth sweep, is said to have been inspired by the mountain of Montserrat, while the apartments themselves resemble eroded cave dwellings. Indeed, there's not a straight line to be seen – hence the contemporary joke that the new tenants would only be able to keep snakes as pets. The self-guided visit includes a trip up to the extraordinary *terrat* (roof terrace) to see at close quarters the enigmatic chimneys – you should note that the roof terrace is often closed if it's raining. In addition, there's an excellent exhibition about Gaudí's life and work installed under the 270 curved brick arches of the attic. **El Pis** ("the apartment"), on the building's fourth floor, re-creates the design and style of a *modernista*-era bourgeois apartment in a series of extraordinarily light rooms that flow seamlessly from one to another. The apartment is filled with period furniture and effects, while the moulded door and window frames, and even the brass door handles, all follow Gaudí's sinuous building design. During the early summer's **Nits d'estiu** (advance booking essential) you can enjoy the amazing rooftop by night with a complimentary glass of *cava* and music, while other concerts are also held at La Pedrera at various times.

Through the grand main entrance of the building there's access to the Pedrera **exhibition hall**, which hosts temporary art shows of works by major international artists.

VINÇON

Pg. de Gràcia 96 Ⓜ Diagonal ☎ 932 156 050, Ⓦ www.vincon.com. Mon–Fri 10am–8.30pm, Sat 10.30am–9pm. MAP P.105, POCKET MAP H2

The Vinçon store emerged in the 1960s as the country's pre-eminent purveyor of household furniture and design, pioneered by Fernando Amat, the "Spanish Terence Conran". There are various separate street entrances, including Carrer de Provença 273 and de Carrer Pau Claris 175, while the extraordinary furniture floor gives access to a terrace with views of La Pedrera. The *Sala Vinçon* gallery (same hours as shop; admission free) puts on shows of graphic and industrial design and contemporary furniture.

PALAU ROBERT

Pg. de Gràcia 107 Ⓜ Diagonal ☎ 932 388 091, Ⓦ www.gencat.cat/palaurobert. Mon–Sat 10am–8pm, Sun 10am–2.30pm. Free. MAP P.105, POCKET MAP H2

Visit the information centre for the Catalunya region for regularly changing exhibitions on all matters Catalan, from art to business. There are several exhibition spaces, both inside the main palace – built as a typical aristocratic residence in 1903 – and in the old coach house. The centre is also an important concert venue for recitals and orchestras, while the gardens around the back are a popular meeting point for local nannies and their charges.

PALAU BARÓ DE QUADRAS

Av. Diagonal 373 Ⓜ Diagonal ☎ 934 678 000, Ⓦ www.llul.cat. Mon–Fri 8am–7.30pm. MAP P.105, POCKET MAP H2

The beautifully detailed Palau Baró de Quadras (a Josep Puig i Cadafalch work from 1904) now serves as the headquarters of the Institut Ramon LLull, an organization that promotes

PALAU BARÓ DE QUADRAS

Catalan language studies at universities worldwide. Though most of the building is closed to the public, visitors can look around its stunningly ornate ground floor during the institute's opening hours. If you first see the building from the Avinguda Diagonal side, be sure walk around to Carrer del Rosselló – this side of the building is decorated in a more subdued, but very lovely, *modernista* style.

CASA DE LES PUNXES

Av. Diagonal 416–420 Ⓜ Diagonal. No public access. MAP P.105, POCKET MAP H2

Cadafalch's largest work, the soaring Casa Terrades, is more usually known as the Casa de les Punxes ("House of Spikes") because of its red-tiled turrets and steep gables. Built in 1903 for three sisters, and converted from three separate houses spreading around an entire corner of a block, the crenellated structure is almost northern European in style, reminiscent of a Gothic castle.

Shops

ANTONIO MIRÓ

Rambla de Catalunya 125 Ⓜ Diagonal
Ⓦ www.antoniomiro.es. Mon–Sat
10.30am–8.30pm. MAP P.105, POCKET MAP G3

The showcase for Barcelona's
most innovative designer, now
also branding accessories and
household design items.

BULEVARD DELS ANTIQUARIUS

Pg. de Gràcia 55–57 Ⓜ Passeig de Gràcia
Ⓦ bulevarddelsantiquaris.com. Mon–Sat
10am–8.30pm; closed Sat in Aug. MAP P.105,
POCKET MAP H3

An arcade with over seventy
shops full of antiques, from
toys and dolls to Spanish
ceramics and African art.

CASA DEL LLIBRE

Pg. de Gràcia 62 Ⓜ Passeig de Gràcia
Ⓦ www.casadellibro.com. Mon–Sat
9.30am–9.30pm. MAP P.105, POCKET MAP H3

Barcelona's biggest book
emporium, with lots of
English-language titles and
Catalan literature in
translation.

COLMADO QUILEZ

Rambla de Catalunya 63 Ⓜ Passeig de
Gràcia Ⓦ www.lafuente.es. Mon–Fri
9.30am–2pm & 4.30–8.30pm, Sat
9.30am–2pm, plus Sat afternoon Sept–Dec.
MAP P.105, POCKET MAP G3

Classic Catalan grocery piled
high with tins, jars and
packets, overseen by sober
gents in collar and tie and
blue smocks.

CUBIÑÀ

C/Mallorca 291 Ⓜ Verdaguer Ⓦ www.cubinya
.es. Mon–Sat 10am–2pm & 4.30–8.30pm.
MAP P.105, POCKET MAP H3

The building is stupendous
– Domènech i Montaner's
modernista Casa Thomas
– while inside holds the very
latest in household design.

MANGO

Pg. de Gràcia 36, plus others Ⓜ Passeig de
Gràcia Ⓦ www .mango.com. Mon–Sat
10am–9.30pm. MAP P.105, POCKET MAP H3, H4

Barcelona is where high-street
fashion chain Mango began.
For last season's gear at
unbeatable prices, head to
Mango Outlet (c/Girona 37).

PURIFICACION GARCIA

C/de Provença 292 Ⓜ Diagonal Ⓦ www
.purificaciongarcia.es. Mon–Sat 10am–8.30pm.
MAP P.105, POCKET MAP G4

A hot designer with an eye for
fabrics – Garcia's first job was
in a textile factory. She's also
designed clothes for film and
theatre, and her costumes were
seen at the opening ceremony
of the Barcelona Olympics.

RESERVA IBÉRICA

Rambla de Catalunya 61 Ⓜ Passeig de
Gràcia ☎ 902 112 641, Ⓦ reservaiberica.com.
Mon–Sat 9.30am–9pm. MAP P.105, POCKET MAP G3

A ham wonderland specializing
in *jamón ibérico de bellota*, the
finest of all of the Spanish cured
hams, which comes from
acorn-fed pigs. Pick up pre-
packaged samplers or tuck into
a plate of paper-thin slices at
one of the marble-topped tables.

DISPLAY AT VINÇON

Cafés

CAFÉ DEL CENTRE

C/Girona 69 Ⓜ Girona ☎ 934 881 101.
Mon–Fri 8am–11pm; closed Aug. MAP P.105,
POCKET MAP J3

This quiet coffee stop is only
four blocks from the main drag
of Passeig de Gràcia. It's been
here since 1873 (a plaque
outside honours its service to
the city) and, with its timeworn
modernista decor, seems
largely unchanged.

FORN DE SANT JAUME

Rambla de Catalunya 50 Ⓜ Passeig de
Gràcia ☎ 932 160 229. Mon–Sat 9am–9pm.
MAP P.105 POCKET MAP G3

Uptown *pastisseria* whose
glittering windows are piled
high with croissants, cakes,
pastries and sweets. The small
adjacent café has *rambla* seats,
or you can take away your
goodies for later.

LAIE LLIBRERIA CAFÉ

C/Pau Claris 85 Ⓜ Passeig de Gràcia ☎ 933
027 310, Ⓦ www.laie.es. Mon–Fri 9am–9pm,
Sat 10am–9pm. MAP P.105, POCKET MAP H4

The city's first and best
bookshop-café is known for its
popular weekday buffet
breakfast spread, set lunch
deals and à la carte dining.

Restaurants and tapas bars

LA BODEGUETA

Rambla Catalunya 100 Ⓜ Diagonal
☎ 932 151 725, Ⓦ www.labodegueta.com.
Mon–Fri 7am–1.45am, Sat 8am–1.45am, Sun
& hols 6.30pm–1.45am; closed mornings in
Aug. MAP P.105, POCKET MAP G2

Long-established *bodega* with
cava and wine by the glass, as
well as ham, cheese, anchovies
and other tapas to soak it up.

CASA CALVET

C/de Casp 48 Ⓜ Catalunya ☎ 934 124 012,
Ⓦ www.casacalvet.es. Mon–Sat 1–3.30pm &
8.30–11.30pm; closed Mon June–Aug.
MAP P.105, POCKET MAP F10

Antoni Gaudí's earliest
commissioned townhouse is a
marvel of interior decoration,
making for a truly glam night
out. It offers a seasonally
changing, modern Catalan
menu, with desserts that are
artworks in themselves, though
with mains around the €30
mark (or tasting menus from
€49 to €70) expect it to be a
wallet-emptying experience.

CIUDAD CONDAL

Rambla de Catalunya 18 Ⓜ Passeig de
Gràcia ☎ 933 181 997. Daily 7.30am–1.30am.
MAP P.105, POCKET MAP G4

This handy city-centre pit stop
is the best of the uptown
tapas-hall-style places.
Breakfast sees the bar groan
under the weight of a dozen
types of crispy baguette
sandwich, plus croissants and
pastries, while the daily
changing tapas selection ranges
far and wide – *patatas bravas* to
octopus. It can be standing
room only at lunch (and not
much of that either), so get

CASA CALVET

there early. Dinner doesn't really have the same buzz, but it's a useful stop for a drink at any time.

ELJ APO NÉS

Ptge. de la Concepció 2 ⓜ Diagonal ☎ 934 872 592, ⓦ grupotragaluz.com. Daily 1–4pm & 8.30–11.30pm (Fri & Sat until 12.30am). MAP P.105, POCKET MAP G2

Designer style – gunmetal grey interior, black-clad staff, sharp service – at moderate prices gives this minimalist Japanese restaurant the edge over its more traditional rivals. Tick your choices from the long menu of sushi, sashimi, noodles and tempura and hand it to the waiter; average cost is around €25 a head.

EL MUSSOL

C/Aragó 261 ⓜ Passeig de Gràcia ☎ 934 876 151; branch at c/de Casp 19 ☎ 933 017 610. Daily 1pm–1am (c/Aragó branch from 8am). MAP P.105, POCKET MAP G3, E10

Chain of big rustic diners, known for their meat and vegetables *a la brasa* (on the grill), most of which run between €6 and €12. They're good places to sample hearty Catalan country cooking, with snails and wild mushrooms on the menu all year round and *calçots* (big spring onions) a spring speciality.

TAPAS, 24

C/Diputació 269 ⓜ Passeig de Gràcia ☎ 934 880 977, ⓦ carlesabellan.com. Mon–Sat 9am–midnight. MAP P.105, POCKET MAP H4

Carles Abellan, king of pared-down designer cuisine at his restaurant *Comerç, 24*, offers a simpler tapas menu at this retro basement bar-diner. There's a reassuringly traditional feel that's echoed in the menu – *patatas bravas*, Andalucian-style fried fish, *bombas* (meatballs), chorizo sausage and fried eggs. But the

TAPAS, 24

kitchen updates the classics too, so there's also *calamares romana* (fried squid) dyed black with squid ink or a burger with *foie gras*. Most tapas dishes cost around €4 to €16. And there's always a rush and bustle at meal times, so be aware that you might well have to queue.

TRAGALUZ

Ptge. de la Concepció 5 ⓜ Diagonal ☎ 934 870 621, ⓦ www.grupotragaluz.com /tragaluz. Daily 1.30–4pm & 8.30pm–midnight. MAP P.105, POCKET MAP G2

A stylish uptown standby that attracts beautiful people by the score, and the classy Mediterranean-with-knobs-on cooking, served under a glass roof (*tragaluz* means "skylight"), doesn't disappoint. The menu ranges from seasonal salads to grilled seabass, with mains costing €16–30. It's a relaxing stop for those fresh off the *modernista* trail (La Pedrera is just across the way).

Sagrada Família and Glòries

If there's one building that is an essential stop on any visit to Barcelona it's Antoni Gaudí's great church of the Sagrada Família (Metro Sagrada Família). In many ways this has become a kind of symbol for the city, representing the glory of Catalan design and endeavour. Most visitors make a special journey out to see the church and then head back into the centre, but it's worth taking in the few blocks south of the area known as Glòries for a further set of attractions, including the city's main concert hall and music museum, and Catalunya's flagship national theatre building.

SAGRADA FAMÍLIA

C/Mallorca 401 Ⓜ Sagrada Família ☎ 935 132 060, ⓦ www.sagradafamilia.org. Daily, April–Sept 9am–8pm; Oct–March 9am–6pm. Tours in English April–Oct 11.15am, 12.30pm, 1.45pm & 3pm; Nov–March 10.15am, 12.15pm & 3pm. €14.80 (under-10s free), or €19.30 including tour; combination ticket with Casa Museu Gaudí at Parc Güell €18.30. MAP P.116–117, POCKET MAP K2

The metro drops you right outside the overpowering church of the Sagrada Família ("Sacred Family"). Begun in 1882 on a modest scale, the project changed the minute that 31-year-old architect Antoni Gaudí took charge in 1884 – he saw in the Sagrada Família an opportunity to reflect his own deepening spiritual feelings. Gaudí spent the rest of his life working on the church and was adapting the plans right up to his untimely death. Run over by a tram on June 7, 1926, his death was treated as a Catalan national disaster, and all of Barcelona turned out for his funeral.

Although the building survived, Gaudí's plans were mostly destroyed during the Spanish Civil War. Work restarted in the 1950s amid great controversy, and has continued ever since – as have the arguments. Some maintained that the Sagrada Família should be left incomplete as a memorial to Gaudí, others that the architect

SAGRADA FAMÍLIA

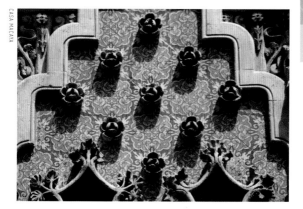

CASA MACAYA

intended it to be the work of several generations. Either way, based on reconstructed models and notes, the project is now moving towards completion (within the next twenty years, it's said), and the building is beginning to take final shape.

The size alone is startling (Gaudí's original plan was to build a church to seat over 10,000 people), while the carved spires, monumental bronze doors and vibrant facades are an imaginative and symbolic *tour de force*. Gaudí made extensive use of human, plant and animal models to exactly produce the likenesses he sought – the spreading stone leaves of the roof in the church interior, for example, were inspired by the city's plane trees. A **lift** (€4.50) up one of the towers provides an unforgettable close-up view of the work, while in the **crypt** (where Gaudí is buried) a fascinating museum traces the construction of the church – you can also view sculptors and model-makers at work.

HOSPITAL DE LA SANTA CREU I DE SANT PAU

C/de Sant Antoni Maria Claret 167 Ⓜ Hospital de Sant Pau ☎ 935 537 801. Ⓦ www.santpaubarcelona.org. Mon–Sat 10am–6.30pm (Nov–March until 4.30pm), Sun & hols 10am–2.30pm. English-language tours Mon–Sat noon, 1pm, 4pm & 5pm (Nov–March noon, 1pm & 4pm), Sun & hols noon & 1pm. €8; tours €14. MAP P.116–117, POCKET MAP M1

Lluís Domènech i Montaner's *modernista* public hospital is possibly the one building that can touch the Sagrada Família for size and invention, its whimsical pavilions, turrets and towers adorned with sculpture, mosaics, stained glass and ironwork. The old buildings have been super-seded by the modern hospital behind, but there are interesting guided tours of the historical complex – and it's an easy stroll up here from the Sagrada Família.

CASA MACAYA

Pg. de Sant Joan 108 Ⓜ Verdaguer. MAP P.116–117, POCKET MAP J2

Just four blocks from the Sagrada Família, Josep Puig i Cadafalch's Casa Macaya (1898–1900) is well known for its imaginative exterior carvings by craftsman Eusebi Arnau – look for the angel holding a camera or the sculptor himself on his way to work by bike.

ACCOMMODATION
Barcelona Urbany 1
Hotel Eurostars
Monumental 2

RESTAURANTS AND TAPAS BARS
Alkimia 1
La Taquería 3
CAFÉ
El Racó del Mercat 2

SHOPS
Centre Comercial
Barcelona Glòries 1

T1 Tram

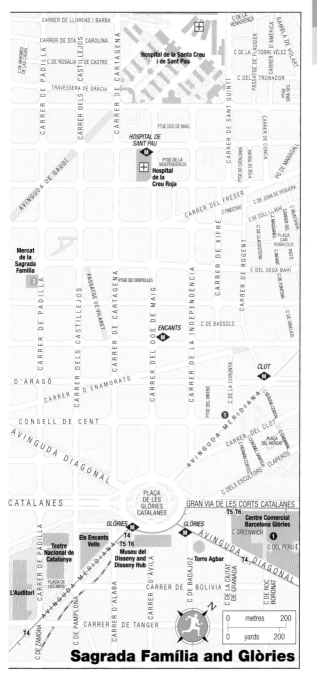

Sagrada Família and Glòries

PLAÇA DE LES GLÒRIES CATALANES

Ⓜ Glòries. MAP P.116–117, POCKET MAP M4

Barcelona's major avenues all meet at Plaça de les Glòries Catalanes, dedicated to the Catalan "glories", from architecture to literature. Glòries is at the centre of the city's latest bout of regeneration. Signature buildings are Jean Nouvel's cigar-shaped **Torre Agbar**, a remarkable aluminium-and-glass tower inspired by Montserrat, and the sleek new Disseny Hub, future home to the city's applied art collections. Nearby **Parc del Clot** shows what can be done in an urban setting within the remains of a razed factory site. Trams speed down Avinguda Diagonal to the Diagonal Mar district, passing the **Parc del Centre del Poble Nou** (10min walk, or tram stop Pere IV), another park on an old industrial site.

MUSEU DEL DISSENY AND DISSENY HUB

Pl. de les Glòries Catalanes 37–38 Ⓜ Glòries Ⓦ museudeldisseny.cat. Check museum website for hours and entrance fee. Disseny Hub ☎ 932 566 713, Ⓦ dhub.cat. Tue–Sun 10am–8pm. Hub free. MAP P.116–117, POCKET MAP M4

The new Museu del Dissney brings together Barcelona's applied art collections inside the Disseny Hub building. At the time of writing the museum was still transitioning into its new home, but in the meantime, the zinc-plated building alone is worth seeing. In addition to the museum, the Hub is also home to temporary exhibition spaces, a public library and the headquarters of local design institutions such as the Foment de les Arts i del Disseny (FAD).

TEATRE NACIONAL DE CATALUNYA

TEATRE NACIONAL DE CATALUNYA

Pl. de les Arts 1 Ⓜ Glòries ☎ 933 065 700, Ⓦ www.tnc.cat. MAP P.116–117, POCKET MAP L4/5

Catalunya's National Theatre features an enterprising programme of classics, original works and productions by guest companies. The building itself makes a dramatic statement, presenting a soaring glass box encased within a Greek temple, and there are guided **tours** for anyone interested in learning more (currently Wed & Thurs; €8; reservations required).

L'AUDITORI

C/Lepant 150 Ⓜ Glòries ☎ 932 479 300, Ⓦ www.auditori.cat. Museu de la Música, c/Padilla 155 ☎ 932 563 650, Ⓦ www .museumusica.bcn.cat. Tues–Sat & hols 10am–6pm, Sun 10am–8pm. €5, free first Sun of the month and every Sun after 3pm. MAP P.116–117, POCKET MAP L5

The city's main contemporary concert hall is home to the Barcelona Symphony Orchestra (OBC), though the programme also includes chamber, choral, jazz and world concerts. There's also the city's entertaining Museu de la Música (Music Museum), which displays a remarkable collection of historic instruments and musical devices.

Shops

CENTRE COMERCIAL BARCELONA GLÒRIES

Av. Diagonal 208 Ⓜ Glòries Ⓦ www.lesglories
.com. Mon–Sat 10am–10pm. MAP P.116–117.
POCKET MAP M4

Anchoring the neighbourhood
is this huge 230-store mall with
all the national high-street
fashion names represented
(H&M, Zara, Bershka, Mango)
as well as a big Carrefour
supermarket and an eight-
screen cinema complex.

ELS ENCANTS VELLS

Av. Meridiana 69; Ⓜ Glòries Ⓦ encantsbcn
.com. Mon, Wed, Fri & Sat 9am–8pm.
MAP P.116–117, POCKET MAP L4

The city's flea market has a shiny
new home next to the Teatre
Nacional de Catalunya. The site
sports multiple levels of open-air
treasure-hunting – all protected
by a large canopy whose metallic
underside reflects the bustling
market below.

Cafés

EL RACÓ DEL MERCAT

Mercat de la Sagrada Família, c/de Padilla
255 Ⓜ Sagrada Família ☏ 934 363 452,

Ⓦ www.mercatsagradafamilia.com. Tues–
Thurs 7am–2.30pm & 5.30–8.30pm, Fri
7am–8.30pm, Sat 7am–2pm. MAP P.116–117.
POCKET MAP L2

Only two blocks east of the
Sagrada Família – and not a
tourist in sight. Browse the
stalls and pick up your picnic
lunch, and make for the
stand-up market bar, which has
pastries, sandwiches and tapas
at local prices.

Restaurants and tapas bars

ALKIMIA

C/Indústria 79 Ⓜ Sagrada Família
☏ 932 076 115, Ⓦ www.alkimia.cat. Mon–Fri
1.30–3.30pm & 8–10.15pm; closed Easter
week and 3 weeks in Aug. MAP P.116–117.
POCKET MAP K2

Ask Barcelona foodies which is
the best Catalan new-wave
restaurant in town, and once
they've all stopped bickering
this is the one they'll probably
plump for. "Alchemy" is what's
promised by the name, and
that's what chef Jordi Vilà
delivers in bitingly minimalist
style. It's a Michelin-starred
operation, so reservations are
vital – expect a bill north of
€100 a head too (though the
€40 lunch is a comparative
bargain).

LA TAQUERÍA

Ptge. del Font 5 Ⓜ Sagrada Família
☏ 931 26 13 59, Ⓦ lataqueria.eu. Tues–Sun
1–4.30pm & 8.30–11.30pm (Fri & Sat until
midnight). MAP P.116–117, POCKET MAP K3

When it comes to Mexican
food in Europe, throwing the
word "authentic" around can
get you in trouble with the
purists, but it's an apt
description for the menu here,
which ranges from *tacos al
pastor* to fresh-made
guacamole (€5–10).

ALKIMIA

Esquerra de l'Eixample

The long streets west of Rambla de Catalunya as far as Barcelona Sants station are perhaps the least visited on any city sightseeing trip. With all the major architectural highlights found on the Eixample's eastern (or right-hand) side, the Esquerra de l'Eixample (left-hand side) was intended by its nineteenth-century planners for public buildings and institutions, many of which still stand. However, the Esquerra does have its moments of interest – not least a couple of excellent museums and an eye-catching public park or two – while it's here that some of the city's best bars and clubs are found, particularly in the gay-friendly streets of the so-called Gaixample district, near the university.

UNIVERSITAT DE BARCELONA

Gran Via de les Corts Catalanes 585, at Pl. de la Universitat ⓂUniversitat. MAP P.122–123. POCKET MAP F4–G4

Built in the 1860s, the grand Neoclassical university building is now largely used for ceremonies and adminis-tration purposes, but you can visit the main hall or the fine arcaded courtyards and extensive gardens. The traditional student meeting point is the *Bar Estudiantil*, outside in Plaça Universitat, where you can usually grab a pavement table.

FUNDACIÓ FRANCISCO GODIA

C/Diputació 250 ⓂPasseig de Gràcia ☎932 723 180, ⓦwww.fundacionfgodia.org. Mon & Wed–Sun 10am–8pm. €6. MAP P.122–123. POCKET MAP G4

The private art collection of aesthete and 1950s racing driver Francisco Godia springs a real surprise, concentrating on medieval art, ceramics and modern Catalan art. Not all of the collection can be shown at any one time, so pieces are

UNIVERSITY COURTYARDS

rotated on occasion, while special exhibitions run in tandem, for which there's usually no extra charge.

MUSEU DEL MODERNISME CATALÀ

C/Balmes 48 ⓜ Passeig de Gràcia ☎ 932 722 896, ⓦ mmcat.cat. Mon–Sat 10am–8pm, Sun & hols 10am–2pm. €10. MAP P.122–123, POCKET MAP G3

Barcelona's traditional "gallery district", around c/Consell de Cent, is a fitting location for the stupendous *modernista* collection housed in the Museu del Modernisme Català. It's the private enterprise of the celebrated Gothsland antiques gallery, and displays a collection forty years in the making – including the famous marble decorative vase by craftsman Eusebi Arnau that was the gallery's symbol for over thirty years. This is just one of 350 works on show across two exhibition floors in a restored former textile warehouse – the grand, vaulted basement contains paintings and sculpture while on the ground floor is *modernista* furniture, from screens to sofas. There are paintings and works by many famous names, from oils by Ramon Casas i Carbó to sinuous mirrors and tables by Antoni Gaudí (originally made for the casas Batlló and Calvet). But above all, this a rare opportunity to examine extraordinary Art Nouveau fixtures and fittings by less familiar artists – wonderful creations by pioneering cabinet-maker Joan Busquets i Jané, for example, the dramatic carved headboards of Gaspar Homar i Mezquida, or the expressive terracotta sculptures of Lambert Escaler i Milà. As a crash course in the varied facets of Catalan *modernisme*,

RAMON CASAS I CARBÓ, *DAMA CON FOULARD ROJO*, MUSEU DEL MODERNISME CATALÀ

beyond the iconic buildings themselves, it's invaluable.

MERCAT DEL NINOT

C/Mallorca 133 ⓜ Hospital Clínic ☎ 934 536 512, ⓦ www.mercatsbcn.com. Mon–Fri 8am–8pm, Sat 8am–3pm. MAP P.122–123, POCKET MAP F2/3

One of the oldest markets in the city is currently undergoing a major refurbishment, but there's a large temporary market building on c/ Casanova, in front of the hospital. You won't find many tourists here and the shops around the market are refreshingly down-to-earth places to buy clothes, jewellery, accessories and homeware.

Around the back of the hospital, it's also worth having a look at the **Escola Industrial**, formerly a textile mill, which boasts a 1920s chapel by Joan Rubió i Bellvér, who worked with Antoni Gaudí. Students usually fill the courtyards, and you're free to take a stroll through to view the highly decorative buildings.

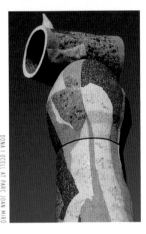

DONA I OCELL AT PARC JOAN MIRÓ

piazza whose only feature is Joan Miró's gigantic mosaic sculpture *Dona i Ocell* ("Woman and Bird"), towering above a shallow reflecting pool. The rear of the park is given over to games areas and landscaped sections of palms and firs, with a kiosk café and some outdoor tables among the trees. The children's playground here is one of the best in the city.

ARENAS DE BARCELONA

Gran Via de les Corts Catalanes 373–385, at Pl. d'Espanya Ⓜ Espanya ☏ 932 890 244, ⓦ www.arenasdebarcelona.com. Daily 10am–10pm. MAP P.122–123, POCKET MAP C4

The landmark building on the north side of Plaça d'Espanya is the fabulous Moorish-style bullring, the Arenas de Barcelona, originally built in 1900 but re-imagined as a swish shopping and leisure

PARC JOAN MIRÓ

C/de Tarragona Ⓜ Tarragona. Daily 10am–dusk. MAP P.122–123, POCKET MAP C3/4–D3/4

Parc Joan Miró was laid out on the site of the nineteenth-century municipal slaughter-house. It features a raised

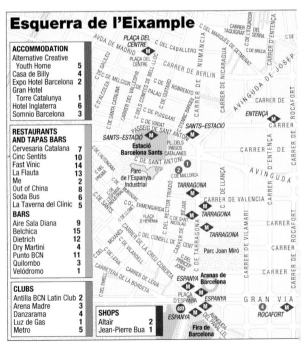

Esquerra de l'Eixample

ACCOMMODATION

Alternative Creative Youth Home	5
Casa de Billy	4
Expo Hotel Barcelona	2
Gran Hotel Torre Catalunya	1
Hotel Inglaterra	6
Somnio Barcelona	3

RESTAURANTS AND TAPAS BARS

Cerveseria Catalana	7
Cinc Sentits	10
Fast Vinic	14
La Flauta	13
Me	2
Out of China	8
Soda Bus	6
La Taverna del Clínic	5

BARS

Aire Sala Diana	9
Belchica	15
Dietrich	12
Dry Martini	4
Punto BCN	11
Quilombo	3
Velódromo	1

CLUBS

Antilla BCN Latin Club	2
Arena Madre	3
Danzarama	4
Luz de Gas	1
Metro	5

SHOPS

Altaïr	2
Jean-Pierre Bua	1

centre that opened in 2011. On top is a walk-around promenade circling the **dome** that offers 360-degree views, while inside are four floors of shopping and entertainment, including cinema, gym and various restaurants (some on the top-floor promenade).

PARC DE L'ESPANYA INDUSTRIAL

C/de Sant Antoni Ⓜ Sants-Estació. Daily 10am–dusk. MAP P.122–123, POCKET MAP B2/3–C2/3

If you have time to kill at Barcelona Sants station, nip around the south side to Basque architect Luis Peña Ganchegui's urban park. Built on the site of an old textile factory, there's a line of concrete lighthouses contrasting with an incongruously classical Neptune, as well as boating lake, café kiosk, playground and sports facilities. It's a decent attempt at reconciling local

On the Miró trail

When you've seen one Miró – well, you start to see them everywhere in Barcelona, starting with the large ceramic mural visible on the facade at the airport. The towering *Dona i Ocell* in the Parc Joan Miró is unmissable, but you should also look down at your feet on the Ramblas for the pavement mural at Plaça de la Boqueria. Miró also designed the *Caixa de Pensions* starfish logo splashed across the Caixa Forum arts centre. In many ways, it's a Miró city, whatever Picasso fans might think.

interests with the otherwise mundane nature of the surroundings, typical of the city's approach to revitalizing unkempt urban corners.

123

Shops

ALTAÏR

Gran Via de les Corts Catalanes 616
Ⓜ Passeig de Gràcia Ⓦ www.altair.es. Mon–Sat
10am–8.30pm. MAP P.122–123, POCKET MAP G4

Europe's biggest travel
superstore has a massive
selection of travel books,
guides, maps and world music,
plus a programme of travel-
related talks and exhibitions.

JEAN-PIERRE BUA

Av. Diagonal 469 Ⓜ Hospital Clinic Ⓦ www
.jeanpierrebua.com. Mon–Sat 10am–8.30pm.
MAP P.122–123, POCKET MAP F1

The city's high temple for
fashion victims: a postmodern
shrine for Yamamoto, Gaultier,
Miyake, Galliano, McQueen,
McCartney, Westwood and
other international stars.

Restaurants and tapas bars

CERVESARIA CATALANA

C/Mallorca 236 Ⓜ Passeig de Gràcia
☎ 932 160 368. Daily 9am–1am. MAP P.122–123,
POCKET MAP G3

A place that is serious about its
tapas and beer – the counters
are piled high, supplemented
by a blackboard list of daily
specials, while the walls are
lined with bottled brews from
around the world. It gets busy
after work and at meal times,
and you might have to wait for
a table.

CINC SENTITS

C/Aribau 58 Ⓜ Universitat ☎ 933 239 490,
Ⓦ www.cincsentits.com. Tues–Sat
1.30–3.30pm & 8.30–10pm; closed two weeks
in Aug. MAP P.122–123, POCKET MAP F3

Jordi Artal's "Five Senses" wows
diners with its contemporary
Catalan cuisine – and the
restaurant now has a Michelin
star to boot, so you'll need to
book. Six- and eight-course
"tasting menus" (€65 and €80,
matching wines available) use
rigorously sourced ingredients
(wild fish, mountain lamb,
seasonal vegetables,
farmhouse cheeses) in elegant,
pared-down dishes that are all
about flavour.

FAST VÍNIC

C/Diputació 251 Ⓜ Passeig de Gràcia
☎ 934 873 241, Ⓦ www.fastvinic.com. Mon–
Sat noon–midnight; closed Aug. MAP P.122–123,
POCKET MAP G4

Emphasis in this designer
sandwich bar is on top-of-the-
range ingredients from
sustainable sources (gourmet
sandwiches, wraps and salads
€5–10), plus a range of more
than twenty Catalan wines
starting at pocket-money
prices. It's the more democratic
outpost of the hallowed
wine-and-foodie temple next
door that is *Monvínic* (Ⓦ www
.monvinic.com).

LA FLAUTA

C/Aribau 23 Ⓜ Universitat ☎ 933 237 038.
Mon–Sat 8am–1am, closed 3 weeks in Aug.
MAP P.122–123, POCKET MAP F4

One of the city's best-value
lunch menus sees diners

CINC SENTITS

LA TAVERNA DEL CLINIC

not *Out of China*. Black-and-red decor, lanterns and jazz-lounge sounds set the tone for a contemporary Chinese menu that's particularly hot on veggie options, from fried aubergine to tofu curry. Lunch is a good deal but even at night prices won't break the bank, with most dishes around €8–10.

SODA BUS

C/d'Aribau 125 Ⓜ Diagonal ☎ 934 531 044, Ⓦ balta1900.com. Mon–Wed 9am–5pm, Thurs 9am–5pm & 10pm–2.30am, Fri 9am–5pm & 10pm–3am, Sat 10pm–3am; closed 2 weeks in Aug. MAP P.122–123, POCKET MAP F2

Formerly known as *El Racó d'en Balta* (it has now joined forces with the century-old *Balta Bar* next door), this funky hangout serves a popular weekday lunch, while at night you can eat for around €30 from a Mediterranean market-led menu, chowing down things like vegetarian ceviche or fish and hand-cut chips.

LA TAVERNA DEL CLÍNIC

C/Rosselló 155 Ⓜ Hospital Clinic ☎ 934 104 221, Ⓦ latavernadelclinic.com. Mon–Sat 1–5pm & 8–11.30pm. MAP P.122–123, POCKET MAP F2

This sleek *taverna*, named for the hospital over the road, is a gourmet tapas spot that concentrates on rigorously sourced regional produce. Snacks at the solid marble bar come in at just a few euros, but the serious food, accompanied by artisan-made olive oil and a high-class wine list, is served at one of the ten tables (book in advance) and runs to more like €10–30 a dish, from crispy suckling pig to sea urchins artfully arranged atop mounds of sea salt.

queuing for tables early – get there before 2pm to avoid the rush. While the name is a nod to the house speciality gourmet sandwiches (a *flauta* is a crispy baguette) there are also tapas-style meals served day and night (dishes €4–10).

ME

C/Paris 162 Ⓜ Provença ☎ 934 194 933, Ⓦ www.catarsiscuisine.com. Tues & Sat 8.45–11.30pm, Wed–Fri 1.45–3.30pm & 8.45–11.30pm. MAP P.122–123, POCKET MAP F2

All the rage for its clever fusion of cuisines from Vietnam and New Orleans by way of Barcelona – all places dear to owner Javier's heart. Expect gumbo and marinated shrimp alongside papaya salad or grilled Saigon rib-eye with lemongrass, all in a stylish neo-Colonial setting. Mains are €15–23 though lunch is a cheaper, simpler affair.

OUT OF CHINA

C/Muntaner 100 Ⓜ Provença ☎ 934 515 555, Ⓦ www.outofchinabarcelona.com. Mon–Sat 1–4pm & 8pm–midnight, Sun 1–4pm. MAP P.122–123, POCKET MAP F3

Most Chinese restaurants in Barcelona are pretty bland, but

Bars

DRY MARTINI

AIRE SALA DIANA

C/de Valencia 236 Ⓜ Passeig de Gràcia
☎ 934 878 342, Ⓦ www.arenadisco.com.
Thurs–Sat 11pm–2.30am. MAP P.122–123,
POCKET MAP G3

The hottest, most stylish lesbian
bar in town is a relaxed place
for a drink and a dance to pop,
house and retro sounds. Gay
men are welcome too.

BELCHICA

C/Villaroel 60 Ⓜ Urgell ☎ 625 814 001.
Mon–Thurs 6pm–2.30am, Fri & Sat 6pm–3am,
Sun 6pm–2am. MAP P.122–123, POCKET MAP F4

Barcelona's first Belgian beer
bar guarantees a range of
decent brews (including
Trappist beers) that you can't
get anywhere else. It's a cosy
haunt, playing electronica, new
jazz, lounge, reggae and other
left-field sounds, and there are
music and poetry nights.

DIETRICH

C/Consell de Cent 255 Ⓜ Universitat
☎ 934 517 707. Thurs 10pm–2.30am, Fri &
Sat 10pm–3am. MAP P.122–123, POCKET MAP F3

Cornerstone of the Gaixample
scene is this well-known music
bar and "teatro-café"
– *tranquilo* during the week,
but ever more hedonistic as the
weekend wears on, with drag
shows, acrobats and dancers
punctuating the DJ sets.

DRY MARTINI

C/Aribau 166 Ⓜ Provença ☎ 932 175 072,
Ⓦ www.drymartinibcn.com. Mon–Fri
1pm–2.30am (opens 6.30pm in Aug).
Sat & Sun 6.30pm–3am. MAP P.122–123,
POCKET MAP F2

White-jacketed bartenders,
dark wood and brass fittings, a
self-satisfied air – it could only
be Barcelona's legendary
uptown cocktail bar. To be fair,
though, no one in town mixes
drinks better.

PUNTO BCN

C/Muntaner 63–65 Ⓜ Universitat ☎ 934 878
342, Ⓦ www.arenadisco.com. Daily 6pm–2.30am.
MAP P.122–123, POCKET MAP F3

Gaixample classic that attracts
a lively crowd for drinks, chat
and music. Wednesday happy
hour is a blast, while Friday
night is party night.

QUILOMBO

C/Aribau 149 Ⓜ Provença ☎ 934 395 406.
Tues–Thurs 9.30pm–3am, Fri & Sat
8.30pm–3.30am. MAP P.122–123, POCKET MAP F2

Unpretentious music bar
that's rolled with the years
since 1971, featuring live
guitarists, Latin American
bands and a clientele that joins
in enthusiastically, maracas
in hand.

VELÓDROMO

C/Muntaner 213 Ⓜ Hospital Clinic
☎ 934 306 022. Daily 6am–2.30am (Fri & Sat
until 3am). MAP P.122–123, POCKET MAP F1

A gleaming facelift has put the
glam back into this lofty,
Parisien-style Art Deco gem.
It's ideal for swish drinks and
cocktails, though with a
breakfast, tapas and bistro

menu by renowned chef Jordi Vilà it's also made for early starts and later dinners.

Clubs

ANTILLA BCN LATIN CLUB

C/Aragó 141–143 Ⓜ Urgell ☎ 934 514 564, Ⓦ www.antillasalsa.com. Wed 10pm–4am, Thurs–Sat 11pm–6am, Sun 7pm–3am. MAP P.122–123, POCKET MAP E3

Latin and Caribbean tunes galore – rumba, son, salsa, merengue, mambo, you name it – for out-and-out good-time dancing. There are live bands, killer cocktails and dance classes most nights.

ARENA MADRE

C/Balmes 32 Ⓜ Passeig de Gràcia ☎ 934 878 342, Ⓦ www.arenadisco.com. MAP P.122–123, POCKET MAP G4

The "mother" club sits at the helm of *Arena*'s gay empire, all within a city block (pay for one, get in to all) – frenetic house at *Arena Madre* (daily 12.30–5.30am), high-disco antics at *Arena Classic* (c/de la Diputació 233; Fri & Sat 2.30–5.30am), more of the same plus dance, r'n'b, pop and rock at the more mixed

Arena VIP (Gran Via de les Corts Catalanes 593; Fri & Sat 1–6am), and vintage chart hits at *Arena Dandy* (same address and hours). Admission is usually €6 on weekdays, including Fridays, and €12 on Saturdays.

DANZARAMA

Gran Vía de les Corts Catalanes 604 Ⓜ Universitat ☎ 933 019 743, Ⓦ www .danzarama.com. Daily 7am–2am (Fri & Sat until 3am). MAP P.122–123, POCKET MAP G4

One of the stalwarts of the uptown gastro-club scene, with a flashy fusion restaurant (open day and night), summer *terrassa* and cool bar and lounge, great for starting the night before some serious dancing elsewhere.

LUZ DE GAS

C/Muntaner 246 Ⓜ Provença ☎ 932 097 711, Ⓦ www.luzdegas.com. Daily 11.30pm–5am, occasional gigs from 9.30pm. MAP P.122–123, POCKET MAP F1

Smart live music venue, housed in a former ballroom, which is popular with a slightly older crowd and hosts live bands (rock, blues, soul, jazz and covers) every night around midnight. Foreign acts appear regularly too, mainly jazz-blues types but also old soul acts and up-and-coming rockers. Admission up to €20.

METRO

C/Sepúlveda 158 Ⓜ Universitat ☎ 933 235 227, Ⓦ www.metrodiscobcn.com. Daily 12.15–5am (Fri & Sat until 6.30am). MAP P.122–123, POCKET MAP A10

A gay institution in Barcelona, with cabaret nights and other events midweek, and extremely crowded club nights at weekends in its two rooms playing either current dance and techno or retro disco.

Gràcia and Parc Güell

Gràcia was a village for much of its early existence, before being annexed as a suburb in the late nineteenth century. It still feels set apart from the city in many ways, and though actual sights are few and far between it's well known for its cinemas, bars and restaurants. The one unmissable attraction, meanwhile, is just on the neighbourhood fringe, nearby Parc Güell, an extraordinary flight of fancy by architectural genius Antoni Gaudí. To get to Gràcia take the FGC train from Plaça de Catalunya to Gràcia station, or the metro to either Diagonal (south) or Fontana (north). From any of the stations, it's around a 500m walk to Gràcia's main square, Plaça del Sol, hub of the neighbourhood's renowned nightlife.

MERCAT DE LA LLIBERTAT

Pl. Llibertat 27 ⓂFontana ☎932 170 995.
ⓌWww.mercatsbcn.com. Mon–Fri
8am–8.30pm, Sat 8am–3pm. MAP P.129
You may as well start where the locals start, first thing in the morning, shopping for bread and provisions in the neighbourhood market. The red-brick and iron structure has been beautifully restored and at *El Tast de Joan Noi* (next to the Joan Noi fish counter) you can sample the breakfast of champions – oysters, grilled razor clams and a glass of *cava*.

CASA VICENS

C/de les Carolines 24 ⓂFontana. No public access. MAP P.129
Antoni Gaudí's first major private commission (1883–85)

VIEW FROM PARC GÜELL

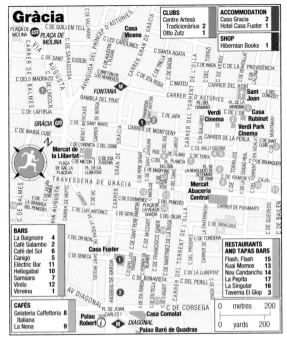

Gràcia

took its inspiration from the Moorish style, covering the facade of the house in green and white tiles with a flower motif. The decorative iron railings are a reminder of Gaudí's early training as a metalsmith (and he also designed much of the mansion's original furniture).

PLAÇA DE LA VIRREINA

Fontana. MAP P.129
This pretty square, backed by the parish church of Sant Joan, is one of Gràcia's favourites, with a couple of bars providing a place to rest and admire the handsome houses, most notably the Casa Rubinat (1909). Nearby streets, particularly **Carrer Verdi**, contain many of the neighbourhood's most fashionable boutiques, galleries and cafés.

VERDI AND VERDI PARK

C/Verdi 32 and c/Torrijos 49 Fontana 932 387 990, www.cines-verdi.com. MAP P.129
Barcelona's favourite art-house cinemas have sister locations in adjacent streets, with nine screens showing original-language movies from around the world. Tickets are €9 at the weekend, €6 on Monday and €8 from Tuesday to Friday (€7 for the first screening of the day).

PLAÇA DE LA VILA DE GRÀCIA

Diagonal. MAP P.129, POCKET MAP H1
The 30m-high clock tower in the heart of Gràcia was a rallying point for nineteenth-century radicals – whose twenty-first-century counter-parts prefer to meet for brunch at the square's popular café *terrassas*.

129

PILLARED WALKWAY IN PARC GÜELL

PARC GÜELL

C/d'Olot Ⓜ Vallcarca/Lesseps. ☎ 902 200 302, ⓦ www.parkguell.cat. Daily: April 8am–8pm; May–Oct 8am–9pm; Nov–March 8.30am–6pm. €7 online or €8 ticket office/ ATMs at Lesseps and Vallcarca metro stations. Advance bookings recommended. MAP P.130

Gaudí's Parc Guell (1900–14) was his most ambitious project after the Sagrada Família, conceived as a "garden city" of the type popular at the time in England, but opened as a public park instead in 1922. Laid out on a hill, which provides fabulous views back across the city, the park is an almost hallucinatory expression of the imagination. Pavilions of contorted stone, giant decorative lizards, meandering rustic viaducts, a vast Hall of Columns, carved stone trees – all combine in one manic swirl of ideas and excesses, like the famous meandering ceramic

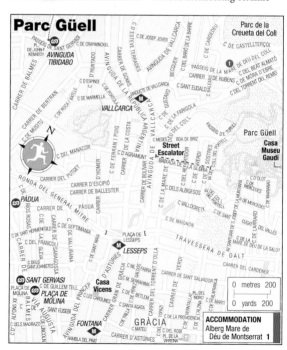

ACCOMMODATION
Alberg Mare de
Déu de Montserrat 1

bench that snakes along the edge of the terrace above the columned hall. Your ticket grants access to these sites, now part of the **monumental zone**. Only 400 visitors are allowed inside this zone each half-hour (once inside you can stay as long as you like), so it's advised to book ahead. The area outside the monumental zone is free.

The most direct route to Parc Güell is on bus #24 from Plaça de Catalunya, Passeig de Gràcia or c/Gran de Gràcia, which drops you at the eastern side gate. From Ⓜ Vallcarca, walk a few hundred metres down Avinguda de Vallcarca until you see the mechanical escalators on your left, ascending Baixada de la Glòria – follow these to the western side park entrance (15min in total). From Ⓜ Lessaps, turn right along Travessera de Dalt and then left up steep c/Larrard, which leads (10min) straight to the main entrance on c/Olot.

CASA-MUSEU GAUDÍ

Parc Güell Ⓜ Vallcarca/Lessaps ☎ 932 193 811, Ⓦ www.casamuseugaudi.org. Daily: April & May 10am–8pm; June–Sept 9am–8pm; Oct–March 10am–6pm. €5.50, combination ticket with Sagrada Família €18.30. MAP P.130

One of Gaudí's collaborators, Francesc Berenguer, designed and built a turreted house within Parc Güell for the architect (though he only lived in it intermittently). This contains a diverting collection of some of the furniture Gaudí designed for other projects – a typical mixture of wild originality and brilliant engineering – as well as plans and objects related to the park and to Gaudí's life. His study and bedroom have been preserved and there's an inkling of his personality, too, in the displayed religious texts and pictures, along with a silver coffee cup and his death mask, made at the Santa Pau hospital where he died.

PARC DE LA CREUETA DEL COLL

Pg. de la Mare de Deu del Coll 89 Ⓜ Vallcarca. Daily 10am–dusk. Free. MAP P.130

For a different kind of experience altogether, combine a trip to Gaudí's extravagant park with this contemporary urban space laid out on the site of an old quarry, whose sheer walls were retained in the landscaping. You're greeted at the top of the park steps by an Ellsworth Kelly metal spike, while suspended by steel cables over water is a massive concrete claw by the Basque artist Eduardo Chillida. There are also palms, promenades and a kiosk-café.

Bus V17 from near Plaça de Catalunya at Via Laietana and Metro Urquinaona, stops 100m from the park, or you can walk from Ⓜ Vallcarca in about twenty minutes (there's a map of the neighbourhood at the metro station). It's worth knowing that if you visit Creueta del Coll first and then take the main Passeig de la Mare de Deu del Coll, there are signposts leading you into Parc Güell the back way.

GAUDÍ'S DESK IN THE CASA-MUSEU GAUDÍ

HIBERNIAN BOOKS

more waiting as you struggle to choose from the twenty-odd flavours.

LA NENA

C/Ramon i Cajal 36 Ⓜ Joanic ☎ 932 851 476. Mon 8.30am–2pm & 4–10.30pm, Tues–Thurs 8.30am–10.30pm, Fri 8.30am–11pm, Sat 9am–11pm, Sun 9.30am–10.30pm; closed Aug. MAP P.129, POCKET MAP J1

Great for home-made cakes, waffles, quiches, organic ice cream, squeezed juices and the like. But parents also like the "little girl" as it's very child-friendly, from the changing mats in the loos to the little seats, games and puzzles.

Restaurants and tapas bars

FLASH, FLASH

C/de la Granada del Penedès 25 Ⓜ Diagonal ☎ 932 370 990, Ⓦ www.flashflashbarcelona .com. Daily 1pm–1.30am (bar open 11am–2am). MAP P.129, POCKET MAP G1

A classic 1970s survivor with a keen sense of style, *Flash, Flash* does tortillas (€6–9) served any time you like, any way you like, from plain and simple to elaborately stuffed, with sweet ones for dessert. If that doesn't grab you, try the reasonably priced menu of salads, steaks, burgers and fish. Either way, you'll love the original white leatherette booths and monotone photo-model cutouts – very Austin Powers.

KUAI MOMOS

C/Martínez de la Rosa 71 ⅯDiagonal ☎ 932 185 327, Ⓦ momosbcn.com. Mon–Wed 8–11.30pm, Thurs–Sat 8pm–midnight. MAP P.129, POCKET MAP H1

"Tapas with chopsticks" reads the motto of this restaurant, which has an intimate vibe best described as sushi bar meets

Shop

HIBERNIAN BOOKS

C/Montseny 17 Ⓜ Fontana Ⓦ www.hibernian -books.com. Mon 4.30–8.30pm, Tues–Sat 10.30am–8.30pm. MAP P.129

Barcelona's only secondhand English bookstore has around 40,000 titles in stock – you can part-exchange, and there are always plenty of giveaway bargains available.

Cafés

GELATERIA CAFFETTERIA ITALIANA

Pl. de la Revolució 2 Ⓜ Fontana ☎ 932 102 339. Sun–Thurs 2pm–1am, Fri & Sat 2pm–2am; Nov–April opens at 4pm. MAP P.129, POCKET MAP H1

For real hand-made Italian ice cream (the shop has been churning it out since 1881), and a stroll around a pretty square in the sun. Expect queues at peak times and then

Catalan tavern. The kitchen rolls out quite the tour of Asia's greatest culinary hits, from pork-and-vegetable *momos* (dumplings) and lacquered duck to fragrant Thai curries and plump fishcakes. Tapas run €5–14 (you'll eat well for around €30).

NOU CANDANCHU

Pl. de la Vila de Gràcia 9 ⓂDiagonal ☎ 932 377 362. Mon, Wed, Thurs & Sun 7am–1am, Fri & Sat 7am–2am. MAP P.129, POCKET MAP H1

Good for lunch on a sunny day or a leisurely night out on a budget, when you can sit beneath the clock tower and soak up the atmosphere in the ever-entertaining local square. There's a wide menu – tapas and hot sandwiches, but also steak and eggs, steamed clams and mussels, or cod and hake cooked plenty of different ways. It's managed by an affable bunch of young guys, and there's a lot of choice for €8–12.

FLASH, FLASH

LA PEPITA

C/Còrsega 343 ⓂDiagonal/Verdaguer ☎ 932 384 893, ⓦlapepitabcn.com. Mon 8pm–1.30am, Tues–Sat 9am–1.30am, kitchen open 1–4.30pm & 7.30pm–midnight. MAP P.129, POCKET MAP H2

There's usually a queue out the door, and deservedly so. The tapas, like roasted chicken croquettes with romesco sauce (€4) or aubergine fritters with goats' cheese, honey and apples (€8), are fantastic, and the atmosphere is chatty and convivial. Hundreds of "love notes" scrawled by customers on the white-tiled walls hint at its popularity. It's a good place for drink if you show up outside of kitchen hours, too.

LA SINGULAR

C/Francesc Giner 50 ⓂDiagonal ☎ 932 375 098. Mon–Thurs 1–4pm & 8.30–11.30pm, Fri 1–4pm & 8.30pm–12.30am, Sat 8.30pm–12.30am. MAP P.129, POCKET MAP H1

The tiny kitchen turns out refined Mediterranean food at moderate prices (most dishes €5–15) – think aubergine and smoked fish salad or chicken stuffed with dates and ham. There's always something appealing on the menu for veggies, too. It's a cornerstone of the neighbourhood, with a friendly atmosphere, but there are only nine tables, so go early or reserve.

TAVERNA EL GLOP

C/Sant Lluís 24 ⓂJoanic ☎ 932 137 058, ⓦwww.tavernaelglop.com. Daily 1pm–1am. MAP P.129

The rusticity (stone-flagged floors, baskets of garlic) stops just the right side of parody and the lunch *menú del dia* is one of the city's best deals; otherwise expect to spend around €25 a head for grills and other tavern specials prepared in front of you on the open kitchen ranges.

Bars

LA BAIGNOIRE

C/Verdi 6 Ⓜ Fontana ☎ 677 408 993. Daily 7pm–1am (Fri & Sat until 3am). MAP P.129, POCKET MAP H1

Cosy little wine bar offering a small corner of sophistication on an otherwise busy street – Ella Fitzgerald on CD, a dozen good wines by the glass and cheesy nibbles.

CAFÉ SALAMBO

C/Torrijos 51 Ⓜ Fontana ☎ 932 186 966, Ⓦ www.cafesalambo.com. Mon–Thurs noon–1am, Fri & Sat noon–3am, Sun noon–midnight. MAP P.129

Where the pre- and post-cinema crowd meets (both Verdi cinemas are on the doorstep). It's a long-standing neighbourhood hangout, with something of a colonial feel, and there are lots of wines and *cava* by the glass, and good food too.

CAFÉ DEL SOL

Pl. del Sol 16 Ⓜ Fontana ☎ 934 155 663, Ⓦ cafedelsol.cat. Daily 1pm–2.30am (Fri & Sat until 3am). MAP P.129, POCKET MAP H1

The grandaddy of the Plaça del Sol scene sees action day and night. On summer evenings, when the square is packed with revellers, there's not an outdoor table to be had, but even in winter this is a popular drinking den – the pubby interior has a back room and gallery, often rammed to the rafters.

CANIGÓ

C/Verdi 2 Ⓜ Fontana ☎ 932 133 049, Ⓦ barcanigo.com. Mon–Thurs 10am–2am, Fri 10am–3am, Sat 8pm–3am. MAP P.129, POCKET MAP H1

Family-run neighbourhood bar now entering its third generation. It's not much to look at, but the drinks are cheap and it's a Gràcia institution with a loyal following, packed out at weekends especially with a young, largely local crowd.

ELÈCTRIC BAR

Trav. de Gràcia 233 Ⓜ Joanic Ⓦ www.electricbarcelona.com. Daily 7pm–2am (Fri & Sat until 3am). MAP P.129, POCKET MAP J1

The regular gigs and eclectic live programming may have stopped, but Gràcia's original grunge-feel boho bar is still a great place for a drink, and Friday night is always a wild Brazilian music thrash. There's an occasional concert too, so keep checking the website or their Facebook page.

HELIOGABAL

C/Ramon i Cajal 80 Ⓜ Joanic Ⓦ www.heliogabal.com. Wed–Sat 9.30pm–2am (Fri & Sat until 3.30am). MAP P.129, POCKET MAP J1

Not much more than a boiler room given a lick of paint, but filled with a cool, twenty-something crowd, here for the live poetry and music – expect something different every night (Catalan versifying, jazz jam sessions and earnest singer-songwriters), starting at 10pm. Admission is usually €5–10, depending on the act, and drinks aren't expensive.

TERRACE AT CAFÉ DEL SOL

SAMSARA

C/Terol 6 Ⓜ Fontana ☎ 932 853 688.
Mon–Thurs 8.30pm–1am, Fri 7.30pm–2am,
Sat 12.30–3.30pm & 7.30pm–2am, Sun
12.30–3.30pm & 7.30pm–1am. MAP P.129,
POCKET MAP H1

It's totally Gràcia – low tables,
low lighting and painted
concrete walls, plus a chillout
soundtrack and a projection
screen above the bar. There's
also contemporary tapas and
"platillos" (little plates) but it's a
bar first and foremost, with DJs
cracking out house and techno
sets at the weekend.

VINILO

C/Matilde 2 Ⓜ Diagonal ☎ 626 464 759.
Mon–Thurs 8pm–2am, Fri & Sat 8pm–3am.
MAP P.129, POCKET MAP H1

Wear a beret, surgically
attached to your iPad? Favour
Blade Runner, Jeff Buckley and
Band of Horses? This bar's for
you – a dive bar with the
lighting set at perpetual dusk,
where time slips easily away.

VIRREINA

Pl. de la Virreina 1 Ⓜ Fontana ☎ 932 379
880. Daily 9am–2am. MAP P.129

Another real Gràcia favourite,
on one of the neighbourhood's
prettiest squares, with a very
popular summer *terrassa*.
Cold beer and sandwiches
are served to a laidback
crowd – it's one of those
places where you drop by for
a quick drink and find
yourself staying for hours.

Clubs

CENTRE ARTESÀ TRADICIONÀRIUS

Trav. de Sant Antoni 6–8 Ⓜ Fontana ☎ 932
184 485, Ⓦ www.tradicionarius.cat. MAP P.129

The best place in town for folk,
traditional and world music by
Catalan, Spanish and visiting

OTTO ZUTZ

performers, including some
occasional big names.
Admission is usually €5–15,
and you can expect anything
from Basque bagpipes to
Brazilian singers. There are
also music and instrument
workshops, while CAT
sponsors all sorts of outreach
concerts and festivals,
including an annual international folk and traditional
dance festival between January
and April.

OTTO ZUTZ

C/de Lincoln 15 Ⓜ Fontana ☎ 932 380 722,
Ⓦ www.ottozutz.com. Tues–Thurs 11pm–3am,
Fri & Sat midnight–6am. MAP P.129

It first opened in 1985, and has
lost some of its erstwhile glam
cachet, but this three-storey
former textile factory still has a
shedload of pretensions. The
sounds are basically hip-hop,
r'n'b and house, and with the
right clothes and face you're in
(you may or may not have to
pay, depending on how
impressive you are, the day of
the week, the mood of the door
staff, etc).

Camp Nou, Pedralbes and Sarrià-Sant Gervasi

On the northwestern edge of the centre, the city's famous football stadium, Camp Nou, draws locals and visitors alike, both to the big game and to the FC Barcelona museum. Nearby, across Avinguda Diagonal, the Palau Reial de Pedralbes is home to serene public gardens (the lush vegetation hides an early work by Gaudí), while a half-day's excursion can be made by walking from the palace, past the Gaudí dragon gate at Pavellons Güell, to the calm cloister at the Gothic monastery of Pedralbes. You can complete the day by returning via Sarrià, to the east, more like a small town than a suburb, with a pretty main street and market to explore. At night, the focus shifts to the bars and restaurants of neighbouring Sant Gervasi in the streets north of Plaça de Francesc Macià.

AVINGUDA DIAGONAL

Ⓜ Maria Cristina. MAP P.138–139

The uptown section of Avinguda Diagonal runs through the heart of Barcelona's flashiest business and shopping district. The giant **L'Illa** shopping centre flanks the avenue – the stepped design is a prone echo of New York's Rockefeller Center. Designer fashion stores are ubiquitous, particularly around **Plaça de Francesc Macià** and Avinguda Pau Casals – at the end of the latter, **Turó Parc** (daily 10am–dusk) is a good place to rest weary feet, with a small children's playground and a

café-kiosk. Meanwhile, behind L'Illa, it's worth seeking out **Plaça de la Concordia**, a surprising survivor from the past amid the uptown tower blocks – the pretty little square is dominated by its church belltower and ringed by local businesses (florist, pharmacy, hairdresser), with an outdoor café or two for a quiet drink.

MUSEU DEL FUTBOL

CAMP NOU AND FC BARCELONA

Av. Arístides Maillol Ⓜ Collblanc/Maria Cristina ☎ 902 189 900 or ☎ 934 963 600 from outside Spain, ⓦ www.fcbarcelona.com. Match tickets (€50–100) also from Ticketmaster ⓦ ticketmaster.es. MAP P.138–139

In Barcelona, football is a genuine obsession, with support for the local giants FC (Futbol Club) Barcelona raised to an art form. "More than just a club" is the proud boast, and during the dictatorship years the club stood as a Catalan symbol around which people could rally. Arch rivals, Real Madrid, on the other hand, were always seen as Franco's club. The swashbuckling team – past European champions and darling of football neutrals everywhere – plays at the magnificent Camp Nou football stadium, built in 1957, and enlarged for the 1982 World Cup semi-final to accommodate 98,000 spectators. A new remodelling (by architect Norman Foster) plans to update the stadium over the next few years, but even today Camp Nou provides one of the world's best football-watching experiences.

The **football season** runs from August until May, with league games usually played on Sundays. Tickets are relatively easy to come by, except for the biggest games, and go on general sale up to a month before each match – buy them online, at the ticket office, or by calling ServiCaixa.

The stadium complex hosts basketball, handball and hockey games with FC Barcelona's other professional teams, and there's also a public ice rink, souvenir shop and café.

CAMP NOU EXPERIENCE

Camp Nou, Av. Arístides Maillol, enter through Gates 7 & 9 Ⓜ Collblanc/Maria Cristina ☎ 902 189 900 or ☎ 934 963 600, ⓦ www.fcbarcelona.com. April & mid-Oct to Dec Mon–Sat 10am–6.30pm, Sun & hols 10am–2.30pm; May to mid-Oct daily 9.30am–7.30pm; tours until 1hr before closing. €23, children 6–13 years €17. MAP P.138–139

No soccer fan should miss the Camp Nou stadium tour and museum, billed as the "Camp Nou Experience". The self-guided tour winds through the changing rooms, onto the pitch and up to the press gallery and directors' box for stunning views. The museum, meanwhile, is jammed full of silverware and memorabilia, while displays and archive footage trace the history of the club back to 1901. Finally, you're directed into the massive **FC Botiga**, where you can buy anything from a replica shirt to a branded bottle of wine.

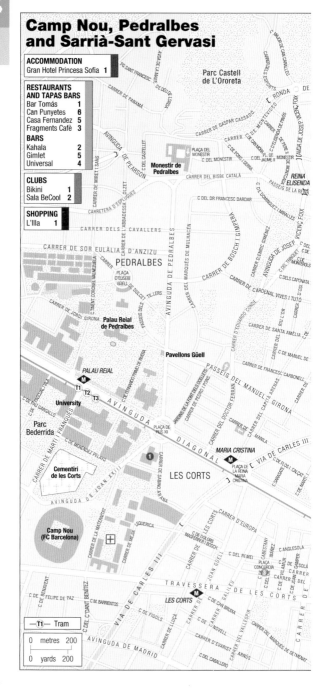

Camp Nou, Pedralbes and Sarrià-Sant Gervasi

ACCOMMODATION
Gran Hotel Princesa Sofia 1

RESTAURANTS AND TAPAS BARS
Bar Tomás 1
Can Punyetes 6
Casa Fernandez 5
Fragments Cafè 3

BARS
Kahala 2
Gimlet 5
Universal 4

CLUBS
Bikini 1
Sala BeCool 2

SHOPPING
L'Illa 1

—T1— Tram

0 metres 200
0 yards 200

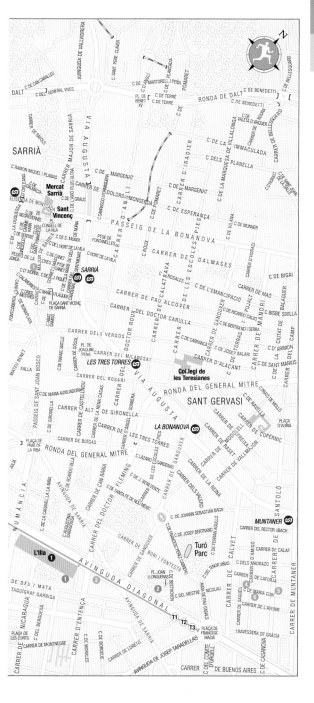

THE PALAU REIAL DE PEDRALBES GARDENS

PALAU REIAL DE PEDRALBES

Av. Diagonal 686 Ⓜ Palau Reial. Gardens daily 10am–dusk. Free. MAP P.138–139

Opposite the university on Avinguda Diagonal, formal grounds stretch up to the Italianate Palau Reial de Pedralbes – basically a large villa with pretensions. It was built for the use of the royal family on their visits to Barcelona, with funds raised by public subscription, and received its first such visit in 1926. However, within five years the king had abdicated and the palace somewhat lost its role. Franco kept it on as a presidential residence and it later passed to the city. The rooms had been used to show off the city's applied art collections, but those collections are being moved to the new Museu del Disseny near Plaça de les Glòries Catalanes. Although the palace is now closed to the public, the gardens – a breezy oasis of Himalaya cedars, strawberry trees and bougainvillea – are worth a visit. Hidden in a bamboo thicket, to the left-centre of the façade, is the "Hercules fountain" (1884), an early work by Antoni Gaudí. He also designed the parabolic pergola, which is covered in climbing plants and is a nice place to sit and rest your feet. In late June, a music festival (Ⓦ festivalpedralbes.com) takes place in the palace's gardens.

PAVELLONS GÜELL

Av. de Pedralbes 7 Ⓜ Palau Reial ☏ 933 177 652, Ⓦ www.rutadelmodernisme.com. Tours Sat & Sun at 10.15am & 12.15pm in English, plus 11.15am & 1.15pm in Spanish/Catalan. €6. MAP P.138–139

As an early test of his capabilities, Antoni Gaudí was asked by his patron, Eusebi Güell, to rework the entrance, gatehouse and stables of the Güell summer residence. The resultant brick and tile buildings are frothy, whimsical affairs, though it's the gateway that's the most famous element.

Here be dragons

The slavering beast on Gaudí's dragon gate at the Pavellons Güell is not the vanquished dragon of Sant Jordi (St George), the Catalan patron saint, but the one that appears in the Labours of Hercules myth, a familiar Catalan theme in the nineteenth century. Gaudí's design was based on a work by the Catalan renaissance poet Jacint Verdaguer, a friend of the Güell family, who had reworked the myth in his epic poem, L'Atlàntida – thus, the dragon guarding golden apples in the Gardens of Hesperides is here protecting instead an orange tree (considered a more Catalan fruit). Gaudí's gate indeed can be read as an homage to Verdaguer, with its stencilled roses representing those traditionally given to the winner of the Catalan poetry competition, the Jocs Floral, which the poet won in 1877.

An extraordinary winged dragon of twisted iron snarls at the passers-by, its razor-toothed jaws spread wide in a fearsome roar. During the week you can't go any further than the gate, but guided visits show you the grounds and Gaudí's innovative stables, now used as a library by the university's historical architecture department.

SARRIÀ

FGC Sarrià, or bus #64 from Pl. Universitat or Pedralbes. MAP P.138–139

The Sarrià district was once an independent small town and still looks the part, with a narrow, traffic-free main street – c/Major de Sarrià – at the top of which stands the much-restored church of Sant Vicenç. The church flanks the main Passeig de la Reina Elisenda de Montcada, across which lies the neighbourhood market, Mercat Sarrià, housed in a 1911 *modernista* red-brick building. You'll find a few other surviving old-town squares down the main street, prettiest of which is Plaça Sant Vicenç de Sarrià (off c/Mañe i Flaquer), where there's a statue of the saint.

MONESTIR DE PEDRALBES

Biaxada del Monestir Ⓜ Palau Reial and 20min walk, or FGC Reina Elisenda and 10min walk, or bus #64 from Pl. Universitat ☎ 932 563 434, Ⓦ www.museuhistoria.bcn. cat. April–Sept Tues–Fri 10am–5pm, Sat 10am–7pm, Sun 10am–8pm; Oct–March Tues–Fri 10am–2pm, Sat & Sun 10am–5pm. €7. MAP P.138–139

Founded in 1326 for the nuns of the Order of St Clare, this is in effect an entire monastic village set within medieval walls on the outskirts of the city. The cloisters in particular are the finest in Barcelona, built on three levels and adorned by the slenderest of columns. Side rooms and chambers give a clear impression of medieval convent life, and also display a selection of the monastery's treasures, while the adjacent church contains the carved marble tomb of the convent's founder, Elisenda de Montcada, wife of King Jaume II. After 600 years of isolation, the monastery was sequestered by the Generalitat during the Civil War. It was turned into a museum in 1983, and a new adjacent convent was built, where the Clare nuns still reside.

MONESTIR DE PEDRALBES

Shopping

L'ILLA

Av. Diagonal 555–559 Ⓜ Maria Cristina
Ⓦ www.lilla.com. Mon–Sat 10am–9.30pm.
MAP P.138–139

The landmark uptown shopping mall is stuffed full of designer fashion, plus Camper (shoes), FNAC (music, film and books), Sfera (cosmetics), Decathlon (sports), El Corte Inglés (department store), Caprabo (supermarket), food hall and much more.

You can get here by metro (Maria Cristina) or tram (from Pl. de Francesc Macià), or on the **Tomb Bus shopping line service**, which also visits other uptown stores on a circular route from Plaça de Catalunya (departures every 6–8min; tickets available on board).

Restaurants and tapas bars

BAR TOMÁS

C/Major de Sarrià 49, FGC Sarrià ☎ 932 031 077. Mon–Sat noon–4pm & 6–10pm; closed Aug. MAP P.138–139

The best *patatas bravas* in Barcelona? Everyone will point you here, to this unassuming, white-Formica-table bar in the suburbs (a 12min train ride from Plaça de Catalunya FGC) for their unrivalled spicy fried potatoes with garlic mayo and *salsa picante*. It's not all they serve, but it might as well be.

They fry noon to 3pm and 6pm to closing, so if it's *patatas bravas* you want, be sure to take a note of the hours.

CAN PUNYETES

C/Marià Cubí 189, FGC Muntaner ☎ 932 009 159, Ⓦ www.canpunyetes.com. Daily noon–3.45pm & 8pm–midnight. MAP P.138–139

BAR TOMÁS

Traditional grillhouse-tavern that offers diners a taste of older times. Simple salads and tapas, open grills turning out *botifarra* (sausage), lamb chops, chicken and pork – accompanied by grilled country bread, white beans and char-grilled potato halves. It's cheap (almost everything under €10) and locals love it.

CASA FERNANDEZ

C/Santaló 46, FGC Muntaner ☎ 932 019 308, Ⓦ www.casafernandez.com. Mon–Sat 1–5pm & 8pm–midnight, Sun noon–4.30pm. MAP P.138–139

The long kitchen hours are a boon for the bar-crawlers in this neck of the woods. It's a contemporary place featuring market cuisine, though they are specialists in – of all things – fried eggs, either served straight with chips or with Catalan sausage, garlic prawns or other variations. Most dishes are in the range of €6 to €15.

FRAGMENTS CAFÈ

Pl. de la Concórdia 12 Ⓜ Les Corts ☎ 934 199 613, Ⓦ fragmentscafe.com. Tues–Wed 12.30pm–1am, Thurs & Fri 12.30–2.30am, Sat 11.30am–2.30am, Sun 11.30am–1am; closed 2 weeks in Aug. MAP P.138–139

A classy yet casual bistro popular with locals for its fresh, classic food that's served in the charming dining room or in the shaded garden. The lunch menu is a steal (€12), with the rest of the dishes, from tapas to fresh pasta, around €5–14.

Bars

GIMLET

C/Santaló 46, FGC Muntaner ☎ 932 015 306, Ⓦ www.gimletbcn.com. Mon–Wed 6pm–1am, Thurs 6pm–2.30am, Fri & Sat 6pm–3am. MAP P.138–139

This favoured cocktail joint is especially popular in summertime, when the streetside tables offer a great vantage point for watching the party unfold. There are also two or three other late-opening bars on the same stretch.

UNIVERSAL

C/Marià Cubí 182, FGC Muntaner ☎ 934 136 362, Ⓦ www.universalbcn.com. Mon–Sat 11pm–3.30am (Fri & Sat until 4.30am). MAP P.138–139

A classic designer music bar that's been part of the Barcelona style scene since 1985. Sounds range from house to back-to-the-80s, but be warned: drinks are fairly pricey and they operate a strict door policy; if your face doesn't fit you might not get in.

KAHALA

Avgda. Diagonal 537 Ⓜ Maria Cristina ☎ 934 309 026, Ⓦ www.kahalabarcelona.com. Mon 10am–6pm, Tues–Fri 10am–1am, Sat 10am–2am. MAP P.138–139

Open since 1971, this Hawaiian-themed bar is a treasure trove of Polynesian kitsch: gurgling waterfalls, bamboo furniture and grimacing tiki masks abound. The drinks – from the *Perla de Vicio* ("Pearl of Vice") to the classic Mai Tai – pack quite the punch and are certain to ready you for an evening of island – pardon – *club* hopping.

Clubs

BIKINI

C/Deu i Mata 105 Ⓜ Les Corts ☎ 933 220 800, Ⓦ www.bikinibcn.com. Thurs–Sat midnight–5am. MAP P.138–139

This traditional landmark of Barcelona nightlife (behind the L'Illa shopping centre) offers a regular diet of great indie, rock, roots and world gigs followed by club sounds, from house to Brazilian, according to the night. Admission usually €15–25, though some big-name gigs up to €40.

SALA BECOOL

Pl. Joan Llongueras 5 Ⓜ Hospital Clínic ☎ 933 620 413, Ⓦ www.salabecool.com. MAP P.138–139

Thumping uptown club venue for local and national rock, indie and electro/techno bands and DJs. Gigs usually Thursday to Saturday nights at around 10pm, followed by DJ sessions from midnight or 1am. Admission for either runs from €10 to €20, depending on who's appearing. They also sponsor Friday-night acoustic nights at the next-door Irish bar *Dublin* (music Fri at 11pm, free admission, bar open daily until 3am).

GIMLET

Tibidabo and Parc de Collserola

The views from the heights of Tibidabo (550m), the peak that signals the northwestern boundary of the city, are legendary. On a clear day you can see across to the Pyrenees and out to sea even as far as Mallorca. However, while many make the tram and funicular ride up to Tibidabo's amusement park, few realize that beyond stretches the Parc de Collserola, an area of peaks, wooded river valleys and hiking paths – one of Barcelona's best-kept secrets. You can walk into the park from Tibidabo, but it's actually better to start from the park's information centre, across to the east above Vallvidrera, where hiking-trail leaflets are available. Meanwhile, families won't want to miss CosmoCaixa, the city's excellent science museum, which can easily be seen on the way to or from Tibidabo.

PARC D'ATRACCIONS

Pl. del Tibidabo ☎ 932 117 942, ⓦ www
.tibidabo.cat. Days and hours vary, but
basically June–Sept Wed–Sun, rest of the year
Sat, Sun & hols only, closed Jan & Feb. Park
open from noon until 7–11pm depending on
season. Skywalk ticket €12.70, full admission
€28.50, plus family/discount tickets. MAP P.145
Barcelona's self-styled "magic
mountain" amusement park
takes full advantage of its
hillside location to offer
jaw-dropping perspectives over
the city. Some of the most
famous rides (like the
aeroplane – spinning since
1928 – and the carousel) are
grouped under the discounted
"Skywalk" ticket. Summer
weekends finish with parades,
concerts and a noisy *correfoc*, a
theatrical fireworks display.

VIEW OVER THE PARC D'ATRACCIONS

Tibidabo and Parc de Collserola

BAIXADA DE VILLVEDRERA

Centre d'Informació
Museu-Casa Verdaguer

ACCOMMODATION
Gran Hotel La Florida 1

BAR
Mirablau 1

Parc   de   Collserola

VALLVIDRERA

Font de Budallera

Torre de Collserola

Sagrat Cor

Parc d'Atraccions

Funicular de Vallvidrera

PEU DEL FUNICULAR

TIBIDABO

Funicular del Tibidabo

RONDA DE DALT

C ISAAC NEWTON

PL. DEL DR ANDREU

REINA ELISENDA

CosmoCaixa

VALLCARCA

PLAÇA D'ALFONSO COMIN

Monastir de Pedralbes

Tramvia Blau

SARRIÀ

AV TIBIDABO

PASSEIG DE SANT GERVASI

SARRIÀ

SANT GERVASI

PL. DE JOHN F. KENNEDY

VALLCARCA

0 metres 500
0 yards 500

SAGRAT COR

Elevator operates daily 10am–8pm & 3–7pm.
€2. MAP P.145

Next to Tibidabo's amusement park climb the shining steps of the Templo Expiatorio de España – otherwise known as the Sagrat Cor (Sacred Heart). This is topped by a huge statue of Christ, and inside the church an elevator climbs to a viewing platform from where the city, surrounding hills and shimmering sea glisten in the distance.

Getting to Tibidabo

Reaching the heights of Tibidabo takes up to an hour, all told, from the city centre. First, take the FGC train (line 7) from Plaça de Catalunya station to **Avinguda Tibidabo** (the last stop), where you cross the road to the tram/bus shelter (the Bus Turístic stops here too). The **Tramvia Blau**, an antique tram service (Jan–April & mid-Oct to Dec Sat, Sun & hols 10am–6pm; May–June & mid-Sept to mid-Oct Sat, Sun & hols 10am–7.30pm; July to mid-Sept & Easter week daily 10am–7.30pm; €4.20 one-way) then runs you up the hill to Plaça Doctor Andreu; out of season there's a bus service instead during the week. Here, you change to the **Funicular del Tibidabo**, with connections every 15min to Tibidabo (operates when the Parc d'Atraccions is open; €7.70 without park admission, €4.10 with park admission). Alternatively, the **Tibibus** runs direct to Tibidabo from Plaça de Catalunya, outside El Corte Inglés (from 10.15am every day the park is open; €2.95, reimbursed with park admission).

TORRE DE COLLSEROLA

Carretera de Vallvidrera al Tibidabo ☎ 932 117 942, ⓦ www.torredecollserola.com. March, April, Nov & Dec Sat & Sun noon–1.45pm & 3.30–5.45pm (May & Oct until 6.45pm); July–Sept Wed–Sun noon–1.45pm & 3.30–7.45pm; closed Jan & Feb. €5. MAP P.145

Follow the road from the Tibidabo car park and it's only a few minutes' walk to Norman Foster's soaring communications tower, built for the 1992 Olympics. This features a glass elevator that whisks you up ten floors (115m) for extensive views – 70km, they claim, on a good day. Note that there's a combo ticket for the tower available at the Tibidabo amusement park.

PARC DE COLLSEROLA

Centre d'Informació, FGC Baixada de Vallvidrera (on the Sabadell or Terrassa line from Pl. de Catalunya; 15min) ☎ 932 803 552, ⓦ www.parcnaturalcollserola.cat. Daily 9.30am–3pm. MAP P.145

Given a half-decent day, local bikers, hikers and outdoor enthusiasts all make a beeline

TORRE DE COLLSEROLA

for the city's ring of wooded hills beyond Tibidabo. The park information centre lies in oak and pinewoods, an easy ten-minute walk up through the trees from the FGC Baixada de Vallvidrera train station. There's a bar-restaurant here with an outdoor terrace, plus an exhibition on the park's history, flora and fauna, while the staff hand out English-language leaflets detailing the various park walks. Some of the well-marked paths – like the oak-forest walk – soon gain height for marvellous views over the tree canopy, while others descend through the valley bottoms to springs and shaded picnic areas. Perhaps the nicest short walk from the information centre is to the **Font de la Budellera** (1hr 15min return), a landscaped spring deep in the woods. If you follow the signs from the *font* to the Torre de Collserola (another 20min), you can return to Barcelona on the funicular from the nearby suburban village of **Vallvidrera** (daily 6am–midnight; every 6–10min), which connects to Peu del Funicular, an FGC train station on the line from Plaça de Catalunya.

MUSEU-CASA VERDAGUER

Villa Joana, Carretera de l'Església 4 ☎ 932 047 805, ⓦ www.verdaguer.cat. Mon & Wed–Sun 10am–1.30pm, Tues 5–7pm (April–Nov Sat 5–7pm). Free. MAP P.145

If you're up at the park at the weekend, it's worth having a quick look inside the country house that sits just below the Collserola information centre. Jacint Verdaguer (1845–1902), the Catalan Renaissance poet, lived here briefly before his death, and the house has been preserved as an example of well-to-do nineteenth-century Catalan life.

COSMOCAIXA

C/Isaac Newton 26 ☎ 932 126 050, ⊕ www
.cosmocaixa.com. Tues–Sun 10am–8pm. €4,
under-16s free. MAP P.145

A dramatic refurbishment in
2005 turned the city's science
museum into a must-see
attraction, certainly if you've
got children in tow – it's an
easy place to spend a couple
of hours and can break the
journey on your way to or
from Tibidabo. Partly housed
in a converted *modernista*
hospice, the museum retains
the original building but has
added a light-filled public
concourse and a huge
underground extension with
four subterranean levels,
where hands-on experiments
and displays investigate life,
the universe and everything,
"from bacteria to Shakes-
peare". The two big draws are
the hundred tonnes of "sliced
rock" in the Geological Wall
and, best of all, the Bosc
Inundat – nothing less than a
thousand square metres of
real Amazonian rainforest,
complete with croc-filled
mangroves, anacondas and
giant catfish. Other levels of
the museum are devoted to
children's and family activities,
which tend to be held at
weekends and during school
holidays – pick up a schedule
when you arrive. There are
also daily shows in the
planetarium (in Spanish and
Catalan only), a great gift shop
and a café-restaurant with
outdoor seating.

The easiest way to reach
CosmoCaixa is by FGC train
from Plaça de Catalunya to
Avinguda del Tibidabo station,
and then walk up the avenue,
turning left just before the ring
road (10min) – or the Tramvia
Blau or Bus Turistíc can drop
you close by.

Bar

MIRABLAU

Pl. del Dr. Andrea, Av. Tibidabo ☎ 934
185 879. Daily 11am–5am. MAP P.145
Unbelievable city views
from a chic bar near the
Tibidabo funicular that
fills to bursting at times.
By day, a great place for
coffee and views, by night
a rich-kid disco-tunes
stomping ground.

Montserrat

The mountain of Montserrat, with its rock crags, vast monastery and hermitage caves, stands just 40km northwest of Barcelona. It's the most popular day-trip from the city, reached in around ninety minutes by train and then cable car or rack railway for a thrilling ride up to the monastery. Once there, you can visit the basilica and monastery buildings and complete your day with a walk around the woods and crags, using the two funicular railways that depart from the complex. There are cafés and restaurants at the monastery, but they are relatively pricey and none too inspiring – you may wish to take a picnic instead.

AERI DE MONTSERRAT

Montserrat Aeri ☎ 938 350 005, Ⓦ www .aeridemontserrat.com. Departures every 15min, March–Oct daily 9.40am–2pm & 2.35–7pm; Nov–Feb daily 10.10am–2pm & 2.35–5.45pm. MAP P.150

For the cable-car service, get off the train from Barcelona at Montserrat Aeri station (52min). You may have to wait in line fifteen minutes or so, but then it's only a five-minute swoop up the sheer mountainside to a terrace just below the monastery – probably the most exhilarating ride in Catalunya. Returning to Barcelona, the line R5 trains depart hourly from Montserrat Aeri (from 9.37am).

CREMALLERA DE MONTSERRAT

Monistrol de Montserrat ☎ 932 051 515, Ⓦ www.cremallerademontserrat.com. Departures every hour, daily 8.48am–5.38/7.38pm (later services at weekends April–Oct, plus daily July–Sept). MAP P.150

The alternative approach to the monastery is by the Montserrat rack railway, which departs from Monistrol de Montserrat station (the next stop after Montserrat Aeri, another 4min), and takes twenty minutes to complete the climb. The original rack railway on Montserrat ran between 1892 and 1957, and this modern replacement recreates the

Getting to Montserrat

To reach the Montserrat cable-car/rack-railway stations, take the **FGC train** (line R5, direction Manresa), which leaves daily from **Plaça d'Espanya** (ⓂEspanya) at hourly intervals from 8.36am. All fare options are detailed at **Plaça d'Espanya**, including return through-tickets from Barcelona (around €20) either for the train/cable car or train/rack railway. There are also two combination tickets available: the **Trans Montserrat** (€27.50), which includes all transport services, including unlimited use of the mountain funiculars, and the audiovisual show; and the **Tot Montserrat** (€43.70), which includes the same, plus monastery museum and a cafeteria lunch. Both tickets are also available at the Plaça de Catalunya tourist office.

majestic engineering that allows the train to climb 550m in 4km. Returning to Barcelona, the line R5 trains depart at least hourly from Monistrol de Montserrat (from 9.21am).

MONESTIR DE MONTSERRAT

Visitor centre ☎ 938 777 701, ⓦ www
.montserratvisita.com. Daily 9am–5.30pm (Sat, Sun & July–Sept until 6.45pm). Walking maps and accommodation advice available. MAP P.150

Legends hang easily upon the monastery of Montserrat. Fifty years after the birth of Christ, St Peter is said to have deposited an image of the Virgin (known as La Moreneta), carved by St Luke, in one of the mountain caves. The icon was lost in the early eighth century after being hidden during the Moorish invasion, but reappeared in 880, accompanied by the customary visions and celestial music. A chapel was built to house it, and in 976 this was superseded by a Benedictine monastery, set at an altitude of nearly 1000m. Miracles abounded and the Virgin of Montserrat soon became the chief cult image of Catalunya and a pilgrimage centre second in Spain only to Santiago de Compostela – the main pilgrimages to Montserrat

take place on April 27 and September 8.

The monastery's various outbuildings – including hotel, post office, souvenir shop and bar – fan out around an open square, and there are extraordinary mountain views from the terrace. The best restaurant is inside the *Hotel Abat Cisneros* (meals around €40), though the finest views are from the cliff-edge *Restaurant de Montserrat* (around €25) – the self-service cafeteria, one floor up, is where you eat with the all-inclusive *Tot Montserrat* ticket.

MONASTERY BUILDING AT MONTSERRAT

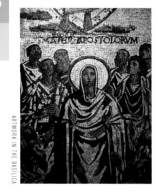

ARTWORK IN THE BASÍLICA

BASÍLICA

Basílica daily 7.30am–8pm. Access to
La Moreneta 8–10.30am & noon–6.30pm
(mid-July to Sept also 7.30–8pm). Free.
MAP P.150

Of the religious buildings, only
the Renaissance basilica, dating
largely from 1560 to 1592, is
open to the public. **La
Moreneta** stands above the
high altar – reached from

behind, by way of an entrance
to the right of the basilica's
main entrance. The approach to
this beautiful icon reveals the
enormous wealth of the monastery, as you queue along a
corridor leading through the
back of the basilica's rich side
chapels. Signs at head height
command "SILENCE" in
various languages, but nothing
quietens the line which waits to
kiss the image's hands and feet.

The best time to be here is
when Montserrat's world-
famous **boys' choir** sings
(Mon–Fri at 1pm & 6.45pm,
Sun at noon & 6.45pm; not Sat;
performance times may vary
during school holidays at
Christmas/New Year and from
late June to mid-Aug). The boys
belong to the Escolania, a
choral school established in the
thirteenth century and
unchanged in musical style
since its foundation.

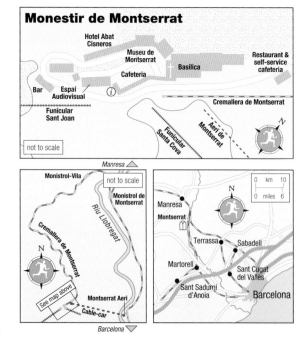

THE HERMITAGE OF SANT JOAN

MUSEU DE MONTSERRAT

☎ 938 777 745. Daily 10am–5.45pm. €7.
MAP P.150

The monastery museum presents a few archeological finds brought back by travelling monks, together with valuable painting and sculpture dating from the thirteenth century onwards, including works by Old Masters, French Impressionists and Catalan *modernistas*. There's also a collection of Byzantine icons, though other religious items are in surprisingly short supply, as most of the monastery's valuables were carried off by Napoleon's troops who sacked the complex in 1811. For more on the history, and to learn something of the life of a Benedictine community, visit the **Espai Audiovisual** (Mon–Fri 9am–5.30pm, Sat & Sun 9am–6.45pm; €5), near the information office.

MOUNTAIN WALKS

Funicular departures vary by season, but mostly every 20min, daily 10am–6pm, weekends only Oct–March. Santa Cova €3.50 return, Sant Joan €9 return, combination ticket €10.

Following the mountain tracks to the caves and hermitages, you can contemplate Goethe's observation of 1816: "Nowhere but in his own Montserrat will a man find happiness and peace." The going is pretty good on all the tracks and the signposting is clear, but you do need to remember that you are on a mountain. Take water if you're hiking far and keep away from the edges.

Two separate funiculars run from points close to the cable-car station. One drops to the path for **Santa Cova**, a seventeenth-century chapel built where the Moreneta icon is said to have been found. It's an easy walk of less than an hour there and back. The other funicular rises steeply to the hermitage of **Sant Joan**, from where it's a tougher 45 minutes' walk to the **Sant Jeroni** hermitage, and another 15 minutes to the Sant Jeroni summit at 1236m. Several other walks are also possible from the Sant Joan funicular, perhaps the nicest being the 45-minute circuit around the ridge that leads all the way back down to the monastery.

Sitges

The seaside town of Sitges, 36km south of Barcelona, is definitely the highlight of the local coast – a great weekend escape for young Barcelonans, who have created a resort very much in their own image. It's also a noted gay holiday destination, with an outrageous annual carnival (February/March) and a summertime nightlife to match. During the heat of the day, though, the tempo drops as everyone hits the beach. Out of season Sitges is delightful: far less crowded, and with a temperate climate that encourages promenade strolls and Old Town exploration.

THE BEACHES

MAP P.153

There are clean sands on either side of the Old Town, though they become extremely crowded in high season. For more space keep walking west from Passeig de la Ribera along Passeig Marítim promenade, past eight interlinked beaches that run a couple of kilometres down the coast as far as the *Hotel Terramar*. Many of the handsome, nineteenth-century seafront mansions were built by successful local merchants (known as "Americanos") who had returned from Cuba and Puerto Rico.

THE OLD TOWN

MAP P.153

The knoll overlooking the town beaches is topped by the landmark Baroque parish church dedicated to Sant Bartolomeu, whose festival is celebrated in the last week of August. The views from the terrace sweep along the coast, while behind in the narrow streets of the Old Town you'll find whitewashed mansions, as well as the town hall and the **Mercat Vell** (Old Market), the latter now an exhibition hall. The pedestrianized shopping street, **Carrer Major**, is the best place for browsing boutiques.

OLD TOWN MANSION

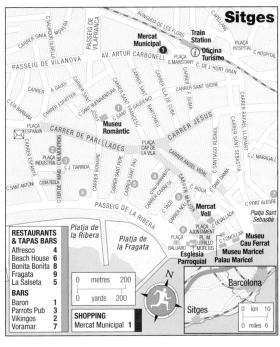

Map: Sitges

RESTAURANTS & TAPAS BARS

Alfresco	4
Beach House	6
Bonita Bonita	8
Fragata	9
La Salseta	5

BARS

Baron	1
Parrots Pub	3
Vikingos	2
Voramar	7

SHOPPING

Mercat Municipal 1

CAU FERRAT, MARICEL AND ROMÀNTIC MUSEUMS

Tues–Sat 9.30am–2pm & 3.30–6.30pm (July–Sept afternoons 4–7pm), Sun 10am–3pm. €3.50 each. MAP P.153

Three museums showcase the town's artistic heritage, not least **Museu Cau Ferrat** (c/Fonollar; closed for renovations), the former house of *modernista* artist Santiago Rusiñol (1861–1931). Next door, the **Museu Maricel** (closed for renovations) contains minor art works, ceramics and sculpture, while in July and August (usually two evenings a week) the main part of the mansion itself is open for guided tours and concerts. Occupying a stately bourgeois house of 1793, the **Museu Romàntic** (c/Sant Gaudenci 1) shows the lifestyle of a rich, nineteenth-century Sitges family (guided tours every hour).

153

Shopping

MERCAT MUNICIPAL

Av. Artur Carbonell ☎ 938 949 777. Mon, Wed & Sat 8.30am–2pm, Tues, Thurs & Fri 8.30am–2pm & 5.30–8.30pm. MAP P.153

The town market is a great place to put together a picnic of cured meats, olives, cheese, fresh bread and fruit.

Restaurants and tapas bars

ALFRESCO

C/Pau Barrabeitg 4 ☎ 938 940 600, ⓦ alfrescorestaurante.es. Daily 8.30pm–midnight (May–June closed Mon). MAP P.153

Exuding romance – from its tucked-away location off a stepped alley to its trellised patio – the restaurant serves Catalan cuisine with Asian influences (green Thai curry, duck breast with glass noodles), with meals for €25–35.

BEACH HOUSE

C/Paseo de la Ribera 33 ☎ 935 168 136, ⓦ www.beachhousesitges.com. Daily 9.30am–2.30am. MAP P.153

Aussie owners have created a highly relaxed seafront restaurant, offering both lunch and dinner menus (from €13 and €20) of the best Mediterra-

BEACH PROMENADE

nean-Asian fusion food, from green Thai curry to black rice with squid and bonito fish flakes. It's a cocktail joint too, while the open-air terrace adds a touch of seaside romance.

BONITA BONITA

C/Major 17 ☎ 932 228 540, ⓦ bonitabonita.es. Mon & Wed–Sun 4pm–2am. MAP P.153

This vibrantly styled and very friendly tapas bar gives small plates an English twist with dishes like chorizo Scotch eggs. Its most memorable offering (though you may not remember much after ordering it) is the giantini, which is big enough for five people to share.

Sitges information

Trains to Sitges leave Passeig de Gràcia or Barcelona Sants stations every twenty minutes, more frequently at peak times (destination Vilanova/St Vicenç), and it's a thirty- to forty-minute ride depending on the service. The main Oficina Turisme (Pl. Eduard Maristany 2 ☎ 938 944 251, ⓦ www.sitgestur.cat; Mon–Fri 10am–2pm & 4–6.30pm, Sat 10am–2pm & 4–7pm, Sun 10am–2pm) is adjacent to the train station. Note that Monday isn't the best day to come, as the museums and many restaurants are closed. As well as Carnival, Sitges is known for its celebrated annual sci-fi, horror and fantasy fest, the Festival Internacional de Cinema (ⓦ www.sitgesfilmfestival.com) every October.

The gay scene and Carnival

The Sitges gay scene is frenetic and ever-changing, but the bulk of the nightlife is centred on Plaça de l'Industria. Summer, of course, sees one long nonstop party, but Carnival time (Feb/March) is also notoriously riotous, with a full programme of parades, masked balls, concerts and beach parties. Highlights are Sunday night's Debauchery Parade and Tuesday's Extermination Parade, in which exquisitely dressed drag queens twirl lacy parasols, while bar doors stand wide open and the celebrations go on till dawn. The other big bash is Gay Pride Sitges (ⓦwww .gaypridesitges.com), a weekend of events plus street parade every July.

FRAGATA

Pg. de la Ribera 1 ☎ 938 941 086, ⓦwww
.restaurantefragata.com. Daily 12.30–4pm &
8.30pm–12.30am. MAP P.153

Typical of the new wave of classy seafood places in town, where catch-of-the-day choices like grilled scallops or wild sea bass cost €17 to €28.

LA SALSETA

C/Sant Pau 35 ☎ 938 110 419, ⓦ lasalseta
.com. Tues–Sat 1.15–3.30pm & 8.30–11pm,
Sun 1.15–3.30pm. MAP P.153

Classic, unpretentious Catalan dishes (cod with garlic confit, seafood paella) made from locally sourced ingredients have kept this 23-year-old restaurant's cosy dining room full of tourists and locals alike.

PARROTS PUB

Bars

BARON

C/Sant Gaudenci 17. Mon–Fri 9am–3pm &
6–11pm, Sat 10am–3pm & 6–11.30pm, Sun
(June–Aug only) 11.30am–3pm. MAP P.153

Definitely not a style bar, but an old tavern that's a real slice of Sitges nonetheless. It's nowhere near the sea, so there's more of a down-to-earth local crowd.

PARROTS PUB

Pl. de l'Industria ☎ 938 941 350,
ⓦ parrotspub.com. Daily 9pm–2am. MAP P.153

The stalwart of the gay bar scene in Sitges, with front-row seats on all the action.

VIKINGOS

C/Marqués de Montroig 7–9 ☎ 938 949 687,
ⓦ www.losvikingos.com. Mon–Wed
1pm–12.30am Fri 1pm–1am, Sat 11am–1.30am,
Sun 11am–12.30am. MAP P.153

Long-standing party-zone bar with a huge air-conditioned interior and streetside terrace. This and the similar *Montroig* next door serve drinks, snacks and meals from morning until night to a really mixed crowd.

VORAMAR

C/Port Alegre 55. Daily 5pm–midnight (Sat &
Sun until 12.30am); closed Wed. MAP P.153

Charismatic seafront bar, away from the main crowds, just right for an ice-cold beer or sundowner cocktail.

ACCOMMODATION

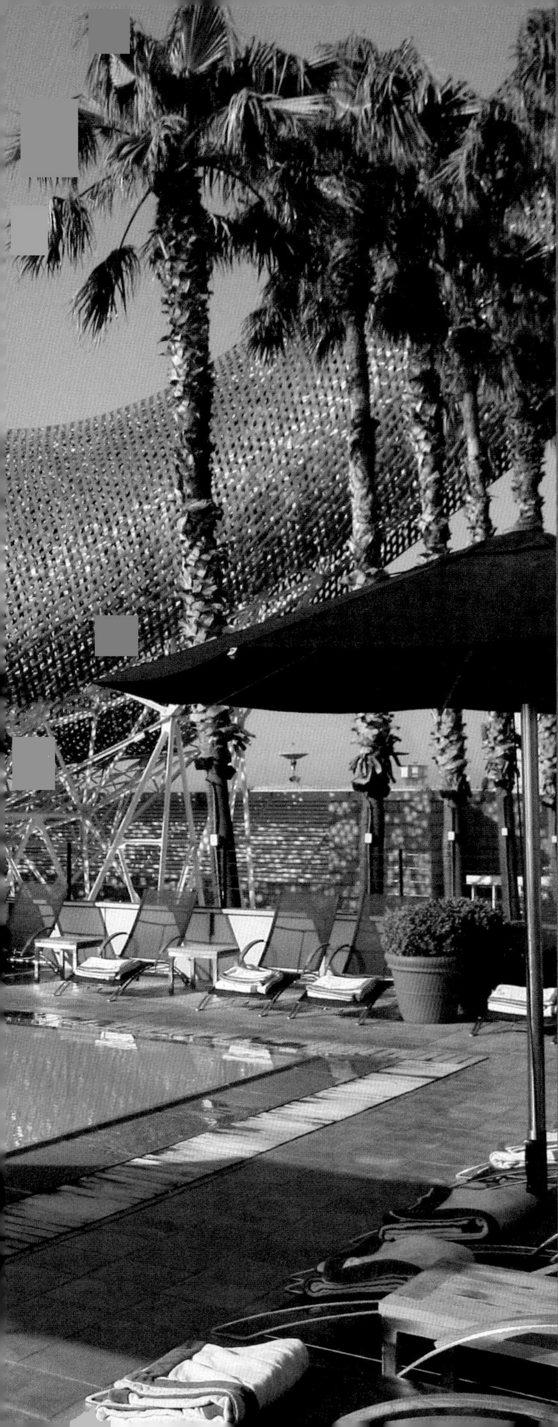

Accommodation

Finding a hotel vacancy in Barcelona at any time of year can be very difficult, so it's best to book in advance. The absolute cheapest rooms in a simple family-run *hostal* or *pension*, sharing a bathroom, cost around €50 (singles from €30), though if you want private facilities €70–80 a night is more realistic. There's a fair amount of choice around the €100 mark, while up to €200 gets you the run of decent hotels in most city areas. For Barcelona's most fashionable hotels count on €250–400 a night, while dorm beds in youth hotels go for €20 to €30 depending on the season. An eight-percent tax (IVA) is added to all accommodation bills (though it's sometimes included in the quoted price), and a new "tourist tax" adds €0.65 to €2.25 per person per night to your bill for stays of up to seven days. Under 17s are exempt, and most tourist establishments in Barcelona fall into the lowest tax band.

Breakfast isn't usually included, unless specifically stated in the reviews. Credit cards are accepted almost everywhere (though American Express isn't always). There's a lot of street noise in Barcelona, so bring earplugs if you're at all concerned.

You can reserve accommodation online with the city tourist board (ⓦ www.hotelsbcn.com) or make same-day bookings in person only at their tourist offices (ⓦ www.barcelonaturisme .com) at Plaça de Catalunya, the airport and elsewhere. Many agencies offer apartment rental, which can be good value for couples and friends.

Along the Ramblas

HOSTAL BENIDORM > Ramblas 37 Ⓜ Drassanes ☎ 933 022 054, ⓦ www .hostalbenidorm.com. MAP P.35, POCKET MAP C13. Refurbished *pension* that offers real value for money, hence the tribes of young tourists. Rooms available for one to five people, and a balcony with a Ramblas view if you're lucky (and prepared to pay a bit more). **€75**

HOTEL 1898 > Ramblas 109 Ⓜ Catalunya ☎ 935 529 552, ⓦ www.hotel1898.com. MAP P.35,
POCKET MAP C11. The former HQ of the Philippines Tobacco Company got an eye-popping boutique refit, adding four grades of rooms (the standard is "Classic") in deep red, green or black, plus sumptuous suites and dramatic public areas, including neocolonial lobby-lounge bar, heated rooftop pool and glam spa facilities. **Special rates from €160, otherwise €250**

HOTEL EUROSTARS RAMBLAS BOQUERIA > Ramblas 91–93 Ⓜ Liceu ☎ 933 435 461, ⓦ www.eurostars ramblasboqueria.com. MAP P.35,

POCKET MAP C12. Snappy little boutique rooms in a small three-star hotel right outside the Boqueria market. There's not much space, but all you need is on the doorstep, and the soundproofing is good so you get a street view without the racket. **€130**

HOTEL ORIENTE > Ramblas 45 Ⓜ Liceu ☎ 933 022 558, Ⓦ www .orienteatiramhotels.com. MAP P.35, POCKET MAP C13. For somewhere on the Ramblas that's traditional but not too pricey, this historic three-star is your best bet – nineteenth-century style in the grand public rooms and tastefully updated bedrooms, some with Ramblas views (though the quieter ones face inwards). **€100**

HOTEL RIVOLI RAMBLAS > Ramblas 128 Ⓜ Catalunya ☎ 934 817 676, Ⓦ www.hotelserhsrivolirambla.com. MAP P.35, POCKET MAP D11. The elegant rooms in this four-star hotel are imaginatively furnished (Art Deco to contemporary), and all come with spacious bathrooms, while the front ones have floor-to-ceiling windows and classic Ramblas views. There's a lovely rooftop terrace and bar. **Special rates from €99, otherwise €150**

Barri Gòtic

HOTEL EL JARDÍ > Pl. Sant Josep Oriol 1 Ⓜ Liceu ☎ 933 015 900, Ⓦ www.eljardi-barcelona.com. MAP P.44–45, POCKET MAP D12. Location is all – overlooking the charming Plaça del Pi – and though rooms can seem a bit bare and plain, some look directly onto the square. You can have breakfast at the hotel, though the *Bar del Pi* below is nicer. **€90, terrace or balcony €105**

HOTEL RACÓ DEL PI > c/del Pi 7 Ⓜ Liceu ☎ 933 426 190, Ⓦ www .hotelh10racodelpi.com. MAP P.44–45, POCKET MAP D12. A stylish three-star hotel in a great location. Rooms – some with balconies over the street – have wood floors and granite-and-mosaic bathrooms. There's a glass of *cava* on check-in and free coffee and pastries during the day in the bar. **€125**

ITACA HOSTEL > c/Ripoll 21 Ⓜ Jaume I ☎ 933 019 751, Ⓦ www .itacahostel.com. MAP P.44–45, POCKET MAP E12. Bright and breezy hostel close to the cathedral offering spacious rooms with balconies. Dorms are mixed, though you can also reserve a private room or apartment (sleeps up to six), and with a capacity of only 30 it feels more house party than hostel. **Dorm beds €27, rooms €70, apartments €120**

NERI HOTEL > c/de Sant Sever 5 Ⓜ Liceu/Jaume I ☎ 933 040 655, Ⓦ www.hotelneri.com. MAP P.44–45, POCKET MAP D12. A delightful eighteenth-century palace close to the cathedral houses this stunning boutique hotel of just 22 rooms and suites, featuring swags of flowing material, rescued timber and granite-toned bathrooms. Catalan designers have created eye-catching effects, like a tapestry that falls four floors through the central atrium, while a beamed library and stylish roof terrace provides a tranquil escape. Breakfast is served bento-box style, either out in the courtyard in summer or in the fine contemporary Mediterranean restaurant. **€285**

PENSIÓ ALAMAR > c/Comtessa de Sobradiel 1 Ⓜ Liceu/Jaume I ☎ 933 025 012, Ⓦ www.pensioalamar.com. MAP P.44–45, POCKET MAP D13. If you don't mind sharing a bathroom, this simply furnished *pension* makes a convenient base. There are twelve rooms (including singles, doubles and triples), most with little balconies, and there's a friendly welcome, laundry service and use of a kitchen. No credit cards. **€45**

PENSIÓN MARI-LUZ > c/del Palau 4, 2° Ⓜ Liceu/Jaume I ☎ 933 173 463, Ⓦ www.pensionmariluz.com. MAP P.44–45, POCKET MAP D13. This old mansion, on a quiet Barri Gòtic street, offers inexpensive rooms (most share bathrooms), plus a more personal touch than many other places of its kind. It can be a tight squeeze when full, but a dozen slick apartments (Ⓦ www .apartmentsunio.com) a few minutes' walk away in the Raval offer more space. **Rooms €70, apartments €95**

What's the neighbourhood like?

If you hanker after a **Ramblas** view, you'll pay for the privilege – generally speaking, there are better deals to be had either side of the famous boulevard, often just a minute's walk away. Alongside some classy boutique choices, most of Barcelona's cheapest accommodation is found in the Old Town, principally the **Barri Gòtic** and **El Raval** neighbourhoods, which both still have their rough edges – be careful (without being paranoid) when coming and going after dark. North of Plaça de Catalunya, the **Eixample** – split into Right (**Dreta**) and Left (**Esquerra**) – has some of the city's most fashionable hotels. Those near **Sants** station are convenient for Montjuïc and the metro system, and those further north in **Les Corts** for the Avinguda Diagonal shopping district. For waterfront views look at **Port Vell** at the end of the Ramblas, and at the **Port Olímpic** southeast of the Old Town – while new four- and five-star hotels abound further out on the metro at the **Diagonal Mar** conference and events site. If you prefer neighbourhood living then **Gràcia** is the best base, as you're only ever a short walk away from its excellent bars, restaurants and clubs.

Port Vell and Barceloneta

BONIC BARCELONA > c/Josep Anselm Clavé 9 Ⓜ Drassanes ⓣ 626 053 434, Ⓦ www.bonic-barcelona.com. MAP P.58–59, POCKET MAP C14. This chic and charming "urban guesthouse" is located just a few steps from port and Ramblas, and features Gothic-Moorish decor and gorgeous tiled floors. The eight rooms are simple, and the three renovated bathrooms are shared. Advance reservations essential; minimum two-night stay required. **€90**

EQUITY POINT SEA > Pl. del Mar 1–4 Ⓜ Barceloneta Ⓦ www.equity-point .com; online bookings only. MAP P.58–59, POCKET MAP H8. The budget beachside choice is this neat little hostel with modern en-suite rooms sleeping four to eight people. The attached café looks right out onto the boardwalk. Dorm beds **€26**, includes breakfast

HOTEL DUQUESA DE CARDONA > Pg. de Colom 12 Ⓜ Drassanes/ Barceloneta ⓣ 932 689 090, Ⓦ www .hduquesadecardona.com. MAP P.58–59, POCKET MAP D14. Step off the busy harbourfront highway into this soothing four-star haven, set in a remodelled sixteenth-century mansion. The rooms are calm and quiet, decorated in earth tones and immaculately appointed. Although not all of the rooms have harbour views, all guests have access to the stylish roof-deck overlooking the harbour. It's great for sundowner drinks, and boasts (if that's the word) probably the city's smallest outdoor pool. **€160**

MARINA VIEW B&B > Pg. de Colom Ⓜ Drassanes ⓣ 678 854 456, Ⓦ www .marinaviewbcn.com. MAP P.58–59, POCKET MAP C14. Six classy rooms featuring bold colours, excellent bathrooms and nice touches, from minibars with normal drinks prices to hospitality trays. Breakfast included (served in the room), and advance reservations essential. **€120**, harbour views **€140**

W BARCELONA > Pl. de la Rosa dels Vents Ⓜ Barceloneta ⓣ 932 952 800, Ⓦ www.w-barcelona.com. MAP P.58–59, POCKET MAP G9. Signature building on the Barceloneta seafront is the stupendously cool, wave-shaped W Barcelona. The open-plan designer rooms offer fantastic views through floor-to-ceiling windows, while facilities are first rate, from iPod docks to an infinity pool. There's a hip, resort feel, with direct beach access, a chill-out lobby bar and rooftop lounge, while dining in Bravo24 is courtesy of hot Catalan chef Carles Abellán. **€260**

El Raval

BARCELÓ RAVAL > Rambla del Raval 17–21 Ⓜ Liceu/Sant Antoni ☎ 933 201 490, Ⓦ www.barcelo.com. MAP P.64–65, POCKET MAP B12. Neighbourhood landmark is this glow-in-the-dark tower whose USP is the 360-degree top-floor terrace with plunge pool and city views. Sophisticated, open-plan rooms have a crisp, space-station-style sheen, plus iPod docks, coffee-makers and other cool comforts, while the slinky lobby "B-lounge" is the place for everything from breakfast to cocktails. **€120**

CASA CAMPER > c/Elisabets 11 Ⓜ Universitat/Liceu ☎ 933 426 280, Ⓦ casacamper.com. MAP P.64–65, POCKET MAP C11. Synonymous with creative, comfy shoes, Barcelona-based Camper has taken a bold step into the hospitality business with this sleek, minimalist hotel. All the rooms are divided by a corridor: the "sleeping" side faces a six-story tall vertical garden; the other part is a "mini-lounge" with a flat-screen TV, hammock and street-facing balcony. Breakfast is included. **€215**

HOSTAL CÈNTRIC > c/Casanova 13 Ⓜ Universitat ☎ 934 267 573, Ⓦ www .hostalcentric.com. MAP P.64–65, POCKET MAP B10. A good upper-budget choice a couple of minutes' walk from the Raval proper. The recently refurbished rooms (2013) offer plenty of light, plus a/c and private bathrooms. Some include balconies. **€94**

HOSTAL GRAU > c/Ramelleres 27 Ⓜ Catalunya ☎ 933 018 135, Ⓦ www .hostalgrau.com. MAP P.64–65, POCKET MAP C10. A really friendly *pension* with attractive, colour-coordinated rooms – superior rooms also have balconies and a touch of modern Catalan style. Two small private apartments in the same building (sleeping two to four, available by the night) offer a bit more independence. **€85, en-suites €105, apartments €150**

HOTEL ESPAÑA > c/de Sant Pau 9–11 Ⓜ Liceu ☎ 935 500 000, Ⓦ hotelespanya.com. MAP P.64–65, POCKET MAP C13. This *modernista* icon has been sumptuously restored, and the gem-like interior – colourful mosaics, sculpted marble, iron swirls and marine motifs – has no equal in Barcelona. Guest rooms are a boutique blend of earth tones and designer style, with rain-showers, iPod docks and the like, while the handsome house restaurant – known as *Fonda España* – offers contemporary Catalan bistro dishes by renowned chef Martín Berasategui. **€165**

HOTEL ONIX LICEO > c/Nou de la Rambla 36 Ⓜ Liceu/Drassanes ☎ 934 816 441, Ⓦ onixliceohotel.com. MAP P.64–64, POCKET MAP B13. Steps from Palau Güell, this four-star hotel features minimalist decor that melds nicely with the building's older architectural elements, such as the grand marble staircase that curves up from the lobby to the second floor. There's a tropical patio and big-for-Barcelona pool on the ground floor and an airy Mozarab-influenced lounge area. **€130**

HOTEL PENINSULAR > c/de Sant Pau 34 Ⓜ Liceu ☎ 933 023 138, Ⓦ www .hotelpeninsular.net. MAP P.64–65, POCKET MAP C13. The interesting old building originally belonged to a priestly order, which explains the slightly cell-like rooms. However, there's nothing spartan about the galleried courtyard (around which the rooms are ranged), hung with tumbling houseplants, while breakfast (included) is served in the arcaded dining room. **€70**

HOTEL SANT AGUSTÍ > Pl. Sant Agustí 3 Ⓜ Liceu ☎ 933 181 658, Ⓦ www.hotelsa.com. MAP P.64–65, POCKET MAP C12. Barcelona's oldest hotel occupies a former convent, with front balconies overlooking a restored square and church. It's of three-star standard, with the best rooms located in the attic, from where there are rooftop views. **€120**

MARKET HOTEL > c/Comte Borrell 68, at Ptge. Sant Antoni Abad Ⓜ Sant Antoni ☎ 933 251 205, Ⓦ www.markethotel .com.es. MAP P.64–65, POCKET MAP E5. The designer-budget *Market* makes a splash with its part Japanese, part neocolonial look – think jet-black rooms with hardwood floors and boxy wardrobes topped with travel trunks. **€100**

ACCOMMODATION

Sant Pere

PENSIÓ 2000 > c/Sant Pere Més Alt 6, 1° Ⓜ Urquinaona ☎ 933 107 466, Ⓦ www.pensio2000.com. MAP P.75, POCKET MAP E11. As close to a traditional family-style B&B as Barcelona gets – seven rooms in a welcoming mansion apartment strewn with books, plants and pictures. A third person could easily share most rooms (€20 extra). **€90**

La Ribera

CHIC & BASIC > c/de la Princesa 50 Ⓜ Jaume I ☎ 932 954 652, Ⓦ www .chicandbasic.com. MAP P.80, POCKET MAP G13. From the babbling blurb ("it's fresh, it's cool, it's fusion") to the all-in-white rooms with adjustable mood lighting, everything is punchily boutique and in-your-face. Chic, certainly – basic, not at all, though the concept eschews room service, mini-bars and tons of staff at your beck and call. Meals are courtesy of the attached – also effortlessly cool – restaurant. There's a more budget *Chic & Basic* on c/Tallers (near Pl. Universitat, El Raval) and apartments peppered around the city centre too (details on the website). **€120**

EQUITY POINT GOTHIC > c/Vigatans 5 Ⓜ Jaume I Ⓦ www.equity-point .com; online bookings only. MAP P.80, POCKET MAP E13. Backpacker heaven, not far from the Picasso museum. There's a great roof terrace, and all sorts of tours available, while each bunk bed gets its own cabinet and reading light. **Dorm beds €25, includes breakfast**

HOSTAL NUEVO COLÓN > Av. Marquès de l'Argentera 19, 1° Ⓜ Barceloneta ☎ 933 195 077, Ⓦ www.hostalnuevocolon.com. MAP P.80, POCKET MAP G14. Run by a friendly family, featuring 24 spacious rooms painted yellow and kitted out with directors' chairs and double glazing. Sunny front rooms all have side views to Ciutadella park, while França station is right opposite. **€55, en-suites €70**

HOTEL BANYS ORIENTALS > c/de l'Argenteria 37 Ⓜ Jaume I ☎ 932 688 460, Ⓦ www.hotelbanysorientals.com. MAP P.80, POCKET MAP E13. Funky boutique hotel with 43 minimalist rooms, plus some duplex suites in a nearby building. Hardwood floors, sharp marble bathrooms and urban-chic decor – not to mention bargain prices for this sort of style – make it a hugely popular choice. The attached restaurant, *Senyor Parellada*, is a great find too. **€115, suites €143**

Port Olímpic

HOTEL ARTS BARCELONA > c/Marina 19–21 Ⓜ Ciutadella-Vila Olímpica ☎ 932 211 000, Ⓦ www .hotelartsbarcelona.com MAP P.101, POCKET MAP K8. Still the city benchmark for five-star designer luxury, service and standards. Effortlessly classy rooms feature floor-to-ceiling windows with fabulous views. Stunning duplex apartments have their own perks (24hr butler service, personal Mini Cooper), and dining options range from the terrace restaurant to Michelin-starred chef Sergi Arola's contemporary tapas place, *Arola*. Seafront gardens encompass an open-air pool and hot tub, while the jaw-dropping Six Senses spa occupies the two top floors. **€295**

Dreta de l'Eixample

EQUITY POINT CENTRIC > Pg. de Gràcia 33 Ⓜ Passeig de Gràcia Ⓦ www.equity-point.com; online bookings only. MAP P.105, POCKET MAP G3. The biggest hostel in the city occupies a refurbished *modernista* building in a swish midtown location. Private twins, doubles, triples and quads available, all with shower room, balcony and views, while dorms (all en suite) sleep up to fourteen. Excellent facilities (bar, laundry, free wifi, common room with TV, music and Wii) include a spectacular roof terrace with views of the famous boulevard and its buildings. **Dorm beds €13, rooms €130, breakfast included**

HOSTAL L'ANTIC ESPAI > Gran Via de les Corts Catalanes 660 Ⓜ Passeig de Gràcia ☏ 933 041 945, Ⓦ www .lanticespai.com. MAP P.105, POCKET MAP H4. Camp and cosy, this beautifully ornate period piece springs a surprise in every room, from mosaic tile floors to antique pendants, with candles and flowers at every turn. Room 102 has an original glassed-in balcony, and 107 opens onto an internal terrace with a candelabra-topped table. Modern bathrooms and DVD players keep comforts up to date. **€120**

HOSTAL GIRONA > c/Girona 24, 1° Ⓜ Urquinaona ☏ 932 650 259, Ⓦ www .hostalgirona.com. MAP P.105, POCKET MAP G10. Delightful family-run *pension* with a wide range of cosy, traditional rooms (some sharing a bathroom, others with a shower or full bath) – the best and biggest have balconies, though you can expect some noise. **€60, full en-suites €85**

HOSTAL GOYA > c/de Pau Claris 74, 1° Ⓜ Urquinaona ☏ 933 022 565, Ⓦ www.hostalgoya.com. MAP P.105, POCKET MAP E10. Boutique-style *pension* that offers stylishly decorated rooms on two floors of a mansion building. There's a fair range of options, with the best rooms opening onto a balcony or terrace. Comfortable sitting areas, and free tea and coffee, are available on both floors. **€95, balcony/terrace €110**

HOTEL CONDES DE BARCELONA > Pg. de Gràcia 73–75 Ⓜ Passeig de Gràcia ☏ 934 450 000, Ⓦ www .condesdebarcelona.com. MAP P.105, POCKET MAP H3. Straddling two sides of c/Mallorca, the *Condes* is fashioned from two former palaces, its rooms all turned out in contemporary style, some with jacuzzi, balcony or private terrace, some with views of Gaudí's La Pedrera. Meanwhile, Michelin-starred Basque chef Martín Berasategui offers fine dining in the hotel's acclaimed *Lasarte* restaurant and a more informal bistro menu in *Loidi*. **€148**

HOTEL MAJESTIC > Pg. de Gràcia 68 Ⓜ Passeig de Gràcia ☏ 934 881 717, Ⓦ www.hotelmajestic.es. MAP P.105, POCKET MAP H3. Traditional grande-dame hotel, first opened in 1918, though refitted in contemporary style and muted colours to provide a tranquil city-centre base. The absolute clincher is the rooftop pool and deck, with amazing views over to the Sagrada Família, while the excellent *Drolma* restaurant is a boon. **€200**

HOTEL OMM > c/Rosselló 265 Ⓜ Diagonal ☏ 934 454 000, Ⓦ www .hotelomm.es. MAP P.105, POCKET MAP H2. The glam designer experience that is *Omm* means minimalist, open-plan rooms, a studiously chic bar, the Michelin-starred *Moo* restaurant, terrace, pool and Spaciomm "relaxation centre", not to mention fearsomely handsome staff. It's not to everyone's taste – it's probably fair to say that the less annoyed you are by the endless Omm/Moo tagging of services and facilities, the more you'll like the hotel. **€200**

MANDARIN ORIENTAL > Pg. de Gràcia 38–40 Ⓜ Passeig de Gràcia ☏ 931 518 888, Ⓦ www.mandarin oriental.com/barcelona. MAP P.105, POCKET MAP H3. The super-sleek *Mandarin Oriental* fills the premises of a former bank building with a soaring white atrium and a serene selection of gorgeously light rooms. There's the obligatory superstar restaurant, *Moments* (under the direction of the world's most Michelin-starred female chef, Carme Ruscalleda), while bar, spa, mimosa garden and rooftop "dipping pool" combine oriental tranquility and Euro cool. **€400**

THE5ROOMS > c/Pau Claris 72, 1° Ⓜ Urquinaona ☏ 933 427 880, Ⓦ www .thefiverooms.com. MAP P.105, POCKET MAP E10. The owner's impeccable taste and fashion background are evident in gorgeous contemporary-styled B&B rooms that are spacious and light-filled, with original artwork above each bed, exposed brick walls and terrific bathrooms. Breakfast is served whenever you like, drinks are always available, and Jessica is happy to sit down and talk you through her favourite bars, restaurants and galleries. Suites and apartments are also available. **€145, apartments €175 for 2 people**

Sagrada Família and Glòries

BARCELONA URBANY > Av. Meridiana 97 Ⓜ Clot ☏ 932 458 414, Ⓦ www.barcelonaurbany.com. MAP P.116–117, POCKET MAP M3. Bumper steel-and-glass 400-bed hostel that's a bit off the beaten track, but on handy metro and airport train routes and with amazing views of Torre Agbar. The rooms are like space-shuttle pods – boxy en-suites with pull-down beds (sleeping two to eight), power-showers and key-card lockers – that are just as viable for couples on a budget as backpackers. There's a bar and terrace, plus free gym, jacuzzi and pool entry in the same building. **Dorm beds €10–30, private rooms €50–85, breakfast included**

HOTEL EUROSTARS MONUMENTAL > c/Consell de Cent 498–500 Ⓜ Monumental ☏ 932 320 288, Ⓦ www.eurostarshotels.com. MAP P.116–117, POCKET MAP K3. An excellent-value four-star choice within walking distance of the Sagrada Família. The 45 rooms are crisply appointed in dark wood and earth tones, staff are really helpful and the top-floor suites boast terrace views of the Gaudí church. **€120, suites €200**

Esquerra de l'Eixample

ALTERNATIVE CREATIVE YOUTH HOME > Ronda Universitat 17 Ⓜ Universitat/Catalunya ☏ 635 669 021, Ⓦ www.alternative-barcelona .com. MAP P.122–123, POCKET MAP G4. The hostel hangout for an art crowd who love the laid-back vibe, projection lounge, cool music and city-savvy staff. The regular hostel stuff is well designed too, with a walk-in kitchen and a maximum of 24 people spread across three small dorms. **Dorm beds €20–36**

CASA DE BILLY > Gran Via de les Corts Catalanes Ⓜ Rocafort ☏ 934 263 048, Ⓦ casabillybarcelona.com. MAP P.122–123, POCKET MAP D4. A welcoming guesthouse in a restored nineteenth-century building near Plaça d'Espanya, with spotless rooms (some en suite) elegantly decorated by Billy himself. It's a rich, refined and utterly charming experience – for an extremely reasonable price. Small breakfast included, two-night minimum, advance reservations essential (contact for directions), over-18s only. **€70**

EXPO HOTEL BARCELONA > c/Mallorca 1–23 Ⓜ Sants-Estació ☏ 936 003 020, Ⓦ www.expohotelbarcelona .com. MAP P.122–123, POCKET MAP C3. Bright, spacious rooms at a good-value four-star hotel. Each has a sliding window onto a capacious terrace and the best have views across to Montjuïc. **€90**

GRAN HOTEL TORRE CATALUNYA > Av. Roma 2–4 Ⓜ Sants-Estació ☏ 936 006 966, Ⓦ www.torrecatalunya.com. MAP P.122–123, POCKET MAP C2. The landmark four-star deluxe hotel outside Sants station features sweeping views from all sides. Breakfast on the 23rd floor is a buzz; there's also a spa with indoor pool, and guests can use the nearby sister *Expo* hotel's outdoor pool. **€110, superior €135**

HOTEL INGLATERRA > c/Pelai 14 Ⓜ Universitat ☏ 935 051 100, Ⓦ www .hotel-inglaterra.com. MAP P.122–123, POCKET MAP C10. The boutique little three-star sister to the Dreta's *Hotel Majestic* has harmoniously toned rooms and snazzy bathrooms. Space is at a premium, but some rooms have cute private terraces, others street-side balconies, while best of all are the romantic roof terrace and pool. **€125**

SOMNIO BARCELONA > c/Diputació 251 2o Ⓜ Passeig de Gràcia ☏ 932 725 308, Ⓦ www.somniohostels.com. MAP P.122–123, POCKET MAP G4. Sisters Lauren and Lee from Chicago bring their passion for Barcelona right into their upscale *pension*, dropping "tips for the day" into your room each morning. Simple but smart rooms with wood-block floors cater for singles, couples and friends. There are four spacious twin rooms, four double rooms (two en suite) and a single. Some have balconies. **Singles €44, doubles €78, en-suites €87**

Gràcia

CASA GRACIA > Pg. de Gràcia 116 Ⓜ Diagonal ☏ 931 874 497, Ⓦ casagraciabcn.com. MAP P.129, POCKET MAP H2. A vibrant and stylish space spread over six floors in a *modernista* building, with bonuses like a concierge, themed dinners and evening concerts. The rooms (from dorms to doubles to six-bed private rooms) have a/c and are en suite, while the deluxe suite pampers with a spa bath, slippers and bathrobes. Though *Casa Gracia* is technically a hostel, you'll feel like you're staying in a (pretty good) hotel. Breakfast included. **Dorms €25, rooms €90**

HOTEL CASA FUSTER > Pg. de Gràcia 132 Ⓜ Diagonal ☏ 932 553 000, Ⓦ www.hotelcasafuster.com. MAP P.129, POCKET MAP H1. *Modernista* architect Lluís Domènech i Montaner's magnificent Casa Fuster (1908) is the backdrop for five-star deluxe luxury with service to match. Rooms are in earth tones, with huge beds, smart bathrooms, and remote-controlled light and heat, while public areas make full use of the architectural heritage – from the magnificent pillared lobby bar, the *Café Vienés*, to the panoramic roof terrace and pool. There's also a contemporary restaurant, *Galaxó*, plus fitness centre, sauna and 24hr room service. **€176**

Les Corts

GRAN HOTEL PRINCESA SOFIA > Pl. Pius XII 4 Ⓜ Maria Cristina ☏ 935 081 050, Ⓦ www.princesasofia.com. MAP P.138–139. A classic – one of the first five-star hotels in town thirty years ago – and well placed for shoppers, with wide-ranging city views from the upper floors. It still exudes old-school charm (the concierges know everything) though the warm-toned rooms, massages and treatments in the Aqua Diagonal Wellness Centre, pool (with retractable roof) and superior club rooms and lounges offer a more contemporary experience – the Barcelona football team stays and eats here before every home match. An immense buffet breakfast is served in the *Contraste* restaurant – which also features an attractive patio for dining in the summer. **€140, club rooms €210**

Montjuïc

HOTEL MIRAMAR > Pl. Carlos Ibañez 3 Ⓜ Paral.lel and Funicular de Montjuïc ☏ 932 811 600, Ⓦ www.hotelmiramar barcelona.com. MAP P.92, POCKET MAP E7. The remodelled *Miramar* has 75 stylish rooms with sweeping views over the city. From the architecture books in the lounge to the terrace jacuzzis, you're in designer heaven, augmented by a stunning pool and tranquil gardens. **€199**

Tibidabo

GRAN HOTEL LA FLORIDA > Ctra. Vallvidrera a Tibidabo 83–93, 7km from the centre ☏ 932 593 000, Ⓦ www .hotellaflorida.com. MAP P.145. This five-star place on Tibidabo mountain recreates the glory days of the 1950s, when *La Florida* was at the centre of Barcelona high society. Its terraces and pools have amazing views, while some of the seventy rooms and suites have private gardens or terraces and jacuzzis. There's also a spa, restaurant, poolside bar and shuttle-bus service to town. **Online advance bookings from €198, otherwise €225**

Horta

ALBERG MARE DE DÉU DE MONTSERRAT > Pg. de la Mare de Déu del Coll 41–51 Ⓜ Vallcarca ☏ 932 105 151, reservations on ☏ 934 838 363, Ⓦ www.xanascat.cat. MAP P.130. A popular hostel, set in a converted mansion with gardens, terrace and great city views, with dorms sleeping six, eight or twelve. It's a long way from the centre (though it's close to Parc Güell) – from the metro, follow Av. República d'Argentina, c/Viaducte de Vallcarca and then the signs, while buses (V17 from Plaça d'Urquinaona, plus night buses) stop just across the street. Reception open 8am–11pm; main door closes at midnight, but opens every 30min thereafter. **Dorms €22, includes breakfast**

Arrival

In most cases, you can be off the plane, train or bus and in your central Barcelona hotel room within the hour. Note that Ryanair flights (and some others) to Barcelona are actually to Girona (90km north) or Reus (110km south), and though there are reliable connecting bus and train services this means up to a 90-minute journey from either airport to Barcelona city centre.

By air

Barcelona's airport (☎902 404 704, ⓦwww.aena.es) is 18km southwest of the city. A **taxi** to the centre costs up to €30, including the airport surcharge (plus other surcharges for travel after 9pm, at weekends or for luggage in the boot). Far cheaper is the **airport train** (5.42am–11.38pm; journey time 18min; €4.10; info on ☎902 240 202), which runs every thirty minutes to Barcelona Sants station (see "By train") and then continues on to Passeig de Gràcia (best stop for Eixample, Plaça de Catalunya and the Ramblas). It departs from Terminal T2, and there's a free shuttle bus to the station from T1 which takes around ten minutes. City travel passes and the Barcelona Card (available at the airport) are valid on the airport train.

Alternatively, the **Aerobús** service (Mon–Sat 6am–1am; €5.90, €10.20 return, departures every 5–10min; ⓦwww.aerobusbcn.es) from T1 and T2 stops in the city at Plaça d'Espanya, Gran Via – Urgell, Plaça Universitat and Plaça de Catalunya (travel time 30min). Aerobus departures back to the airport leave from in front of El Corte Inglés in Plaça de Catalunya – note that there are separate services to Terminals T1 and T2.

By train

The national rail service is operated by RENFE (☎902 320 320, ⓦwww.renfe .com). The city's main station is **Barcelona Sants**, 3km west of the centre, with a metro station (Ⓜ Sants Estació) that links directly to the Ramblas (Ⓜ Liceu), Plaça de Catalunya and Passeig de Gràcia. The high-speed AVE line between Barcelona and Madrid has cut the fastest journey between the cities to under three hours. These services also arrive at and depart from Barcelona Sants, though a second high-speed station for the city is under construction in the north of the city.

Some Spanish intercity services and international trains also stop at **Estació de França**, 1km east of the Ramblas and close to Ⓜ Barceloneta.

Regional and local commuter train services are operated by Ferrocarrils de la Generalitat de Catalunya, or **FGC** (☎932 051 515, ⓦwww.fgc .cat), with stations at **Plaça de Catalunya**, at the top of the Ramblas (for trains from coastal towns north of the city); **Plaça d'Espanya** (for Montserrat); and **Passeig de Gràcia** (Catalunya provincial destinations).

By bus

The main bus terminal is the **Estació del Nord** (☎902 260 606, ⓦwww .barcelonanord.com; Ⓜ Arc de Triomf) on c/Ali-Bei, three blocks north of Parc de la Ciutadella. Various companies operate services across Catalunya, Spain and Europe from here – it's a good idea to reserve a ticket in advance on long-distance routes (a day before at the station is usually fine, or buy online). Some intercity and international services also make a stop at the bus terminal behind Barcelona Sants station. Either way, you're only a short metro ride from the city centre.

Getting around

Barcelona has an excellent integrated transport system which comprises the metro, buses, trams and local trains, plus a network of funiculars and cable cars. The local transport authority has a useful website (Ⓦ www.tmb.cat, English-language version available) with full timetable and ticket information, while a city transport map and information is posted at major bus stops and all metro and tram stations.

Tickets and travel passes

On all the city's public transport (including night buses and funiculars), you can buy a **single ticket** every time you ride (€2.15), but it's much cheaper to buy a **targeta** – a discount ticket card. They are available at metro, train and tram stations, but not on the buses.

Best general ticket deal is the T-10 ("tay day-oo" in Catalan) *targeta* (€10.30), valid for ten separate journeys, with changes between methods of transport allowed within 75 minutes. This card (also available at newsagents' kiosks) can be used by more than one person at a time – simply validate it the same number of times as there are people travelling.

Other useful (single-person) *targetes* include the T-Dia (1 day's unlimited travel; €7.60), and there are also multi-day combos (HolaBCN!) for up to five days (€30.50). Prices given are for passes valid as far as the Zone 1 city limits, which in practice is everywhere you're likely to want to go except Montserrat and Sitges. For trips to these and other out-of-town destinations, buy a specific ticket.

The metro

The quickest way of getting around Barcelona is by **metro**, which currently runs on six main lines. A few stations on a new line, L9, are also now open – on its completion, this will be the longest underground line in Europe (almost 50km) and will run between the airport, city centre and high-speed Sagrera train station.

There's a limited network of stations in the Old Town, but you can take the metro directly to the Ramblas (Catalunya, Liceu or Drassanes), and to the edge of the Barri Gòtic, El Raval and La Ribera.

Metro entrances are marked with a red diamond sign with an "M". Its **hours of operation** are Monday to Thursday, plus Sunday and public holidays 5am to midnight; Friday 5am to 2am; Saturday and the day before a public holiday, 24hr service. The system is safe, but some of the train carriages are heavily graffitied, and buskers and beggars are common.

Trams

The **tram** system (Ⓦ www.tram.cat) runs on six lines, with departures every eight to twenty minutes throughout the day from 5am to midnight. Lines **T1, T2 and T3** depart from Plaça Francesc Macià and run along the uptown part of Avinguda Diagonal to suburban destinations in the northwest – useful tourist stops are at L'Illa shopping and the Maria Cristina and Palau Reial metro stations. **Line T4** operates from Ciutadella-Vila Olímpica (where there's also a metro station) and runs up past the zoo and TNC (the National Theatre) to Glòries, before running down the lower part of Avinguda Diagonal to Diagonal Mar and the Fòrum site. You're unlikely to use the more suburban lines T5 and T6.

Buses

Most **buses** operate daily, roughly from 4am or 5am until 10.30pm, though some lines stop earlier and some run on until after midnight. Night bus services fill in the gaps on all the main routes, with services every twenty to sixty minutes from around 10pm to 4am. Many bus routes (including all night buses) stop in or near Plaça de Catalunya, but the full route is marked at each bus stop, along with a timetable.

Trains

The FGC **commuter train line** has its main stations at Plaça de Catalunya and Plaça d'Espanya, used when going to Sarrià, Vallvidrera, Tibidabo and Montserrat. The national rail service, RENFE, runs all the other services out of Barcelona, with local lines designated as **Rodiales/ Cercanías**. The hub is Barcelona Sants station, with services also passing through Plaça de Catalunya (heading north) and Passeig de Gràcia (south). Arrive in plenty of time to buy a ticket, as queues are often horrendous, though for most regional destinations you can use the automatic vending machines instead.

Funiculars and cable cars

As well as the regular city options, Barcelona also has some fun transport trips and historic survivors. A few **funicular railways** are still widely used, particularly up to Montjuïc and Tibidabo, while summer and year-round weekend visits to Tibidabo also combine a funicular trip with a ride on the clanking antique tram, the **Tramvia Blau**. Best of all, though, are the two **cable car** (*telefèric*) rides: from Barceloneta across the harbour to Montjuïc, and then from the top station of the Montjuïc funicular right the way up to the castle.

Taxis

There are taxi ranks outside major train and metro stations, in main squares, near large hotels and at places along the main avenues. To call a taxi in advance (few of the operators speak English, and you'll be charged an extra €3 or €4), try: Barna Taxis ☎ 933 222 222; Radio Taxi ☎ 933 033 033; Servi-Taxi ☎ 933 300 300; or Taxi Amic ☎ 934 208 088.

A fun way to get around the Old Town, port area and beaches is by **Trixi** (ⓦwww.trixi.com), a kind of love-bug-style bicycle-rickshaw. They tout for business between 11am and 8pm near the Columbus statue at the bottom of the Ramblas, and outside La Seu cathedral in the Barri Gòtic, though you can also flag them down if one cruises by. Fares are fixed (from €15 for 30min, longer tours also available) and the *trixistas* are an amiable, multilingual bunch for the most part.

Cycling and bike rental

The city council is investing heavily in cycle lanes and bike schemes, notably the **Bicing** pick-up and drop-off scheme (ⓦwww.bicing.cat), which is touted as Barcelona's new public transport system. You'll see the red bikes and bike stations all over the city, but Bicing is not aimed at tourists, rather at locals who are encouraged to use the bikes for short trips (users can register online or at the **Oficina de la Bicicleta**, Pl. Carles Pi i Sunyer 8–10, Barri Gòtic, between c/Canuda and c/Duran i Bas).

There are plenty of **bike rental** outfits more geared to tourist requirements. Rental costs around €20 a day with companies all over town, including Un Coxte Menys (ⓦwww.bicicletabarcelona.com) and Biciclot (ⓦwww.bikingin barcelona.net).

Currently there are around 200km of **cycle paths** throughout the city, with plans to double the network in the future. Not all locals have embraced the bike yet, and some cycle paths are still ignored by cars or clogged with pedestrians, indignantly reluctant to give way to two-wheelers. But, on the whole, cycling around Barcelona is not the completely hairy experience it was just a few years ago, while you can always get **off-road** in the Parc de Collserola, where there are waymarked trails through the woods and hills.

City tours

The number of available tours is bewildering, and you can see the sights on anything from a Segway to a hot-air balloon. A good place to start is the official Barcelona Turisme website (⊚ www.barcelona turisme.com), which has a dedicated tours section offering online sales and discounts.

Highest profile are the two tour-bus operators with daily board-at-will, open-top services (1 day €27, 2 days €35), which drop you outside every attraction in the city. The choice is between **Barcelona City Tour** (⊚ www.barcelonatours.es) or the **Bus Turístic** (⊚ www.barcelona turisme.com), with frequent departures from Plaça de Catalunya and many other stops – tickets are available on board.

Advance booking is advised (at Pl. de Catalunya tourist office) for **Barcelona Walking Tours**, two-hour historical Barri Gòtic tour (daily all year, in English at 9.30am;

€15.50). There are also "Picasso", "*Modernisme*" and "Gourmet" walking tours on selected days.

The guides at **My Favourite Things** (⊚ www.myft.net) reveal Barcelona in a new light, particularly on the signature tour "My Favourite Fusion", which gives an insider's view of the city. Tours (in English, flexible departures) cost from €26 per person and last around four hours, and there's always time for diversions, workshop visits and café stops. Altogether more idiosyncratic is **Follow the Baldie** (contact through website, ⊚ www.followthebaldie. com), with whom you can variously tour anarchist Barcelona, track tarantulas near Sitges or stagger from bar to tavern in rural Catalunya.

Bike tours now infest the city, with follow-the-leader cycle packs careering through the Old Town alleys. There are flyers and bike outfits everywhere and you'll pay around €25 for a guided 3hr tour.

At any time of year, the sparkling harbour waters invite a cruise and **Las Golondrinas** (☎ 934 423 106, ⊚ www .lasgolondrinas.com) daily sightseeing boats depart (at least hourly June–Sept, less frequently Oct–May) from the quayside opposite the Columbus statue, at the bottom of the Ramblas (Ⓜ Drassanes). Two separate services visit either the port (40min; €7.20), or port and local coast (1hr 30min; €15).

There are also afternoon catamaran trips around the port with **Catamaran Orsom** (⊚ www.barcelona-orsom.com; Easter week & June–Sept daily, May & Oct daily except Tues & Wed; €15.50) plus summer evening jazz cruises (daily June–Aug; €17.50).

Emergency numbers

Call ☎ 112 for emergency ambulance, police and fire services; for the national police service call ☎ 091.

Directory A–Z

Addresses

The main address abbreviations are Av. (for Avinguda, avenue), c/ (Carrer, street), Pg. (Passeig, boulevard/street), Bxda. (Baixada, alley), Ptge. (Passatge, passage) and Pl. (Plaça, square). The address "c/Picasso 2, 4°" means: Picasso street, number two, fourth floor.

Crime

Take all the usual precautions and be on guard when on public transport or on the crowded Ramblas and the medieval streets to either side. Easiest place to report a crime is the Güardia Urbana (municipal police) station at Ramblas 43, opposite Pl. Reial (Liceu; ☎ 932 562 430, www.bcn.cat/guardiaurbana; 24hr, English spoken). For a police report for your insurance go to c/Nou de la Rambla 80, El Raval (Paral.lel ☎ 933 062 300).

Electricity

The electricity supply is 220v and plugs come with two round pins – bring an adapter (and transformer) to use UK and US cell phone chargers etc.

Embassies and consulates

Australia, Av. Diagonal 433, Eixample, Diagonal ☎ 933 623 792, www.spain.embassy.gov.au; Britain, Av. Diagonal 477, Eixample, Hospital Clinic ☎ 902 109 356, or from outside Spain ☎ 913 342 194, www.ukinspain.fco.gov.uk; Canada, Pl. Catalunya 9, Catalunya ☎ 932 703 614, www.canadainternational. gc.ca; Republic of Ireland, Gran Via Carles III 94, Les Corts, Maria Cristina/Les Corts ☎ 934 915 021, irelanda.es; New Zealand, Trav. de Gràcia 64, Gràcia, FGC Gràcia, ☎ 932 090 399, www.nzembassy .com; USA, Pg. de la Reina Elisenda 23, Sarrià, FGC Reina Elisenda, ☎ 932 802 227, barcelona .usconsulate.gov.

Gay and lesbian travellers

Epicentre of the gay scene is the so-called Gaixample, an area of a few blocks near the university in the Esquerra de l'Eixample. The annual Pride festival runs for ten days in June (www.pride barcelona.org). General listings magazine *Guia del Ocio* can put you on the right track for bars and clubs. The single best English-language website is 60by80.com /Barcelona. For other information, contact the lesbian and gay city telephone hotline on ☎ 900 601 601 (daily 6–10pm only).

Health

The following central hospitals have 24hr accident and emergency services: Centre Perecamps, Av. Drassanes 13–15, El Raval, Drassanes ☎ 934 410 600; Hospital Clinic i Provincial, c/Villaroel 170, Eixample, Hospital Clinic ☎ 932 275 400; Hospital del Mar, Pg. Marítim 25–29, Vila Olímpica, Ciutadella-Vila Olímpica ☎ 932 483 000.

Usual pharmacy hours are 9am to 1pm and 4 to 8pm. At least one in each neighbourhood is open 24hr (and marked as such).

Lost property

Anything recovered by police, or left on public transport, is sent to the Oficina de Troballes (municipal lost property office) at Pl. Carles Pi Sunyer 8–10, Barri Gòtic Jaume I/Catalunya (Mon–Fri 9am–2pm; ☎ 010). You could also try the transport office at Universitat.

Money

Spain's currency is the euro (€), with notes issued in denominations of 5, 10, 20, 50, 100, 200 and 500 euros, and coins in denominations of 1, 2, 5, 10, 20 and 50 cents, and 1 and 2 euros. Normal banking hours are Monday to Friday from 8.30am to 2pm, and there are out-of-hours exchange offices down the Ramblas, as well as at the airport, Barcelona Sants station and the Pl. de Catalunya tourist office. ATMs are available all over the city, and you can usually withdraw up to €300 a day.

Museums and passes

Many museums and galleries offer free admission on the first or last Sunday of the month, and most museums are free on the saints' days of February 12, April 23 and September 24, plus May 18 (international museum day). The useful Barcelona Card (2 days €34, 3 days €44, 4 days €52 or 5 days €58; ⓦwww.barcelonaturisme.com) offers free public transport, plus museum and attraction discounts. The Articket (€30; valid three months; ⓦwww.articketbcn.org) covers free admission into six major art galleries, while the Ruta del Modernisme (€12; valid one year; ⓦwww.rutadel modernisme.com) is an excellent English-language guidebook and discount-voucher package that covers 116 modernista buildings, plus other benefits.

Opening hours

Basic working hours are Monday to Saturday 9.30 or 10am to 1.30pm and 4.30 to 8 or 9pm, though many offices and shops don't open on Saturday afternoons. Local cafés, bars and markets open from around 7am, while shopping centres, major stores and large supermarkets tend to open all day from 10am to 9pm, with some even open on Sunday. Museums and galleries often have restricted Sunday and public holiday hours, while on Mondays most are closed all day.

Phones

Public telephones accept coins, credit cards and phone cards (the latter available in various denominations in tobacconists, newsagents and post offices). The cheapest way to make an international call is to go to a locutorio (phone centre); these are scattered throughout the old city, particularly in the Raval and Ribera. You'll be assigned a cabin to make your calls, and afterwards you pay in cash.

Post

The main post office (Correus) is on Pl. d'Antoni López, at the eastern end of Pg. de Colom, in the Barri Gòtic (Mon–Fri 8.30am–9.30pm, Sat 8.30am–2pm; ⓜBarceloneta/ Jaume I). For stamps it's easier to visit a tobacconist (look for the brown-and-yellow tabac sign), found on virtually every street.

Public holidays

Official holidays are: Jan 1 (Cap d'Any, New Year's Day); Jan 6 (Epifanía, Epiphany); Good Friday & Easter Monday; May 1 (Dia del Treball, May Day/Labour Day); June 24 (Dia de Sant Joan, St John's Day); Aug 15 (L'Assumpció, Assumption of the Virgin); Sept 11 (Diada Nacional, Catalan National Day); Sept 24 (Festa de la Mercè, Our Lady of Mercy, Barcelona's patron saint); Oct 12 (Día de la Hispanidad, Spanish National Day); Nov 1 (Tots Sants, All Saints' Day); Dec 6 (Dia de la Constitució, Constitution Day); Dec 8 (La Imaculada, Immaculate Conception); Dec 25 (Nadal, Christmas Day); Dec 26 (Sant Esteve, St Stephen's Day).

Tickets

You can buy concert, sporting and exhibition tickets with a credit card using the ServiCaixa (ⓦ www .servicaixa.com) automatic dispensing machines in branches of La Caixa savings bank. You can also order tickets online through ServiCaixa or TelEntrada (ⓦ www .telentrada.com). For advance tickets for all city council (Ajuntament) sponsored concerts visit the Palau de la Virreina, Ramblas 99.

Time

Barcelona is one hour ahead of the UK, six hours ahead of New York and Toronto, nine hours ahead of Los Angeles, nine hours behind Sydney and eleven hours behind Auckland. This applies except for brief periods during the change-overs to and from daylight saving (in Spain the clocks go forward in the last week in March, back again in the last week of Oct).

Tipping

Locals leave only a few cents or round up the change for a coffee or drink, and a euro or two for most meals, though fancier restaurants will expect ten to fifteen percent. Taxi drivers normally get around five percent.

Tourist information

The city's tourist board, Turisme de Barcelona (ⓣ 807 117 222 from within Spain, ⓣ 932 853 834 from abroad, ⓦ www.barcelonaturisme .com), has its main office in Plaça de Catalunya (daily 9.30am–9.30pm; ⓜ Catalunya), down the steps in the southeast corner of the square, where there's a tours service and accommodation desk. There's also an office in the Barri Gòtic at Plaça de Sant Jaume, entrance at c/Ciutat 2 (Mon–Fri 8.30am–8.30pm, Sat 9am–7pm, Sun & hols 9am–2pm; ⓜ Jaume I), and staffed information booths dotted across the city. The city's ⓣ 010 telephone enquiries service (available 24hr; some English-speaking staff available) can help with questions about transport, public services and other matters. The city hall (Ajuntament; ⓦ www .bcn.cat) and regional government (Generalitat; ⓦ www.gencat.cat) websites are also mines of information about every aspect of cultural, social and working life in Barcelona. Concerts, exhibitions and festivals are covered in full at the walk-in office of the Institut de Cultura at the Palau de la Virreina, Ramblas 99, ⓜ Liceu (ⓣ 933 161 000, ⓦ www.bcn.cat/cultura; daily 10am–8.30pm). The most useful listings magazine is the Spanish-language *Guia del Ocio* (out every Thursday; ⓦ www.guiadelociobcn.es), available at any newspaper kiosk.

Travellers with disabilities

Barcelona's airport and Aerobús are fully accessible to travellers in wheelchairs. On the metro only lines 1, 2 and 11 are fully accessible, with elevators at major stations (including Pl. de Catalunya, Universitat, Pg. de Gràcia and Sagrada Família) from the street to the platforms. However, all city buses have been adapted for wheelchair use, while the city information line – ⓣ 010 – has accessibility information for museums, galleries, hotels, restaurants, museums, bars and stores. Many Old Town attractions have steps, cobbles or other impediments to access.

Water

Water from the tap is safe to drink, but generally doesn't taste very nice. You'll be given bottled mineral water in a bar or restaurant.

Festivals and events

Almost any month you visit Barcelona you'll coincide with a festival, event or holiday. The best are picked out below, but for a full list check out the Ajuntament (city hall) website Ⓦ www.bcn.cat/cultura.

FESTES DE SANTA EULÀLIA

Mid-February Ⓦ www.bcn.cat/santaeulalia
Winter festival around February 12 in honour of the young Barcelona girl who suffered a beastly martyrdom at the hands of the Romans. There are parades, concerts, fireworks and *sardana* dancing.

CARNAVAL/CARNESTOLTES

Week before Lent (Feb or March)
Costumed parades and other carnival events across every city neighbourhood. Sitges, down the coast, has the most outrageous celebrations.

DIA DE SANT JORDI

April 23
St George's Day celebrates Catalunya's patron saint, with hundreds of book and flower stalls down the Ramblas and elsewhere.

PRIMAVERA SOUND

Usually late May
Ⓦ www.primaverasound.com
The city's hottest music festival attracts top names in the rock, indie and electronica world.

SÓNAR

June Ⓦ www.sonar.es
Europe's biggest, most cutting-edge electronic music, multimedia and urban art festival presents three days of brilliant noise and spectacle.

VERBENA/DIA DE SANT JOAN

June 23/24
The "eve" and "day" of St John herald a "night of fire", involving bonfires and fireworks (particularly on Montjuïc) and watching the sun come up on the beach.

FESTIVAL DE BARCELONA GREC

From end June to August
Ⓦ grec.bcn.cat
This is the city's main performing arts festival, with many events staged at Montjuïc's Teatre Grec.

FESTES DE LA MERCÈ

End September Ⓦ www.bcn.cat/merce
The city's main festival is celebrated for a week around September 24, with costumed giants, firework displays and human tower competitions.

FESTIVAL INTERNACIONAL DE JAZZ

October/November
Ⓦ www.barcelonajazzfestival.com
The annual jazz festival attracts big-name artists to the clubs, as well as smaller-scale street concerts.

Celebrating Catalan-style

Central to any traditional Barcelona festival is the parade of *gegants*, five-metre-high giants with papier-mâché or fibreglass heads. Also typically Catalan is the *correfoc* ("fire-running"), where drummers, dragons and demons cavort in the streets. Meanwhile, teams of *castellers* – "castle-makers" – pile person upon person to see who can construct the highest tower.

Chronology

c230 BC > Carthaginians found the settlement of "Barcino", probably on the heights of Montjuïc.

218–201 BC > Romans expel Carthaginians from Iberian peninsula in Second Punic War. Roman Barcino is established around today's Barri Gòtic.

304 AD > Santa Eulàlia – the city's patron saint – is martyred by Romans for refusing to renounce Christianity.

c350 AD > Roman city walls are built, as threat of invasion grows.

415 > Visigoths sweep across Spain and establish temporary capital in Barcino (later "Barcelona").

711 > Moorish conquest of Spain. Barcelona eventually forced to surrender (719).

801 > Barcelona retaken by Louis the Pious, son of Charlemagne. Frankish counties of Catalunya become a buffer zone, known as the Spanish Marches.

878 > Guifré el Pelós (Wilfred the Hairy) declared first Count of Barcelona, founding a dynastic line that was to rule until 1410.

985 > Moorish sacking of city. Sant Pau del Camp – the city's oldest surviving church – built after this date.

1137 > Dynastic union of Catalunya and Aragón established.

1213–76 > Reign of Jaume I, "the Conqueror", expansion of empire and beginning of Catalan golden age.

1282–1387 > Barcelona at the centre of an aggressively mercantile Mediterranean empire. Successive rulers construct most of Barcelona's best-known Gothic buildings.

1348 > The Black Death strikes, killing half of Barcelona's population.

1391 > Pogrom against the city's Jewish population.

1410 > Death of Martí el Humà (Martin the Humane), last of Catalan count-kings. Beginning of the end of Catalan influence in the Mediterranean.

1469 > Marriage of Ferdinand of Aragón and Isabel of Castile.

1479 > Ferdinand succeeds to Catalan-Aragón crown, and Catalunya's fortunes decline. Inquisition introduced to Barcelona, leading to forced flight of the Jews.

1493 > Christopher Columbus received in Barcelona after his triumphant return from New World. The shifting of trade routes away from Mediterranean and across Atlantic further impoverishes the city.

1516 > Spanish crown passes to Habsburgs and Madrid is established as capital of Spanish empire.

1640–52 > The uprising known as the "Wars of the Reapers" declares Catalunya an independent republic. Barcelona is besieged and eventually surrenders to the Spanish army.

1714 > After War of Spanish Succession, throne passes to Bourbons. Barcelona subdued on September 11 (now Catalan National Day); Ciutadella fortress built, Catalan language banned and parliament abolished.

1755 > Barceloneta district laid out – gridded layout is an early example of urban planning.

1778 > Steady increase in trade; Barcelona's economy improves.

1814 > After Peninsular War (1808–14), French finally driven out, with Barcelona the last city to fall.

1859 > Old city walls demolished and Eixample district built to accommodate growing population.

1882 > Work begins on Sagrada Família; Antoni Gaudí takes charge two years later.

1888 > Universal Exhibition held at Parc de la Ciutadella. *Modernista* architects start to make their mark.

1893 > First stirrings of anarchist unrest. Liceu opera house bombed.

1901 > Pablo Picasso's first public exhibition held at *Els Quatre Gats* tavern.

1909 > Setmana Trágica (Tragic Week) of rioting. Many churches destroyed.

1922 > Parc Güell opens to the public.

1926 > Antoni Gaudí is run over by a tram; Barcelona stops en masse for his funeral.

1929 > International Exhibition held at Montjuïc.

1936–39 > Spanish Civil War. Barcelona at the heart of Republican cause, with George Orwell and other volunteers arriving to fight. City eventually falls to Nationalists on January 26, 1939.

1939–75 > Spain under Franco. Generalitat president Lluís Companys executed and Catalan language banned. Emigration encouraged from south to dilute Catalan identity. Franco dies in 1975.

1977 > First democratic Spanish elections for 40 years.

1978–80 > Generalitat re-established and Statute of Autonomy approved. Conservative nationalist government elected.

1992 > Olympics held in Barcelona. Rebuilding projects transform Montjuïc and the waterfront.

1995 > MACBA (contemporary art museum) opens, and signals the regeneration of El Raval district.

2004 > Diagonal Mar hosts Universal Forum of Cultures, heralding the transformation of the Poble Nou district.

2006 > New statute of autonomy agreed with Spain.

2008 > Montjuïc castle symbolically handed over from state to city, to become a peace museum.

2011 > FC Barcelona are European football champions for fourth time.

2014 > Constitutional Court of Spain deems the Catalan government's 2013 declaration of sovereignty to be unconstitutional.

Catalan

In Barcelona, Catalan (Català) has more or less taken over from Castilian (Castellano) Spanish as the language on street signs and maps. On paper it looks like a cross between French and Spanish and is generally easy to read if you know those two. Few visitors realize how important Catalan is to those who speak it: never commit the error of calling it a dialect. Despite the preponderance of the Catalan language you'll get by perfectly well in Spanish as long as you're aware of the use of Catalan in timetables, on menus, and so on. However you'll generally get a good reception if you at least try communicating in the local language.

Pronunciation

Don't be tempted to use the few rules of Spanish pronunciation you may know – in particular the soft Spanish Z and C don't apply, so unlike in the rest of Spain, the city is not Barthelona but Barcelona, as in English.

a as in hat if stressed, as in alone when unstressed.

e varies, but usually as in get.

i as in police.

ig sounds like the "tch" in the English scratch; lleig (ugly) is pronounced "yeah-tch".

o a round, full sound, when stressed, otherwise like a soft U sound.

u somewhere between the U of put and rule.

ç sounds like an English S; plaça is pronounced "plassa".

c followed by an E or I is soft; otherwise hard.

g followed by E or I is like the "zh" in Zhivago; otherwise hard.

h is always silent.

j as in the French "Jean".

l.l is best pronounced (for foreigners) as a single L sound; but for Catalan speakers it has two distinct L sounds.

ll sounds like an English Y or LY, like the "yuh" sound in million.

n as in English, though before F or V it sometimes sounds like an M.

ny corresponds to the Castilian Ñ.

qu before E or I sounds like K; before A or O, or if the U has an umlaut (Ü), sounds like KWE, as in quit.

r is rolled, but only at the start of a word; at the end it's often silent.

t is pronounced as in English, though sometimes it sounds like a D; as in viatge or dotze.

v at the start of a word sounds like B; in all other positions it's a soft F sound.

w is pronounced like a B/V.

x is like SH or CH in most words, though in some, like exit, it sounds like an X.

z is like the English Z in zoo.

Words and phrases
BASICS

Yes, No, OK	Si, No, Val
Please, Thank you	Si us plau, Gràcies
Hello, Goodbye	Hola, Adéu
Good morning	Bon dia
Good afternoon /night	Bona tarde/nit
See you later	Fins després
Sorry	Ho sento
Excuse me	Perdoni
I (don't) understand	(No) Ho entenc
Do you speak English?	Parleu anglès?
Where? When?	Dónde? Cuando?
What? How much?	Què? Quant?
Here, There	Aquí, Allí/Allá
This, That	Això, Allò
Open, Closed	Obert, Tancat
With, Without	Amb, Sense
Good, Bad	Bo(na), Dolent(a)
Big, Small	Gran, Petit(a)
Cheap, Expensive	Barat(a), Car(a)
I want	Vull (pronounced "wwee")
I'd like	Voldria
Do you know?	Vostès saben?
I don't know	No sé
There is (Is there?)	Hi ha(?)
What's that?	Què és això?
Do you have...?	Té...?
Today, Tomorrow	Avui, Demà

ACCOMMODATION

Do you have a room?	Té alguna habitació?
...with two beds/ double bed	...amb dos llits/ llit per dues persones
...with shower/bath	...amb dutxa/bany
It's for one person (two people)	Per a una persona (dues persones)
For one night (one week)	Per una nit (una setmana)
It's fine, how much is it?	Esta bé, quant és?
Don't you have anything cheaper?	En té de més bon preu?

DIRECTIONS AND TRANSPORT

How do I get to...?	Per anar a...?
Left, Right	A la dreta, A l'esquerra
Straight on	Tot recte
Where is...?	On és...?
...the bus station	...l'estació de autobuses
...the train station	...l'estació
...the nearest bank	...el banc més a prop
...the post office	...l'oficina de correus
...the toilet	...la toaleta
Where does the bus to...leave from?	De on surt el autobús a...?
Is this the train for Barcelona?	Aquest tren va a Barcelona?
I'd like a (return) ticket to...	Voldria un bitlet (d'anar i tornar) a...
What time does it leave (arrive in)?	A quina hora surt (arriba a)?

NUMBERS

1	un(a)
2	dos (dues)
3	tres
4	quatre
5	cinc
6	sis
7	set
8	vuit
9	nou
10	deu
11	onze
12	dotze
13	tretze
14	catorze
15	quinze
16	setze
17	disset
18	divuit
19	dinou
20	vint
21	vint-i-un
30	trenta
40	quaranta
50	cinquanta
60	seixanta
70	setanta
80	vuitanta
90	novanta
100	cent
101	cent un
200	dos-cents (dues-centes)
500	cinc-cents
1000	mil

DAYS OF THE WEEK

Monday	dilluns
Tuesday	dimarts
Wednesday	dimecres
Thursday	dijous
Friday	divendres
Saturday	dissabte
Sunday	diumenge

MONTHS OF THE YEAR

January	Gener
February	Febrer
March	Març
April	Abril
May	Maig
June	Juny
July	Juliol
August	Agost
September	Setembre
October	Octobre
November	Novembre
December	Desembre

Menu reader

BASIC WORDS

Esmorzar	To have breakfast
Dinar	To have lunch
Sopar	To have dinner
Ganivet	Knife
Forquilla	Fork
Cullera	Spoon
Taula	Table
Ampolla	Bottle
Got	Glass
Carta	Menu
Sopa	Soup
Amanida	Salad
Entremesos	Hors d'oeuvres
Truita	Omelette
Entrepà	Sandwich
Torrades	Toast
Tapes	Tapas
Mantega	Butter
Ous	Eggs
Pa	Bread
Olives	Olives
Oli	Oil
Vinagre	Vinegar
Sal	Salt
Pebre	Pepper
Sucre	Sugar
El compte	The bill
Sóc vegetarià/ vegetariana	I'm a vegetarian

COOKING TERMS

Assortit	Assorted
Al forn	Baked
A la brasa	Char-grilled
Fresc	Fresh
Fregit	Fried
A la romana	Fried in batter
All i oli	Garlic mayonnaise
A la plantxa	Grilled
En escabetx	Pickled
Rostit	Roast
Salsa	Sauce
Saltat	Sautéed
Remenat	Scrambled
Del temps	Seasonal
Fumat	Smoked
A l'ast	Spit-roasted
Al vapor	Steamed
Guisat	Stewed
Farcit	Stuffed

FISH AND SEAFOOD/PEIX I MARISC

Anxoves/Seitons	Anchovies
Calamarsets	Baby squid
Orada	Bream
Cloïsses	Clams
Cranc	Crab
Sípia	Cuttlefish
Lluç	Hake
Llagosta	Lobster
Rap	Monkfish
Musclos	Mussels
Pop	Octopus
Gambes	Prawns
Navalles	Razor clams
Salmó	Salmon
Bacallà	Salt cod
Sardines	Sardines
Llobarro	Sea bass
Llenguado	Sole
Calamars	Squid
Peix espasa	Swordfish
Tonyina	Tuna

MEAT AND POULTRY/CARN I AVIRAM

Bou	Beef
Embotits	Charcuterie
Pollastre	Chicken
Xoriço	Chorizo sausage
Pernil serrà	Cured ham
Llonganissa	Cured pork sausage
Costelles	Cutlets/chops
Ànec	Duck
Pernil dolç	Ham
Xai/Be	Lamb
Fetge	Liver
Llom	Loin of pork
Mandonguilles	Meatballs
Porc	Pork
Conill	Rabbit
Salsitxes	Sausages
Cargols	Snails
Bistec	Steak
Llengua	Tongue
Vedella	Veal

VEGETABLES/VERDURES I LLEGUMS

Carxofes	Artichokes
Albergínia	Aubergine/eggplant
Faves	Broad/lima beans
Carbassó	Courgette/zucchini
All	Garlic
Mongetes	Haricot beans
Llenties	Lentils
Xampinyons	Mushrooms
Cebes	Onions
Patates	Potatoes
Espinacs	Spinach
Tomàquets	Tomatoes
Bolets	Wild mushrooms

FRUIT/FRUITA

Poma	Apple
Plàtan	Banana
Raïm	Grapes
Meló	Melon
Taronja	Orange
Pera	Pear
Maduixes	Strawberries

DESSERTS/POSTRES

Pastís	Cake
Formatge	Cheese
Flam	Crème caramel
Gelat	Ice cream
Arròs amb llet	Rice pudding
Tarta	Tart
Yogur	Yoghurt

DRINKS

Cervesa	Beer
Vi	Wine
Xampan/cava	Champagne
Cafè amb llet	Large white coffee
Cafè tallat	Small white coffee
Descafeïnat	Decaf
Te	Tea
Xocolata	Drinking chocolate
Granissat	Crushed ice drink
Llet	Milk
Orxata	Tiger nut drink
Aigua	Water
Aigua mineral	Mineral water
Zumo	Juice

CATALAN SPECIALITIES

Amanida Catalana Salad served with sliced meats (sometimes cheese)

Arròs a banda Rice with seafood, the rice served separately

Arròs a la marinera Paella: rice with seafood and saffron

Arròs negre "Black rice", cooked in squid ink

Bacallà a la llauna Salt cod baked with garlic, tomato and paprika

Botifarra (amb mongetes) Grilled Catalan pork sausage (with stewed haricot beans)

Calçots Large char-grilled spring onions

Canelons Cannelloni, baked pasta with ground meat and béchamel sauce

Conill all i oli Rabbit with garlic mayonnaise

Crema Catalana Crème caramel, with caramelized sugar topping

Escalivada Grilled aubergine/eggplant, pepper/capsicum and onion

Espinacs a la Catalana Spinach cooked with raisins and pine nuts

Esqueixada Salad of salt cod with peppers/capsicums, tomatoes and olives

Estofat de vedella Veal stew

Faves a la Catalana Stewed broad beans, with bacon and botifarra

Fideuà Short, thin noodles (the width of vermicelli) served with seafood

Fuet Catalan salami

Llenties guisades Stewed lentils

Mel i mató Curd cheese and honey

Pa amb tomàquet Bread (often grilled), rubbed with tomato, garlic and olive oil

Pollastre al cava Chicken with *cava* sauce

Pollastre amb gambes Chicken with prawns

Postres de músic Cake of dried fruit and nuts

Salsa Romesco Spicy sauce (with chillis, nuts, tomato and wine), often served with grilled fish

Samfaina Ratatouille-like stew (onions, peppers/capsicum, aubergine/eggplant, tomato), served with salt cod or chicken

Sarsuela Fish and shellfish stew

Sípia amb mandonguilles Cuttlefish with meatballs

Suquet de peix Fish and potato casserole

Xató Mixed salad of olives, salt cod, preserved tuna, anchovies and onions

PUBLISHING INFORMATION

This third edition published April 2015 by **Rough Guides Ltd**

80 Strand, London WC2R 0RL

11, Community Centre, Panchsheel Park, New Delhi 110017, India

Distributed by Penguin Random House

Penguin Books Ltd, 80 Strand, London WC2R 0RL

Penguin Group (USA) 345 Hudson Street, NY 10014, USA

Penguin Group (Australia) 250 Camberwell Road, Camberwell, Victoria 3124, Australia

Penguin Group (NZ) 67 Apollo Drive, Mairangi Bay, Auckland 1310, New Zealand

Penguin Group (South Africa) Block D, Rosebank Office Park, 181 Jan Smuts Avenue, Parktown North, Gauteng, South Africa 2193

Rough Guides is represented in Canada by

Tourmaline Editions Inc., 662 King Street West, Suite 304, Toronto, Ontario, M5V 1M7

Typeset in Minion and Din to an original design by Henry Iles and Dan May.

Printed and bound in China

© Rough Guides, 2015

Maps © Rough Guides

No part of this book may be reproduced in any form without permission from the publisher except for the quotation of brief passages in reviews.

192pp includes index

A catalogue record for this book is available from the British Library

ISBN 978-0-24100-934-5

The publishers and authors have done their best to ensure the accuracy and currency of all the information in **Pocket Rough Guide Barcelona**; however, they can accept no responsibility for any loss, injury, or inconvenience sustained by any traveller as a result of information or advice contained in the guide.

1 3 5 7 9 8 6 4 2

MIX
Paper from responsible sources
FSC™ C018179
www.fsc.org

ROUGH GUIDES CREDITS

Text editors: Rebecca Hallett, Lara Kavanagh, Edward Aves

Layout: Nikhil Agarwal, Sachin Tanwar

Photography: Roger d'Olivere Mapp, Chris Christoforou, Tim Kavenagh

Cartography: James MacDonald, Ed Wright, Katie Bennett

Picture editors: Michelle Bhatia, Nicole Newman, Rhiannon Furbear

Proofreader: Susannah Wight

Production: Linda Dare

Cover design: Nikhil Agarwal, Dan May, Nicole Newman, Chloë Roberts

THE AUTHORS

Jules Brown first visited Barcelona in 1985. Apart from this book he has also written half a dozen other Rough Guides, and contributed as researcher and editor to many others. But he's beginning to think he's left it too late to play for Huddersfield Town.

Laurie Isola is a California-based writer and researcher whose work has appeared in various magazines and newspapers, as well as online. During the nearly three years she lived in Barcelona, she could be found treasure hunting at Els Encants Vells or sipping a *tallat* on a sunny *terrassa*.

ACKNOWLEDGEMENTS

Laurie would like to thank Montse Planas of Turisme de Barcelona, and Jules Brown for all his hard work on the previous edition of this guide.

HELP US UPDATE

We've gone to a lot of effort to ensure that the third edition of **Pocket Rough Guide Barcelona** is accurate and up-to-date. However, things change – places get "discovered", opening hours are notoriously fickle, restaurants and rooms raise prices or lower standards. If you feel we've got it wrong or left something out, we'd like to know, and if you can remember the address, the price, the hours, the phone number, so much the better.

Please send your comments with the subject line "**Pocket Rough Guide Barcelona Update**" to 📧 mail@roughguides.com. We'll credit all contributions and send a copy of the next edition (or any other Rough Guide if you prefer) for the very best emails.

Find more travel information, connect with fellow travellers and book your trip on 🌐 www .roughguides.com

PHOTO CREDITS

Index

Maps are marked in **bold**.

185

SO NOW WE'VE TOLD YOU
ABOUT THE THINGS NOT TO
MISS, THE BEST PLACES TO
STAY, THE TOP RESTAURANTS,
THE LIVELIEST BARS AND THE
MOST SPECTACULAR SIGHTS,
IT ONLY SEEMS FAIR TO
TELL YOU ABOUT THE BEST
TRAVEL INSURANCE AROUND

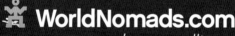
WorldNomads.com
keep travelling safely

RECOMMENDED BY ROUGH GUIDES

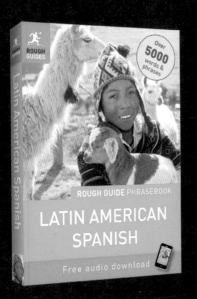